Praise for Previous Editions of *Sell Your Specialty Food*

"*Wow!* All this information in one place. I can't put it down.
Thank you for your book. I cannot wait to read every page."
—Deanna Ansell, Ana-de Country Kitchen

"Hall tells readers how to break into the specialty food industry.
It's all between the covers of this excellent guide."
—Bookviews.com

"The gourmet food industry is perfect for entry-level food distribution
in this country: it lends to testing new products, it doesn't require large
start-up investment, and it's a fast-growing industry. To enter, consult
Food Marketing International president Stephen F. Hall's latest edition:
it outlines and analyzes all kinds of food marketing opportunities for small
cottage industries new to the business, discussing everything from building
a product's concept using trade shows, brokers, and more. A 'must' for
any newcomer cook who would market a product."
—*Midwest Review of Books*

"Hall takes the reader step by step through the entire marketing process,
offering guidelines on market research, packaging, pricing, and advertising.
Interesting vignettes on actual successes and failures allow a realistic view
of possible scenarios. The appendixes, which make up a good portion of
the book and list trade shows, journals, associations, sample forms, and
so forth, are terrific quick resources that significantly enhance this
already strong and well-written guide."
—*Library Journal*

"Practical and strategic. I use the guide as the text for the weekend class that
I teach through University of California Davis Extension, Getting Started
in the Specialty Food Business. You won't be guaranteed success just because
you make a great tasting product; Hall discusses how you need to package,
market and distribute your product effectively."
—Shermain D. Hardesty, PhD, University of California—Davis

**Market, Distribute, and Profit
from Your Kitchen Creation**

sell your specialty food

Stephen F. Hall

PUBLISHING

New York

This publication is designed to provide accurate and authoritative information in regard to the subject matter covered. It is sold with the understanding that the publisher is not engaged in rendering legal, accounting, or other professional service. If legal advice or other expert assistance is required, the services of a competent professional should be sought.

Published by Kaplan Publishing, a division of Kaplan, Inc.
1 Liberty Plaza, 24th Floor
New York, NY 10006

Printed in the United States of America

10 9 8 7 6 5 4 3 2 1

Library of Congress Cataloging-in-Publication Data

Hall, Stephen F.
    Sell your specialty food : market, distribute, and profit from your kitchen creation / Stephen F. Hall.
        p. cm.
    Rev. ed. of: From kitchen to market : selling your gourmet food specialty. 2005.
    Includes index.
    ISBN 978-1-4277-9826 8
    1. Food industry and trade--United States. 2. Food service--United States. I. Hall, Stephen F. From kitchen to market. II. Title.
    HD9004.H25 2008
    664.0068'8--dc22

Kaplan Publishing books are available at special quantity discounts to use for sales promotions, employee premiums, or educational purposes. Please email our Special Sales Department to order or for more information at *kaplanpublishing@kaplan.com* or write to Kaplan Publishing, 1 Liberty Plaza, 24th Floor, New York, NY 10006.

Contents

. . . .

Chapter Six
Taking Your Product to Market 99

Chapter Seven
Running Your Business 145

Contents

Introduction

· ·

The specialty food industry has exploded. A combination of factors has led to exciting opportunities for food entrepreneurs. Retail sales of all specialty foods are generating revenues of more than $48 billion a year and averaging annual growth of more than 8 percent. To some, this means great opportunity. To others, it represents a formidable challenge.

Your ability to grab a slice of this pie and make your mark, establish your independence, achieve success, and acquire wealth will depend on how effectively you prepare—and prepare you must!

How to prepare for the opportunities and challenges of taking your food products to the appropriate store shelves is the subject of this guide. You need not know the basics of small business operations just yet. For now, success will depend on your personal and business vision, drive, talent, and the amount of capital you can raise.

Let's put that last item into perspective: the average cost of getting national grocery store shelf exposure for a new product by a branded manufacturer has been estimated at more than $6 million.

Still reading? Take heart. There is a proven alternative: the specialty food industry. It has become the proven vehicle for entry-level food distribution in the United States. Different market segments and new products can be tested in the specialty food industry without the initial investment required of the major food producers. The secret has to do with superior execution of often ordinary ideas.

How Long Does It Take to Be Successful?

Here are the *Food Entrepreneur eZine* 2008 survey responses in order of prevalence:

- Four to five years (28%)
- One to two years (21%)
- Less than one year (21%)
- Five to six years (7%)
- Four to five years (2%)
- Six to ten years (2%)

How Much Will It Cost You?

Depending on your approach, you can expect to incur minimum start-up costs of approximately $35,000 to $100,000 and more each year for the first three to five years. This includes production, packaging, labeling, advertising, and promotion of one product. It does *not* include the cost of success. Many firms that won "Outstanding Product Awards" were ill prepared for the next move. Not all of them succeeded in profiting from their good fortune. This estimated cost also assumes that you will be doing a lot of the leg work (administrative, invoicing, database management, sales calls, and so on).

Our purpose is to explore the inner workings of niche marketing. Niche marketing entails finding the best combination of product packaging, pricing, positioning, and promotion that will

Life Before Specialty Food Marketing

What food entrepreneurs did before starting a specialty food firm (in order of prevalence):

- Other business, non-food-related (52%)
- Other food-related business (14%)
- Medical profession (11%)
- Education (8%)
- Nonprofit charity (8%)
- Law and government service (3.6%)

—*Food Entrepreneur eZine* 2008 survey responses

encourage the consumer to purchase a product not otherwise offered by the major suppliers. Imagination is a key ingredient, but adequate funding is essential.

In addition to the above, a successful undertaking requires you to center your activities on your competitive strengths, control your costs, know your competition, and learn how to manage the entire process effectively and professionally. As with most new food entrepreneurs, you will have to learn to deal with finding resources, motivating employees, developing a compelling vision, and even handling family issues.

We are not addressing what you can do with a several-million-dollar budget. Rather, this guide deals with the essence of entrepreneurship. There is a lot of "ready, fire, aim" in the gourmet food-marketing process that leads to some success and frequent failure. This guide helps you accomplish most of the "aiming" during the "ready" phase.

Specialty food marketing requires creative responses. As soon as you adopt a successful marketing strategy, you may learn of another entrepreneur who is just as successful but who has implemented an entirely different marketing scheme!

How to Use This Guide

Sell Your Specialty Food helps you learn all the secrets about profitably marketing food, a process that generally entails everything from product concept and production to after-sales service. This edition addresses important and developing aspects of specialty food marketing not addressed in any other book, such as the growing role of the Internet and the place for information technology, and provides up-to-date resources for getting your business off the ground.

In addition to explaining packaging, labeling, pricing, storage, and shipping, *Sell Your Specialty Food* tells you how to advertise, promote, and sell your product. Flowcharts describe how to process the orders you generate. Major sections include "Guidelines for Success," which you can use as you prepare to take your product to market. New sections deal with how to exploit overseas opportunities, the personal characteristics of an entrepreneur, business management software, risk management and liability insurance, order processing and accounting software, and how to grow your enterprise.

"Recipes for Success" are used throughout the book to highlight experiences of specialty food entrepreneurs. In this edition, "Recipes for Success" identify the successes—and failures—of many winners of the National Association for the Specialty Food Trade (NASFT) Specialty Outstanding Food Innovation ("sofi") Awards with the purpose of showing you that it takes more than an award to ensure your success.

Sell Your Specialty Food is designed for both small cottage industries new to the food business and for large food processors and overseas food companies interested in learning how the U.S. specialty food trade functions.

Specialty food marketing is addressed in a straightforward, logical manner. The book begins with introductory comments, followed by a general discussion of the industry. It proceeds to discuss the issues relevant to understanding your readiness to be an entrepreneur, preparing your product for the market, and taking your product to market. The appendixes offer information about additional sources of assistance along with useful data regarding trade shows, trade journals, professional associations, etc. Most, if not all, of the resource listings are regularly updated on our website: *www.specialtyfoodresource.com.*

You will probably not need this guide if your name is Paul Newman or Wolfgang Puck. Deep pockets can make the difference between success or failure for a high-quality product. However, if like the rest of us, you have neither the funding to support a major marketing effort nor the clout to see it through, then this guide is for you.

> ## Where Does Capital Come From?
>
> What revenue source did you initially use to finance your venture?
>
> - Personal savings/inheritance (70%)
> - Credit card(s) (10%)
> - Family and friends (5%)
> - Second mortgage/commercial loan (5%)
> - Venture capital (5%)
> - Small Business Administration (SBA) or other government-financed loan (5%)
>
> —*Food Entrepreneur eZine* 2008 survey responses

Before you begin: Do you want your food operation to be a full-time occupation or a sideline business?

One of the following scenarios may describe your circumstances and could help you respond to the important issue of just how involved you would like to become in the business. All four of these scenarios have played out, with varying degrees of success, in the gourmet food industry.

Scenario 1

You have just returned from another successful church bazaar where your homemade supply of organic, sugar-free apple-cranberry chutney sold out. Your chutney is based on a family recipe handed down for generations. Your friends and neighbors urge you to sell your chutney to Whole Foods, where they think it will be a great hit. You think it's a wonderful idea, but you haven't the foggiest idea of where to begin.

In this scenario, the entrepreneur has to decide, after significant investigation, whether to continue in the sideline mode or to take the risk of turning the operation into a full-time business.

On the one hand, the owner has a product that has been tested, in a fashion, with positive reactions from customers, friends, and neighbors. There is reason to believe that success, at least initially, might be achieved with a reasonable expectation of profit. On the other hand, what level of funding is required for the venture? If the owner has an outside source of income, then the venture may be undertaken. Otherwise, the possibilities for negative cash flow (more money going out than coming in) are quite high.

Scenario 2

Your specialty food store is doing a lot of business. You are especially pleased with the success of your prepared foods section, in which one item is your home-baked, seasoned breadsticks. You note that there seems to be a growing interest in this product from a broad segment of your customer base. You wonder if it would be possible to sell the breadsticks to a wider audience in other markets in your region. Where to begin?

Interest in Green, Organic, and Local Foods Is Exploding

Organic foods, locally sourced foods, and sustainable living or "green" enterprises have become part of our mainstream lifestyles. Organic foods are produced without the use of conventional pesticides, artificial fertilizers, human waste, or sewage sludge and are processed without ionizing radiation or food additives. There is a growing belief that eating organic is better for our bodies and better for the planet. Green food producers and processors are becoming increasingly environmentally friendly. More importantly, data suggest that these markets have exceeded 60 percent in compound annual growth. This suggests a significant demand that specialty food entrepreneurs can meet.

If the second scenario fits, then your food marketing venture could be supported by revenues from the existing retail operation. This makes market entry more attractive, because many initial costs of operation could be absorbed by the retail store sales of other products. Nevertheless, you will have to devote substantial time to developing markets for the breadsticks, which will take away from time spent in the store. If this can be accommodated, then a full-time sales and marketing operation can be adopted.

Scenario 3

You have recently taken over a small, local chocolate-manufacturing concern. Until now, revenues have come from bulk sales to walk-in and mail-order customers. You think there are substantial opportunities for developing a retail packaged version, and you want to begin distributing it to stores all over the country. How do you proceed?

This scenario offers some of the same challenges as Scenario 2. Both require investing substantial time at the existing business. Scenario 3, however, offers a chance to expand an existing base of sales to customers located outside of the local area. It also provides an existing source of revenue (from retail packaged sales) on which to base some of the expansion costs. It would appear, then, that turning the chocolate operation into a full-time sales and marketing operation might be an appropriate alternative.

Scenario 4

Your family and friends love your honey-and-pecan mustard. You have been very successful in selling it at the local women's exchange and farmers' market and at area school fairs. You also ran an ad in a slick "upscale" magazine that cost you a fortune but produced results in Internet sales sufficient to cover the cost. Your life is too busy to contemplate going into a food business full-time. What do you need to know about this business to make a little money on the side?

The challenge in Scenario 4 is to transform your hobby into a sideline business. You can take your talent, your recipes, your promotional genius, and your money and have your product produced, packaged, warehoused, and marketed by another company. You will definitely need the supporting funds and the knowledge of how specialty food marketing works.

Your situation may differ from these scenarios but still have the opportunity to turn your food ideas into an endeavor that gains you financial independence. The specialty food business is one way of obtaining a significant shot at achieving success and acquiring wealth.

Now that you are armed with a sense of how your situation fits into the range of possible scenarios, read on to learn how to take the next step in the exciting and challenging world of specialty food marketing.

Chapter 1

Do You Have What It Takes for Long-Term Success?

A lthough you are just getting started, now is the time to think about your long-term vision for your business.

Long-term success boils down to being customer directed and process oriented, and making decisions based on facts. Long-term success is not ensured by wholly intuitive, seat-of-the-pants marketing. Of course, there have been, and always will be, exceptions to prove this rule.

The Importance of Formulating a Future: Vision

In the food business, the exceptions are usually based on products that are in high demand—ones that consumers will do or pay anything to get—or those that are associated with, and introduced by, marketers with deep pockets. Even then, if the product does not meet a specific consumer need at the right quality and right price, it will be short-lived.

We can no longer simply afford to think up a new food product, prepare it, and try to market it. Instead, use the information from Figure 3.1: Checklist to Refine Your Focus to focus your efforts.

How does all this connect to the food entrepreneur? How does the entrepreneur, wearing all the hats at once, maintain focus? The answer is *vision*. Simply put, your vision is what and where you envision yourself being (as food entrepreneur, professional, spouse, parent, neighbor, citizen, etc.) in about five to ten years. It is your dream. As a food entrepreneur, your vision should be a positive and inspiring statement of where your business will be at that time. A clearly articulated vision will help you and all your stakeholders (anyone with an interest in your venture) keep on track. Important elements of your organizational vision might include reputation, products to offer, values, types of customer, working environment, manner in which your people would work together, and how you and you team would handle both good and bad times.

You will want to share your dream with, and solicit input from, these stakeholders to develop the strongest possible vision. Revisit your vision from time to time. See how it can be constantly refined. Your vision will help you determine if the task or activity you are doing now is adding value to getting from where you are to where you envision yourself being in five or ten years.

Abraham Lincoln

President Abraham Lincoln was a success in politics but a failure in small business. In his case, failure was due mostly to temperament and disposition. As the saying goes, "He had no head for business." Would he have fared differently with the wisdom in this book? We can only guess.

What you are doing, or about to do, in food marketing is part of a system. This system consists of inputs, actions, and outputs. If you can develop the right supplier partnering (inputs), understand variation in your process (actions), and be able to set measurable quality standards (outputs), you have a substantially greater chance of delighting your customer.

To delight your customers, everyone involved must devote sufficient time to education and training in developing a quality philosophy. This is probably the most difficult part of this process: taking assets away from what we do best—firefighting—and focusing them on long-term thinking.

In fact, food marketing, and the business supporting it, *cannot* continue in the same vein as it has in the past. The food industry is notoriously product driven. We are being snookered out of profit-generating opportunities because we lack vision—a vision based on perceived customer quality standards. Make the bold move. Cut the waste. Set aside a half hour or more each week to think about your vision. See if the path you have selected is headed in the desired direction.

Your vision—your dream for the future—is just one important element to consider in your continuous improvement effort. Other elements include the mission (what you do to realize your vision), guiding principles (standards of how you do business, your values and goals), and strategic objectives.

A Vision Example

"[In the year 20xx], our company is internationally recognized as the premier supplier of [your food products]. We regularly exceed customer expectations by providing innovative and valuable [your food products]."

The Importance of Understanding Your System

Assumption: You want to develop, produce, administer, market, and sell food that is valued and wanted by customers. As the quality of your work improves, so does your productivity—and costs go down. Knowing how to make this happen requires knowing something about *continuous process improvement*. The term is self-explanatory. All of the processes you want to improve all the time are part of a *system*. What you do as a food entrepreneur should be understood in context of this system.

Your system consists of the following components:

- **Inputs:** Customer needs/feedback, ingredients, packaging materials, trained employees, etc.

- **Food processes:** What you do to formulate and prepare your food product (your response to the customer need)

- **Outputs:** The packaged, labeled, priced, and positioned product

- **Outcomes:** Many satisfied repeat customers (or the opposite)

Managing your system from a broad perspective necessitates developing your company's vision, mission, guiding principles, and strategic goals and objectives.

Why Do You Need to Think about a Mission?

Once you have articulated and shared your vision with everyone in your firm, you will need to figure out what you are going to do to realize it. The result is called your mission.

How to Develop a Mission Statement

The first and last rule is to know your customer. This presumes that you have people who want to buy and consume your food. It also presumes that you know something about your customer's needs. This information is then compared with

A Mission Example

"Our company produces the best [your food products] that offer outstanding value and result in regular and repeat sales. We do this in a working environment that is customer oriented and in which our employees are fully involved team members. We make decisions based on facts. We continually plan, track, and measure performance. Our mission success is every employee's business. Management relies on team members—who know the work better than anyone else—to tell management how to help do the job better. We strive to produce the right product, the first time and every time, at a price both we and our customer can afford."

your "bag of tricks"—your distinctive creative and production capabilities—which you utilize to formulate a response to the perceived customer needs. This process can be accomplished by brainstorming ideas.

A clearly defined organizational mission will go a long way in building your employees' pride, dedication, and team effort. The key to this is to organize for quality.

Brainstorming Is a Useful Tool

RECIPE FOR SUCCESS

M. J.'s Fine Foods Inc.'s cofounder Margaret Sarrasin, in business for eight years, believes that a 24/7 mentality is absolutely required to succeed. The company's NASFT award-winning Margaret's Chives and Garlic Artisan Flatbread took three months to roll out with a dollar investment of just $1,000. It also has a 2008 entry, Onion Confit with Fennel.

Sarrasin's advice: "You will have to challenge conventional thinking and turn existing resources into new opportunities, and at the same time you will add value to your organization."

Organize your mission team. This should consist of five to seven members from various departments in your company. As a small business, this might be everyone. Gather them for a brainstorming session. Brainstorming involves each member and encourages open thinking. There are a variety of brainstorming types. We suggest the following (from Peter R. Scholtes, Brian L. Joiner, and Barbara J. Streibel, *The Team Handbook* (3rd ed.) [Madison, WI: Oriel, 2003]: 2-38 to 2-39):

The rules for conducting a brainstorming session are as follows:

- Encourage everyone to freewheel. Don't hold back on any ideas, even if they seem silly at the time. The more ideas the better.
- No discussion should take place during brainstorming. That will come later.
- Let people "hitchhike"; that is, build upon ideas generated by others in the group.
- Write *all* ideas on a flipchart so the whole group can easily scan them.

The general sequence of events in a brainstorm is as follows:

1. Review the topic, defining the subject of the brainstorming session. Often this is done best as a why or what question (e.g., "What are possible ways to inform and train supervisors and hourly workers on all three shifts?" "How can we get all the information we need on a regular basis to complete these forms on time?")
2. Give everyone a minute or two of silence to think about the question.
3. Invite everyone to call out their ideas. The meeting facilitator should enforce the ground rules ("No discussion! Next idea . . .").
4. Have one team member write down all ideas on the flipchart, pausing only to check accuracy.

Feel free to modify this procedure to fit the group and the topic. For instance, you could have everyone write down their own ideas, then go around the group and have each person say one idea, continuing in this way until everyone's list is voiced. Or you could do the entire sequence in stages: (1) have everyone think of the minimal or partial solutions to a problem; (2) then have them think of the most outrageous, unconventional, or expensive solutions; and (3) finally try to meld the two together into reasonable alternatives. Be particularly alert for ways to combine suggestions.

Brainstorming will help you define your mission and will clarify how you will go about meeting, even exceeding, perceived customer needs and expectations. This is your mission. It's what you do, the nature of your business.

Values and Beliefs

Before taking a trip with a group of like-minded people, you have to ask yourselves: "Why do we want to go on the journey? What is our common purpose?" It is important that fellow travelers focus on "Why this particular caravan? Why as a fledgling food entrepreneur?"

This set of values and beliefs helps you decide how comfortable you will be on your journey with others. This set of behaviors forms the culture of the team traveling together. This culture helps you establish your expectations for yourself and others. This way, you know how to work and play together.

Key Results Areas

As part of setting up your company for the journey, ask the following questions: "What do we need to give constant care and attention to throughout our journey? In which areas do we need to achieve results to optimize our resources and be most effective? How will we measure ourselves in each of these areas?" By addressing these "key results areas," you establish your own goals and measurement system to ensure you get where you want to go in the manner you want to get there.

You can now envision the whole picture of what your journey will be like, with whom you are traveling, what to expect of each other, and why you have chosen to travel together. This strategic framework is what you will communicate to others if asked why you have chosen to travel in this caravan. Think of the strategic framework as a road map for a journey that you want to take.

Each part of this strategic framework—the vision, mission, values and beliefs, and key results areas—plays an important part in guiding a successful journey for everyone involved.

Your Strategic Framework

Food entrepreneurs often wonder what the value is in investing all the time and energy required to develop a strategic framework—vision, mission, values/beliefs, and key result areas. Once created, it is only occasionally seen in business documents. However, leveraging these elements to optimize your performance and the performance of others throughout your enterprise will result in you and your staff having a sense of fulfillment, as well as building a strong, united culture.

Creating Your Strategic Framework

The process of creating a strategic framework differs with each firm. However, there are some key factors to keep in mind. First, there must be a leader to champion the process, one who has both the authority and influence to approve and implement the framework once it has been created.

The wider the participation in developing the framework, the more likely advisors and staff will understand and buy into it. Creating a strategic framework is best viewed as an educational and a change management process with the goal of improving overall company performance.

RECIPE FOR SUCCESS

Celebrating ten years in business, Jean Marie Brownson stated that Frontera Foods Inc.'s original goal was 300 cases of gourmet salsa, then 500 cases. As it grew, it expanded its line from the first 5 original salsas to 11 salsas and has developed product extensions with Frontera's Guacamole Mix and Black Bean Chili Mix.

Frontera's vision is to bring the dynamic, vibrant flavors of Mexico to the American consumer.

Brownson's advice: "Listen to consumers. They will tell you what they want and need and what they are willing to pay."

Once the framework has been created to your satisfaction, there follows the challenge of implementing it as a working document throughout your firm. The initial rollout can be referred to as "sharing the vision." Here, you inform others both inside and outside your company (key stakeholders) about why and how the document was created and how it will be used throughout the business. This working document is best left unaltered for at least six months so that its effectiveness can be tested.

Applying Your Strategic Framework

Your strategic framework has several direct applications for both day-to-day and long-term decision making. These are some of the most obvious:

- Developing policy and procedures
- Hiring and orienting new employees

- Performance management—forming and achieving goals, self-discipline, and collaboration
- Career development
- Supplier/vendor relations

The above activities must align with your mission, values, and beliefs and other elements of your strategic framework to drive you towards the results you seek to achieve. A worthwhile test of the alignment of your strategy and your organization's behavior would be to take each of the above and discuss how your strategic framework applies to it.

Chapter 2
Understanding the Food Industry

To understand the industry, you will need a solid understanding of the primary sales territories and segments of the specialty food market. In this chapter, you will gain this knowledge and learn about transition products; that is, those that make the transition from gourmet to grocery (the "big time"). You'll also learn about a typical gourmet retail store operation.

Defining the Territory

The food industry in general, and the specialty food industry in particular, has yet to sanction specific guidelines for the use of many industry terms. As a result, the process of tracking and understanding the myriad elements of specialty food sales and marketing activity has posed additional challenges to those trying to understand the industry. Because few industry terms have been standardized, here is a list of terms as defined in this book.

- **Gourmet:** This guide uses the term *gourmet* sparingly as a synonym for *specialty*.

- **Specialty food:** The National Association for the Specialty Food Trade (NASFT) has adopted the following description of specialty foods:

  Specialty food products . . . [are] foods and beverages that exemplify quality, innovation and style in their category.

  Their specialty nature derives from some or all of the following characteristics: their originality, authenticity, ethnic or cultural origin, specific processing, ingredients, limited supply, distinctive use, extraordinary packaging or specific channel of distribution or sale. By virtue of their differentiation in their categories, such products maintain a high perceived value and often command a premium price.

  Specialty food is the traditionally accepted term meaning food products that fit the following criteria:

  - *High quality:* Above all, the specialty food product must be of the highest quality in both content and form. As a rule, only the best ingredients are used, whether the product is a premium ice cream or a mustard with peppercorns. Specialty food products sold at retail must also look the part—a high price demands that the product appear to be fancy and high tone.

  - *High price:* Most specialty foods are priced higher than staple food products because of costly ingredients and labor used in their preparation. Others are high in cost because of high demand and limited supply. Still others are sold at high prices because of the low turnover they generate in retail stores. (The longer they remain on the shelf, the more they cost the retailer.)

  - *Limited availability:* Many specialty foods have appeal because they are not generally available. Such foods often gain a cult status—fresh caviar is an example—in that they offer the consumer a cachet not offered by products sold everywhere.

- *Imported or unique:* Imported specialty foods no longer maintain a strong hold on the market. Many high-quality products are now produced in this country yet retain the "imported" distinction that first brought them to U.S. consumers' attention.

- **Food producer/processor:** The producer is usually the grower, and the processor adds value by turning the raw commodity into a table-ready food product.

- **Food broker:** A commissioned sales representative, usually with broad experience in the food industry, generally calls mostly on distributors and large retail chains.

- **Specialty food distributor:** A company buys in volume for its own account and sells to retailers (and to other distributors).

- **Store-door delivery:** This means delivery made to stores by distributors.

- **Direct store distributor:** This distributor performs many of the same services as a jobber (described below).

- **Wholesaler:** A company contracts with, for example, a chain supermarket to warehouse and deliver a product that has been sold by the food producer to the supermarket. Wholesalers usually buy the product only when the producer has sold it to the supermarket chain. It is highly unlikely that you will have to deal with wholesalers, because most of them are not equipped to handle the very detailed nature of specialty food merchandising.

- **Rack jobber:** These are the people you see in supermarkets stocking shelves. (They are the ones with the suits and ties as opposed to supermarket employees.) They price the incoming merchandise with price stickers (in those states where this is still required), fix shelf labels, follow schematic diagrams approved by the store, remove damaged and returned merchandise, and stock and dust the shelves.

- **Customers:** These are retailers and distributors.

- **Consumers:** "Consumers are our reason for existing."

Product Segments

The following definitions and brand examples of 41 specialty food segments are courtesy of the National Association for the Specialty Food Trade, Inc. For additional information, please visit *www.specialtyfood.com*.

- **Baking Mixes, Supplies, and Flours:** Gourmet, ethnic, and natural brands. *Natural:* Bob's Red Mill, Sunspire. *Specialty:* Ghirardelli, King Arthur.

- **Beans, Grains, and Rice:** Gourmet and ethnic; includes rice mixes and couscous. *Natural:* Lundberg, Ancient Harvest, Arrowhead Mills. *Specialty:* Riceselect, Goya, Nishiki.

- **Bread and Baked Goods:** Artisanal, primarily fresh; frozen is included. *Natural:* Rudi's Organic, Food For Life, French Meadow. *Specialty:* Masada Bakery, Just Desserts, Tumaro's.

- **Candy and Individual Snacks:** Gourmet, ethnic; includes jerky items. *Natural:* Green and Black, Endangered Species, Dagoba. *Specialty:* Lake Champlain, Lindt, Divine.

- **Carbonated, Functional, and RTD (ready-to-drink) Tea/Coffee Beverages:** Gourmet, ethnic, and natural sodas; sparkling juice drinks from traditional water companies; sparkling nonalcoholic juices or celebration drinks. *Natural:* GT Kombucha, Izze, Tazo Tea. *Specialty:* Boylan Natural, San Pellegrino, Orangina.

- **Cheese and Cheese Alternatives:** *Natural:* Organic Valley, Horizon, Tofutti. *Specialty:* Tillamook, Cabot, Athenos.

- **Chips, Pretzels, and Individual Snacks:** *Natural:* Kettle Foods, Garden of Eatin', Terra Chips. *Specialty:* Food Should Taste Good, Route 11.

- **Coffee, Coffee Substitutes, and Cocoa:** Premium whole-bean and ground coffees sold in supermarkets. *Natural:* Equal Exchange, Green Mountain, Teecino. *Specialty:* Peet's Coffee, Caffe Sanora, Starbucks.

- **Cold Cereals:** Gourmet and ethnic items. *Natural:* Nature's Path, Kashi, Barbara's Bakery. *Specialty:* Familia, Weetabix, Heartland.

- **Condiments:** Mustard, mayonnaise, ketchup, olive, marinades, soy sauces, pickled vegetables, and barbecue sauces; includes Asian ethnic varieties. *Natural:* Annie's Naturals, Bragg, Thai Kitchen. *Specialty:* Soy Vay, Chatham Village, Kikkoman.

- **Conserves, Jams, and Nut Butters:** Gourmet and ethnic items. *Natural:* Maranatha, Woodstock Farms, Bionaturae. *Specialty:* Stonewall Kitchen, Dickinson's.

- **Cookies and Snack Bars:** Gourmet and ethnic items. *Natural:* Newman's Own Organics, Kashi. *Specialty:* Almondina, Matt's Cookies, Walkers.

- **Crackers and Crispbreads:** Gourmet and ethnic items. *Natural:* Blue Diamond Nut Thins, Late July. *Specialty:* Dr. Kracker, Wasa, San J.

- **Eggs:** Certified organic and premium products such as free-range and Omega-3 fatty acid enhanced. *Natural:* Organic Valley, Chino Valley Ranchers. *Specialty:* Farmer Jon, New Zealand Speckled Hen.

- **Energy Bars:** Lifestyle, wellness, and athletic bars. Inherently part of the natural product industry. *Natural:* Lära Bar, Odwalla, Kashi.

- **Entrées and Mixes:** Grain-based rice and couscous mixes, tabouli, pasta dishes, macaroni and cheese. Also shelf-stable ethnic items. *Natural:* Annie's Homegrown, Annie Chun, Back to Nature. *Specialty:* Near East, Simply Asia, A Taste of Thai.

- **Frozen Desserts:** Gourmet ice creams, organic and nonorganic; gelatos, Italian ices; high-end frozen desserts. *Natural:* Turtle Mountain, Stonyfield Farm, Tofutti. *Specialty:* Häagen-Dazs, Whole Fruit, Ciao Bella.

- **Frozen Entrées and Pizzas and Convenience Foods:** Pizzas, soups, pasta, and convenience foods. *Natural:* Amy's Kitchen, Cedar Lane, Ethnic Gourmet. *Specialty:* Tandoor Chef, Vicolo, Bertoli, Wolfgang Puck.

- **Frozen Fruits and Vegetables:** Organic, premium, and ethnic brands. *Natural:* Cascadian Farms, Woodstock Farms, Alexia. *Specialty:* Wyman, Willamette Valley Fruit, Remlinger.

- **Frozen Juices and Beverages:** Organic, premium, natural brands. *Natural:* Cascadian Farms, Tree of Life. *Specialty:* Just Pikt, Seneca.

- **Frozen/Refrigerated Meat, Poultry, and Seafood:** Prepackaged; sold in standard, uniform weights with UPC codes. Does not include random weight products sold at butcher/seafood counters or retailer packed. Also does not include jerkies.

- **Hot Cereals:** Rolled oats, grits, farina (both instant and non-) from regional or imported producers; premium natural companies. *Natural:* Bob's Red Mill, Kashi, Nature's Path. *Specialty:* McCann's, Old Wessex, Red River.

- **Milk, Half and Half, Cream:** Organic, sheep, goat, and small-craft creameries. *Natural:* Organic Valley, Horizon, Meyenberg. *Specialty:* Valley View, Humboldt Creamery, Oberweis.

RECIPE FOR SUCCESS

Mr. and Mrs. T's Bloody Mary Mix, introduced by Taylor Foods in 1960, became a big hit. Now the brand is owned by Mott's (a U.S. division of Cadbury Schweppes) and marketed everywhere. This is a successful example of a transition product.

- **Nuts, Seeds, Dried Fruits, and Trail Mixes:** Organic and natural brands; includes Asian ethnic foods such as dried seaweed. *Natural:* Just Tomatoes, Eden Foods, Himalania. *Specialty:* Delightfully Turkish, San Joaquin, Poindexter Nut.

- **Oils (cooking):** Olive, flavored, and sesame oils. *Natural:* Spectrum Naturals, Napa Valley, Bionaturae. *Specialty:* Colavita, Lucini Italia, Bertolli.

- **Other Dairy:** Premium and imported products. European and organic butters, ricotta cheese, and crème fraîche. *Natural:* Organic Valley, Horizon, Earth Balance. *Specialty:* Tillamook, Cabot, Kerrygold.

- **Puddings and Shelf-Stable Desserts:** Gourmet and ethnic brands; syrups and toppings. *Natural:* Zensoy, Ah!laska, Natural By Nature. *Specialty:* Oetker, Elyon, Fudge Fatale.

- **Refrigerated Juices and Functional Beverages:** Premium fresh juices; enhanced, functional drinks. *Natural:* Odwalla, Naked Juice, Bossa Nova. *Specialty:* Simply Orange, Zeiglers, Champlain Orchards.

- **Refrigerated Sauces, Salsas, and Dips:** Includes pasta sauces, hummus, and baba gannoush. *Natural:* Emerald Valley Kitchen, Blue Moose, Yorgos. *Specialty:* Cibo, Basha Foods, Athenos Tribe.

- **Rice Cakes:** All-natural brands, full-size and mini bite-sized; inherently part of the natural product industry. *Natural:* Lundberg, Mother's, Real Foods Australia.

- **Seasonings:** Spices, spice mixes (foil packets), baking flavors, salt. *Natural:* Frontier, Simply Organic, Spice Hunter. *Specialty:* Morton and Bassett, Magic Seasoning Blends, Celtic Sea.

- **Shelf-Stable Fruits and Vegetables:** Gourmet, ethnic, and natural canned vegetables, beans, and fruit; also fruit sauces. *Natural:* Muir Glenn, Westbrae, Eden. *Specialty:* Wyman, Leroux Creek, Goya.

- **Shelf-Stable Juices and Functional Drinks:** Premium, natural, and organic brands plus kosher brands. *Natural:* R.W. Knudsen, Lakewood, Santa Cruz Organic. *Specialty:* Martinelli's, Volcano, Looza.

- **Shelf-Stable Meat, Poultry, and Seafood:** Gourmet and premium canned fish and shellfish, caviar, etc., imported and domestic. *Natural:* Natural Sea, Wild Planet. *Specialty:* Crown Prince, Bela Olhao, Geisha.

- **Shelf-Stable Pastas:** Imported and domestic, gourmet ethnic and natural items. *Natural:* Bionaturae, Tinkyada, Hodgson Mill. *Specialty:* De Cecco, Al Dente, Barilla.

- **Shelf-Stable Sauces, Salsas, and Dips:** Includes pasta sauce, hummus, and baba gannoush. *Natural:* Muir Glenn, Green Mountain Gringo, Amy's Kitchen. *Specialty:* Desert Pepper, Classico, Emeril's.

- **Soup:** Ready-to-serve, cups, mixes, and instant. Also includes miso, bouillon, and ramen-type items. *Natural:* Pacific Natural Foods, Amy's Kitchen, Health Valley. *Specialty:* Wolfgang Puck, Bear Creek, Better Than Bouillon.

- **Sweeteners:** Pure maple syrups; honey; and alternative sweeteners such as agave, sucanat, turbinado. *Natural:* Spring Tree, Wholesome Sweeteners, Madhava. *Specialty:* Anderson's Maple Syrup, Kallas, Uwharrie.

- **Teas:** All-natural as well as premium and exotic varieties, including African Red (Rooibos) and mate from South America; also brands that offer imported varietals, such as Assam or oolong. *Natural:* Yogi Tea, Traditional Medicinals, Tazo. *Specialty:* Bigelow, Twinings, Taylors of Harrogate.

- **Water:** Premium brands as well as functional, enhanced waters that don't contain artificial ingredients. *Natural:* Penta, Fiji, Metromint. *Specialty:* San Pellegrino, Gerolsteiner, Sanfaustino.

- **Yogurt and Kefir:** Ethnic and cultured dairy and nondairy products; sheep, goat, and water buffalo yogurts. *Natural:* Stonyfield, Brown Cow, Lifeway. *Specialty:* Fage, Woodstock Water Buffalo, Emmi.

Identifying Your Primary Markets

Sales of specialty foods tend to be concentrated in the more affluent market areas, both in the United States and abroad, because of their relatively high retail prices. There are about 40 primary U.S. trade areas of this type, and the majority of your prospective clients will fall within them (see figures 2.1 and 2.2).

Figure 2.1: Primary U.S. Specialty Food Markets

This map of primary U.S. specialty food markets provides a visual representation that will assist you in directing your marketing efforts. Note that entire states can be virtually ignored during your initial introductory efforts.

A variety of retail outlets have the potential to handle specialty food products. So-called "gourmet shops" are the most obvious, but there are also cheese shops, delicatessens, gift stores, and, in increasing numbers, supermarkets and department stores.

Supermarkets throughout the country are playing a stronger role in the specialty food trade than in the past. Their imported, ethnic, or specialty foods sections are often quite large and offer a diversified selection of items. Market research from Mintel/ACNielsen shows that, in 2007, sales of specialty food by retail channel were distributed as follows:

- Supermarkets: $21 billion (70%)
- Specialty Food Stores: $5.2 billion (19%)
- Natural Food Stores: $3.5 billion (12%)

Many independent chains in all major trading areas have taken on specialty foods. Over the past 25 years, some of the nation's largest supermarket chains, such as Safeway (including Vons), Kroger (including Ralphs, King Supers, QFC, City Market, Dillons, Gerbes, Owen's, JC, Smith's, and Fry's), and Giant Foods (now owned by Royal Ahold), have invested significantly in expanding their shelf space to carry specialty foods. Giant opened a separate specialty food store in Northern Virginia—called Someplace Special—which was eclipsed in 2006 by Sutton Place Gourmet (now Balducci's), Whole Foods Markets, and megastore Wegmans. Von's has a specialty food chain called Von's Pavilions. Each offers a mix of high-quality staples, "picture perfect" fresh produce, frozen foods, and specialty items. The industry is watching these ventures with an eye to adopting new directions in distributing specialty foods.

In 2006, there were approximately 34,000 traditional supermarkets, each with sales of over $2 million, offering a full line of groceries, meat, and produce. Of these, 75 percent were operated by a chain of supermarkets that owned 11 or more grocery stores. The rest were operated by independent owners with fewer than 11 grocery stores. In addition, approximately 13,000 small grocery stores with limited selections generated sales of under $2 million each. There are many more convenience stores than grocery stores, but they employ only a few workers per store. Many convenience stores are independently owned and are often franchises of convenience store chains.

Of the approximately 155,000 food stores in the United States, only 26,000 of them can be considered prime prospects for specialty food products. This figure results from careful, conservative paring down of the raw data presented in business directories. The total of prime prospects is composed of approximately 4,800 gourmet shops; 7,300 cheese shops and health food stores; 7,500 delicatessens; and 34,400 chain supermarket outlets, warehouse clubs, gift shops, and major department stores. In 2007, sales of specialty food at retail (all stores) amounted to more than $48 billion, of which specialty food retail stores accounted for more than $6 billion (25 percent more than in 2006).

It would be unlikely for you to reach all of these prime prospects without national distribution capability, either on your own or through a major specialty food distributor.

In view of the "upscale" nature of specialty food product lines, primary marketing targets can be identified by using weighted rankings of *The New Yorker* magazine's Selected Marketing System. It identifies and ranks markets for quality, premium-priced products rather than simply ranking markets by total population and income data.

RECIPE FOR SUCCESS

Owner Tanya Nueske of Nueske's Applewood Smoked Meats, in business for over 75 years, feels that true success is an elusive thing. "We keep learning and growing every day, focusing on doing the best we can in everything that comes at us. And interestingly . . . people notice and appreciate it and business comes your way."

She offers this advice to new to industry companies. "Invest the time and effort to dig deeply to honestly determine who it is you want to be and how that fits into the marketplace and the present economic conditions. The only thing worse than being too late . . . is being too early. Don't compromise your standards, culture, or quality."

Figure 2.2: Primary Trade Areas (in approximate order of primacy)

1. New York	14. Cleveland/Akron	27. Honolulu
2. Los Angeles	15. Minneapolis/St. Paul	28. Tampa/St. Petersburg
3. Chicago	16. San Diego	29. Hartford
4. San Francisco	17. Denver	30. New Orleans
5. Detroit	18. Baltimore	31. Sacramento
6. Washington, DC	19. Atlanta	32. Columbus
7. Philadelphia	20. Pittsburgh	33. Indianapolis
8. Houston	21. St. Louis	34. Oklahoma City
9. Boston	22. Milwaukee	35. San Antonio
10. Miami/Fort Lauderdale	23. Portland	36. Salt Lake City
11. Dallas/Fort	24. Kansas City	37. Charlotte
12. Seattle/Tacoma	25. Riverside/San Bernadino	38. Allentown/Bethlehem
13. Phoenix	26. Cincinnati	39. Buffalo
		40. West Palm Beach

The 40 primary trade areas listed in figure 2.2 are the most important U.S. markets for quality merchandise. About 20,000 of the 25,000 prime prospects are located in these areas. The listing is an accurate reflection of the trade in general. Although a strictly specialty food ranking would include all of those listed, the order in which they are listed would be somewhat different.

Market Segments

Our identification of geographic/demographic markets for specialty food represents one of the first elements of the marketing process. Matters of consumer preference, ethnic concentration, population movement, taste, and historical trends further segment these markets.

To illustrate, hot and spicy foods, once only available in the Southwest, have gained a strong foothold in almost every market. In southern California and Arizona, everybody eats outdoors where barbecue products reign. And it is difficult to introduce a new product to people in Florida and southern Arizona in the summer when specialty food business tends to fall off drastically.

An overall understanding of these differing market segments and varying distribution requirements will be helpful to you as you plan your marketing and distribution strategy. Please note that all references to dollar figures are mostly "poetry," in that specific numbers are difficult to obtain; hence, please view them as magnitudes and trends rather than as exact measurements.

Health and Natural Food Stores

The mounting importance of health food stores, such as Whole Foods, should be taken into account. Annual sales of natural and health food sales are more than $10 billion. Distribution channels for health foods vary. Some distributors carry only health food lines, while others only service the more upscale channels of distribution (e.g., fancy specialty food stores). This segment is one of the fastest growing, and there are profitable opportunities to be explored if your product meets its criteria (e.g., organic).

Organic Foods

Related to health and natural foods, yet much broader in scope, organic foods have become a huge fad because of their reported nutritional superiority. The challenge appears to be in meeting growing demand for a finite number of organically produced foods. Industry organizations report that annual retail sales of certified organic food and beverage products represent nearly $4 billion. Take note, though: consumers appear to be wary of paying the high price for organic. They also do not perceive much difference between organic and non-organic foods, and about a third of consumers are concerned about organic produce safety.

The Gift Trade

The gift trade is also playing a greater part in specialty food marketing, partly due to the widespread use of slotting fees in regular food distribution channels. There are more than 70,000 gift or gift-type stores in the country. This figure includes both upscale and standard outlets. As with health food stores, distribution channels can differ in that segment.

Food reps (brokers) who maintain a showroom, attend and exhibit at gift shows, and call extensively on retail accounts serve much of the gift trade. Such brokers are paid a 15 percent commission of the invoice value of all sales to retailers made in accordance with the broker contract.

> ## RECIPE FOR SUCCESS
>
> In business since 1996, Julie Jeremy of Kjalii Foods offers this advice: "To start a business today, you must believe in your product and be in it for the long haul. There is no fast money in this business."
>
> Kjalii's Native Spice Peanut Sauce is a finalist in the 2008 NASFT Sofi Awards.

Military Exchanges

If you can make the right connection, the Army and Air Force Exchange Service, the Navy Exchange, and the commissaries (military supermarkets) offer interesting possibilities for substantial sales. These stores serve the military families located in many parts of the world. Such families have many of the same needs and wants as do families in any of the major continental U.S. trade areas. I have seen a wide assortment of fancy and specialty foods available at these outlets.

Ethnic Foods

For our purposes, *ethnic foods* means retail and food service packaged food products that can be described generally as either Italian, Hispanic, kosher, Asian, or Greek. A variation of this is the so-called "fusion" style. A key fusion-style trend exists in Asian and pan-Asian foods, wherein one might encounter dishes made of combined food and flavor types from Thailand, Japan, China, Vietnam, and Indonesia. Asian and Hispanic foods drive the ethnic food market.

Italian-style foods continue to comprise one of the largest categories (nearly $12 billion), and Italian ingredients have become one of the basics of our everyday cuisine. Because of this, there is an enormous market for Italian foods. But is there room for another olive oil?

The United States is said to be the fifth-largest Spanish-speaking country in the world. Our Hispanic population exceeds 37 million and is the fastest growing consumer market. Annual Hispanic, particularly Mexican, food sales amount to more than $3.2 billion. The best products for growth will be staples advertised and promoted in Spanish by the major food producer/processors. Your opportunity will lie in the growing interest in Hispanic and Hispanic-style foods and cooking.

According to Mintel International Group, the kosher food market exceeds $100 billion, and it is expected to continue its 10 percent plus annual growth. The broad appeal of kosher foods beyond those mandated by Jewish dietary practice is based on the quality associated with such foods. More than 75 percent of kosher food consumers are non-Jewish. To be certified kosher, a food product must pass an exacting inspection by an authorized rabbinical agency.

American consumer interest in health and fitness has spurred growth of foods that are unprocessed and fresh. This includes a great number of Asian foods. The market for this category exceeds $62 billion at retail. Among the leading Asian food products are vegetables, sauces, and dry mixes. Increasing home use of stir-fry is also encouraging Asian food consumption. Today, once exotic foods such as ginger root, Asian vegetables, tempura sauce, and bean sprouts are readily available.

Greek foods, also referred to as "Mediterranean" cuisine, are growing in popularity because of their traditional reliance on freshness. Some examples include olives, olive oil, cheese, honey, dressings, and baked goods.

Your opportunity with the ethnic food category may be twofold: (1) produce and market traditional ethnic food products not otherwise available to consumers, and/or (2) market new ethnic-style products to both ethnic and nonethnic consumers.

Taking Advantage of Export Markets

The following quotation comes from a recent guide to commercial food production: "The last thing you should consider . . . is the potential for overseas marketing of your product."

That kind of thinking forms the basis of why the United States has failed so miserably in capturing profitable food-marketing opportunities overseas. Aside from the product-oriented nature of U.S. food marketing, this narrow-minded approach simply opens the door to foreign competition.

Instead of just looking in your own backyard, try instead to identify the world markets where your product would have the greatest comparative advantage. It may be that, indeed, your region in the States is the best place for you to start. There are, however, lots of reasons to consider nontraditional markets. Not the least of these is the weak dollar, which means American-made products are very competitive overseas. Additionally, there is a commonality in food marketing, regardless of the market.

Despite language and taste differences, you can profit from exploring markets abroad. Ask your State Department of Agriculture and the U.S. Foreign Agricultural Service for information about current promotional support. This includes trade shows and other overseas market development services.

Initially, your primary overseas markets will be the major trade areas in Canada, Europe, and Japan with potential in Latin America and the Middle East. (See the section on exporting in Chapter 6: Taking Your Product to Market.)

Going for the Big Win with Transition Products

Many specialty food producers are attracted to the idea that their product will capture the public imagination and sell like crazy. They envision the day when everyone will beat a path to their door demanding their product! When, and if, this happens (and it can happen), the product will reach a transition stage from up-market specialty food distribution to down-market grocery trade.

In some markets, your product will continue to be merchandised as a specialty item, while in others, it will be sold solely on grocery/supermarket shelves. Recent examples of transition products include Dave's Gourmet sauces, Jeff Foxworthy Jerky, and Tazo Teas among others.

Understanding Specialty Food Store Concerns

Your understanding of how your product is merchandised (placed before the consumer in the retail store) will influence the direction of all your marketing efforts. Figure 2.3 shows some of the classifications of specialty food stores. Having some knowledge of how a typical retail gourmet food store operates will enable you to work more effectively with your distributors, brokers, and store managers. Figure 2.4 illustrates the product mix an average store may carry.

Product selection will depend on store type and on a variety of demographic conditions. In the past, certain food products have been in higher demand in certain regions. If you were selling your version of a hot salsa, then you probably had better luck by introducing it to New England fancy food stores than to

Figure 2.3: Specialty Food Store Classifications

Type	Classification
Upscale Deli	Delicatessen foods and associated condiments
Specialty	Gourmet foods, sometimes with specific upscale product lines (e.g., coffee)
Cheese	All kinds of cheese and related items
Gift	Gift baskets
Housewares	Gourmet pots and pans and other cookware, with some impulse and companion food items
Department	Upscale with heavy emphasis on cookware and some confectionery (Demonstrations play a key role in cookware sales.)
General	Combination of all of the above, including some traditional staples

Figure 2.4: Product Mix in Typical Gourmet Store

Product Line	Approximate Percentage of Sales
Condiments	35%
Beverages (including bottled water)	5%
Coffee and Tea	5%
Cheese	5%
Pâtés and Meats	10%
Prepared Foods	20%
Confection	10%
Other	10%
Total	**100%**

those in the Southwest, where a "million" such products were well established in grocery distribution. Today, almost any food type is available in each of the 40 primary trade areas, though one still finds more tortillas in the Southwest than in other parts of the country.

As a rule, the manager of a small specialty food store works very long hours, in effect "marrying" the store. Many of the most successful retail specialty food enterprises are operated by families for obvious reasons. You may be interested in knowing how "average" managers spend their time:

8:00 AM–noon	Ordering/opening/training
	Food preparation
Noon–2:00 PM	Luncheon sales
2:00 PM–7:00 PM	General administration/baking
	Supplier meetings (this is you)

Your role is to operate for the convenience of the retailer, who, in turn, operates for the convenience of the consumer.

Your Role as Supplier

- **Become involved:** Get to know the particular challenges confronting each key retailer.
- **Educate the buyer:** Provide point-of-purchase materials. Arrange to spend some time with the sales staff.
- **Follow up on deliveries:** Determine if all went well.
- **Follow up on shortages:** Ascertain if merchandise is still needed and fill orders.
- **Develop seasonal guidelines:** Find out what works best and where.
- **Agree to minimum orders:** Be prepared to "break" cases.
- **Try to allow exclusivity:** Try not to sell same product to a competitor across the street.

Average Opening Costs for a 1,000-Square-Foot Store

Leasehold, Improvements	$59,000
Equipment	$45,000
Start-Up	$23,000
Inventory	$23,000
Total	$150,000

Understanding the Specialty Food Consumer

A good resource for learning more about the specialty food consumer is the National Association for the Specialty Food Trade (NASFT). Its 2008 report "The State of the Specialty Food Industry" provides useful demographics about the magnitude of and trends in the specialty food industry. NASFT also has gathered data from market research sources and combined some 20 specialty food brands into one list where it examines the demographics of consumers who purchased those products.

Topics about specialty food consumers covered in the research included the following. (As an example, I have appended results to each category that show the demographic segment most likely to purchase specialty foods.)

Demographic	Most Likely to Purchase
With whom they live	Two persons
How much they earn	$60,000–$75,999
How old they are	35–44
Their racial background	White
Age of children	No children
Home owners or renters	Owners
Level of formal education	College graduate
Where they live (U.S. Census division)	Pacific and South Atlantic

The report continues with an in-depth discussion of specialty food consumer lifestyles and provides data about the specialty cookie consumer, specialty tea consumer, and specialty chocolate consumer.

Chapter 3
Getting Ready to Market

Before you undertake a large production run for your product, you will want to understand start-up costs, consumer demand, and the market research. You will also learn how to position and produce your product. A description of warehousing, inventory, and shipping is included in this chapter as well.

Define Your Focus

Use the checklist in figure 3.1 to sharpen your focus before proceeding.

Determining Start-Up Costs

Here's an important piece of advice that is based on over 30 years of specialty food sales and marketing experience: you must have an independent source of income to start successfully your own specialty food marketing business! You should have sufficient capital available to cover all your costs for the first three to five years. This includes all normal living expenses.

Figure 3.1: Checklist to Refine Your Focus

What to Do	How to Do It
1. Identify your prospective customers (retailers, distributors, etc.).	Visit stores where like products are sold; attend food-related trade shows; contact NASFT and regional food trade associations; contact state associations/agencies.
2. Determine customer needs (distinguish between customer and consumer needs).	Consumers are the ultimate users of your product; they will determine the quality of your product. Retailers and distributors will determine the quality of your service. Each category has specific needs. Survey them to determine the quality characteristics of their specific needs.
3. Prepare a product in response to those needs.	Many of you most likely already have a product in mind. Make sure it conforms with your findings in #2 above.
4. Test the product (trade shows are good vehicles for this).	This is extremely important. Test for taste acceptance, label and packaging effect, etc. Make sure your product meets, or exceeds, your customers' needs.
5. Refine the product based on data from the tests (change flavor, size, container, labels, etc.).	There will *always* be room for improvement.
6. Return to #2 and repeat the cycle.	This process is the basis of what we call the PDCA cycle: Plan, Do, Check, and Act.

Your start-up costs will depend on your circumstances and on the type of product you plan to market. And even with such information, your specific start-up costs will be difficult to peg. As you will see in the following pages,

Table 3.1: Cost Elements of New Product Introduction by a Major Producer	
Element	**Percent of Costs**
Advertising and consumer promotion*	46
Trade deals and allowances	16
Market research and product development	18
Other	20

* This means mostly promotions, such as mailing, trade show exhibition, in-store tastings, etc.

Source: "Managing the Process of Introducing and Deleting Products in the Grocery and Drug Industry," Joint Industry Task Force, Grocery Manufacturers of America Inc.

our estimate ranges from $40,000 to $100,000 per year for the first three years. Start-up costs encompass production, packaging, warehousing, administration, and product advertising and promotion costs. The specific cost categories include those listed in the accompanying "Guidelines for Success."

If you will be using your own kitchen facility, you can save money until your production requirements outstrip your kitchen's capacity. After that, you will want to negotiate with a food packer/processor to have your product produced to meet the increased demand. The same goes for other overhead and administrative costs. You should take advantage of existing office space and equipment, and you might be able to use friends to help out part-time. The people referred to in Scenarios 2 and 3 at the beginning of this book had offices, production facilities, and administrative capability. They were also operating an existing business.

The data in table 3.1 can give you an idea of cost elements used by the major leaguers. They cover costs of obtaining nationwide grocery distribution of warehouse-sourced products, and they do not include costs of direct-store delivered items. Your cost percentages will be lower in advertising and consumer promotion, while higher by about 15 percent in the trade deals and allowances segment. In the end, trade advertising, promotion, and deals will constitute the major portion of your costs.

GUIDELINES FOR SUCCESS

Start-Up Cost Analysis

Use these guides to determine your start-up costs.

Item	Cost Savings Considerations	Monthly Cost Estimate
Postage	Almost all your mail will be first-class. If you plan to do a lot of mail-order selling, then ask the post office for information about postage-paid and bulk-mail privileges.	$100
Travel	You can reduce your travel costs by carefully planning your itinerary. Expect to make no more than four sales calls per day. Use a phone and e-mail whenever possible.	$800
Office Supplies	You will need a computer (Pentium IV) with a minimum of 320GB hard drive and 3 GB RAM; flat-screen monitor; word processing, spreadsheet, database and accounting, and account management software; color laser printer; forms; bond paper; file cabinets; etc.	$100
Promotion	Business cards, catalog sheets, price lists, neck tags, point-of-purchase materials (possibly). Prepare your own press releases (at first). Do not advertise to the consumer unless you do mail order. Consider using WEBPR.COM. Restrict trade ads to a complete— well-managed—promo campaign. Otherwise, save your money to make sales calls.	$60
Telephone	If you do any trade advertising, for example, the telephone company will require you to install a business, instead of personal, line. Toll-free numbers are being replaced by cellular phones. Of course, a cell phone is now de rigueur.	$100

Start-Up Cost Analysis *(continued)*

Item	Cost Savings Considerations	Monthly Cost Estimate
Fax	You will not require a dedicated fax line. Instead, purchase a scanner with fax capability.	$10
Utilities	Prorate your current utility cost (in your home) to cover that used by the business (if office is in-home).	$75
Website	Costs for developing a good website have come down significantly in the past decade.	$75
Rent	If your office will be in your home, take a percentage of your monthly mortgage equal to the space occupied by your office. That will be your monthly rent.	$900
Product Ingredients	Try to arrange minimum bulk shipments. Ask your supplier(s) to store the ingredients and to invoice you only when you draw down supply.	
Product Packaging	Find other companies that are producing a product in a container similar to yours. Try to realize economies of scale by ordering a large quantity and splitting the shipment between, or among, the other companies.	Product Dependent
Labels	Labeling by hand during your initial stage will save you money. It will also allow you to experiment with different labels without having to order 10,000 of one kind, only to find out they won't work. You will require the talents of a good graphic artist.	Product Dependent
Misc.	All the rest: figure about 10 percent of total costs.	Product Dependent

(continued)

Start-Up Cost Analysis *(continued)*

Notes to start-up cost analysis: These costs do not include labor, most of which will be borne by you. Other costs of production, including inventory management, site selection, and quality control, should be considered if you will be establishing your own production facility. Also, the office rent figure ($900 per month) can be deferred, since you will be paying yourself. The same goes for utilities.

The office supplies include initial purchase of a computer, word processing and related software, telephone answering machine (or voice messaging service, which is preferred), color laser printer, adding machine, etc. The conservative, annualized estimate is $3,600. You may be able to do better with used equipment or something other than top-of-the-line brands.

The grand total estimate, not including production (ingredients, packaging, labeling, and labor) or miscellaneous, comes to just over $32,400. This allows approximately $8,000 to $75,000 to cover the production element, bringing the estimated total requirement in the range of $25,000 and $100,000 for each of the first three years.

How Long Does It Take, and How Much Does It Cost?

Producers Respond

Sauces 'n Love founder Tessa Edick, 2004 winner for Mint Pesto, says her idea for this sauce grew from her garden overrun with mint. She became tired of pairing the bountiful mint with sweet things and tried it with basil instead. After a six-month rollout, it was introduced as an Easter alternative to mint jelly and was successfully launched. This product was introduced at the height of the pesto craze, and buyers needed little education to see its many applications.

A second version, Pink Pesto with tomatoes and cream, has taken a little longer to become as successful, and Tessa cites a greater investment of time to educate the consumer. Both rollouts cost the same.

Her advice: Follow your culinary dream and your gut instinct. All problems have solutions—find them. Innovative ideas change peoples' minds, and differentiation is key.

Internet sales: Sauces 'n Love has not experienced the helping hand of the Internet with regards to ordering, tracking, or sales, but it does allow customers to buy its products directly online. Brand awareness is up.

Producers Respond

Laxmi's Delights' gourmet cook, food writer, and entrepreneur Laxmi Hiremath started her business in 2001 and states her goal is to replicate what she learned in her mother's kitchen. Her product, Organic Flaxseed Spread with Dates and Orange Juice, was a NASFT finalist in 2007. She used her personal savings of $15,000 to start up.

Her advice: "It is a competitive market, and you will encounter frustrations. Only hard work and perseverance will keep you going. Never give up, stay on top, always take business classes to enhance your skills. Talk to other small business owners."

Producers Respond

Dave's Gourmet's hugely successful product line has brought acclaim from NASFT and other associations on numerous occasions. Owner David Hirschkop developed Insane Mary Bloody Mary Mix and rolled it out in a few months with an investment of less than $10,000.

RECIPE FOR SUCCESS

Caley & Cobb Fine Foods co-owner Polly Scholl states that her 11-year-old company is a small company with a determination to stay that way. It even managed to make a sale at its first show in San Francisco, even though the SUV was stolen with every bit of product. "After that, it was all uphill!"

Scholl defines success as industry recognition for superior products "and the satisfaction reorders from our retailers and responses from actual customers."

The NASFT award-winning soup, Asparagus Bisque with Lemon and Dill, took approximately $5,000 to develop and a few months of tastings.

His 2008 innovation is an Adjustable Hot Sauce. Dave describes it as "a mist/spray bottle that allows the consumer to change the heat level of the sauce by turning a dispenser cap either left or right. The sauce goes form slightly spicy to pretty darn hot."

In business since 1993, Dave offers this advice: success does "not have to take very long if you have the right idea and execute it really well. Put yourself in the consumer's shoes. Why would they buy your item over the competition or at all? Do tastings with impartial people. Most people make mediocre items with decent packaging, do average promotion, and wonder why business is not flooding in to them."

Researching the Market to Identify Consumer Demand

One of your first and most important forays into the marketplace will be to determine the strength of demand for your product. You will also want to see who else is marketing a similar product (the competition) and at what price, in what packaging, and with what sort of promotional support.

Weigh the following market research considerations and keep your findings in mind as you make your production, packaging, labeling, pricing, inventory, and shipping arrangements. Explore the issues of how the industry works and acquire a solid foundation of information about the following:

- Major participants
- Recent trends
- Prospects for a product such as yours
- Technical and production requirements
- Regulatory influence (food and drug laws)
- Competitive situation
- Industry advertising and promotion methods

GUIDELINES FOR SUCCESS

Market Research

What to Do	**How to Do It**
Define and analyze the specialty food industry.	Visit major specialty food industry trade shows, especially those sponsored by NASFT.
Identify industry participants: producers, distributors, brokers, retailers, and consumers.	Visit shows and review this guide. Gather information from NASFT.
Develop an overview of major trends. Understand current changes in consumer requirements for specialty foods, in general, and for the food category you have in mind, in particular.	Review industry trade journals (see appendix A).
Describe important suppliers, especially those with whom you will be competing. Understand the various sales, marketing, and distribution strategies they employ.	Visit food shows. Ask questions. Take notes.
Review the impact of technology on the entire marketing process, including production, packaging, and order processing. What are the technological implications for your application?	For example, will your ingredients require special machinery to process them? Will the package you have selected require special orders from high-tech packaging companies? Contact the Institute of Food Technologists, 525 W. Van Buren St., Suite 1000, Chicago, Illinois 60607; (312) 782-8424; *www.ift.org.*
Describe regulatory influence on the production, packaging, labeling, and marketing of your intended product.	Check your state's regulations and the FDA for sanitary certification. Check Title 21 of the Code of Federal Regulations (CFR) for labeling and ingredient statements. Most states prohibit the use of your own kitchen; a separate facility is required.

Be prepared to gather as much information and data as possible about the potential for your product. Do not underestimate the value of networking. A lot of specialty food producers and marketers will be happy to share their experiences and insights with you. If they can't answer your question, ask them for the names of three other participants who might be able to respond.

Developing Your Product

Marketing strategies will differ depending on whether your product is fresh, refrigerated, or frozen. Also, matters of shelf life—the time it takes for your product to deteriorate—will have to be considered. For example, chocolate products are traditionally sold and shipped during cooler seasons. Otherwise, the cost of shipping can escalate and place your chocolate product out of a competitive price range. A product with a short shelf life will have to move off the shelf faster. To ensure this happens may require a considerable promotional expenditure.

A comprehensive market profile appears in Appendix O. The profile discusses major specialty food product categories in terms of configuration, types, recent trends, size, market share, and other considerations. You will find it useful to review the category in which you hold an interest to become better informed about your prospects for success.

An ever-changing listing of upscale products rated with the highest growth potential appears in figure 3.2. The products with the least potential for growth are in figure 3.3. Those products with the greatest growth potential tend to be high-quality convenience foods. They are foods that are perceived, for the most part, as being healthy, or healthier than others, while offering the benefit of a special treat.

There are many exceptions to the above listings. For example, almost any food that claims it is organic is probably carving out a profitable niche. Other "hot" aspects include genetically modified organisms, soy, organic and natural foods, orange, smoky, and sweet potatoes. Also, even though alcoholic beverages appear to be on the wane, there has been a mushrooming of so-called microbreweries. Ommegang Brewery's Rare VOS Belgian-style beer is just one

Figure 3.2: Upscale Products with the Greatest Growth Potential

- Candy and snacks
- Refrigerated juices and functional beverages
- Milk
- Energy bars and gels
- Cold cereals
- Chips, pretzels
- Yogurt and kefir
- Frozen and refrigerated entrées
- Hot cereals
- Frozen fruits and veggies
- Frozen and refrigerated meats
- Entrées and mixes
- Refrigerated sauces, salsas, and dips

Here is a list of somewhat more interesting foods that are either a trend or a fad:

- Soy protein
- Prunes to dried plums
- Organic frozen meats
- Steak with bacterial analysis
- Organic beer
- Vitamin water
- Chicken sausage on a stick
- Chocolate with trace elements and vitamins
- Carrot- and potato-colored chips
- Winter tea
- Canned Hungarian goulash
- Cheese matured in earthenware jars with Tuscan wine
- Vintage olive oil
- Smoked salmon with black truffles
- Cooked, peeled chestnuts
- Apples suited to children's mouths and hands

Figure 3.3 Upscale Products with the Least Growth Potential

- Shelf-stable meats
- Teas
- Other dairy
- Frozen desserts
- Condiments
- Shelf-stable juices

such exception. The Stonewall Kitchen line of jams and preserves is another exception, in this case to the slower growing jams/jellies and preserves category, and Peace Works's Meditalia All Natural Pesto Sauces and Spreads also seem to be in high demand.

Positioning Your Product

The term *product positioning* covers the overall concept of how your product will be marketed. It includes pricing, packaging, labeling, and advertising and promotion considerations. For example, a Cajun-style food might be better positioned as a gift/souvenir when sold in New Orleans—to

> ## RECIPE FOR SUCCESS
>
> Sable & Rosenfeld President Myra Sable runs this extremely successful Canadian gourmet food company serving the retail, gift, and food service segments of the market. With 30 years in the business and products too numerous to list, Myra offers this advice: success has come by "working hard at keeping up with the trends, developing innovative and unique products, and strengthening brand identity." Sable & Rosenfeld stands behind its products 100 percent and works very closely with national sales and marketing managers to help retail customers with innovative promotional programs.

attract the attention of tourists—than as merely as a food product. Successful positioning has to do with your best assessment of what benefit you will be providing to your prospective consumer. How to appeal to this consumer is the point of product positioning.

There are many examples. Who knew that bottled water would make such a splash in the United States? Our tap water is supposed to be perfectly safe and wholly acceptable for all of our water needs. Then, in the 1970s, Source Perrier invested an estimated $3 million to position its bottled sparkling water as an alternative to tap water and, even more importantly, as an alternative to alcohol in bars and restaurants. Perrier is bottled in a unique container, imported from France, and commands a higher price than its competition. Yet it has developed a commanding lead in its market—all by effective product positioning. The point of positioning is to differentiate your product.

Everyone knows about the apple. Yes, it is healthy. Yes, it is inexpensive. Yes, it is available at every grocery in the nation. So if you have a new "apple," then you will have to differentiate it from the others. Doing this is called product positioning. Think hard about novel means of packaging and promoting it. Remember the "pet rock"? Read "Pliskin's Phables," which follows, for an effective and amusing description of product positioning.

Pliskin's Phables: How Positioning Began

With thanks to Mr. Pliskin.

In the beginning, the woman Eve was shopping in the Garden of Eden. As she was browsing through the fresh produce section, a serpent appeared unto her. "Psst, woman!" said the Serpent, "Try this."

"What is it, O Serpent?" asked Eve.

And the Serpent spake unto her, "It is a fruit, as yet unnamed. It grows on the tree of paradise, and it's mostly roughage, so it's good for what aileth you. And it's a product of nature: 85 percent water, vitamins A and C, calcium, thiamin, riboflavin, iron, and niacin."

"I've never heard of vitamins," said Eve, "and I don't aileth. I feel great."

"Try a bite. Just a bite," urged the Serpent, holding an apple before her. "It's just what you needeth."

"Who needeth anything that's good for them?" retorted Eve, as she headed for the heavenly hash ice cream.

"Curses!" spake the Serpent unto himself. "I was sure she'd fall for it." And he slithered away to thinketh. "I know I've got a great product here. Yea, verily, the projected sales figures are out of this world. Maybe my segmentation aileth. Maybe I barketh up the wrong tree. Hmmmeth. Hallelujah! The woman Eve is also a mother. Maybe this product is for kids!"

And so the Serpent hired unto him a $100,000-a-year copywriter. And this copywriter delivered unto the Serpent a terrific advertising slogan: "An apple a day keepeth the doctor away."

"Who needeth a doctor in paradise?" laughed Eve. "Besides my kids eateth only peanut butter and jelly."

"Double curses!" hissed the serpent, as he slithered off to thinketh again. He thought and he thought and he thought. And his thinking begat an idea. He decided to undertaketh giant systematic research.

First he spake unto consumers in Kansas City, Rochester, and Des Moines. And they spake unto him of their desires. Then he called in Yankelovich to checketh the demographics. And Yankelovich spake unto the truth of the Serpent's findings in a 16-volume report. Then he handed the word of Yankelovich over to a new-product consulting firm, and he awaited their suggestions. And those of the firm spake unto him of the target market and communications thereto, and the Serpent did as he was told. He painted the apple bright red. He polished it until it shone even as the sun. He garnished it with a stem and a little green leaf. And he saw that it was good. Then he placed it in the center of the fruit section and crawled off to waiteth.

The next day, the woman Eve came byeth pushing her shopping cart. The beautiful apple caught her eye, and she spake. "O Serpent," she asked, "What's this?"

And the Serpent knew great joy, and he spake unto her, "It's something new. It's a tempting dessert. It's a little sinful, and all natural, and very, very indulgent, and loweth in calories, and it's called 'Fatal Apple.' You probably can't afford it."

"Sayeth who?" snapped Eve. "I'll take a bushel." And lo, the Serpent and Eve begat positioning, which dwelleth among us, even unto this day.

Carving Out Your Share of Market

Market share is the percentage of a given market that a food producer is said to control. For example, XYZ Tea Company may claim a 75 percent share of the market for "imported retail packaged British tea." This means that of all the retail packaged British Tea sold in the United States, 75 percent is sold by XYZ Tea Company.

It will be unlikely for you to start out as the product leader in your category; therefore, you should think seriously about not being number two, but rather, becoming a market niche competitor. This is precisely why the specialty food industry works. Why is this? The leading seller of mustard, for example, may have a 30 percent share of the total mustard market, with a 10 percent net profit margin.

You, on the other hand, could carve out a 1 to 2 percent share of the mustard market, with a 20 percent net profit margin. The idea is to focus on overall profitability rather than beating the product leader in the market-share race.

Market share is generally of little consequence to the entry-level food entrepreneur; however, you should know that major food processors seem to "allow" small companies about 1 percent share of a given market before launching a competitive campaign.

General Foods, for example, claimed a 38 percent share of the estimated $440 million specialty coffee market. If your new specialty-coffee roasting business can sell up to $4 million per year, then you can expect some attention from General Foods. Otherwise, you will face most of your competition from other coffee roasters looking for a niche.

Actually, if you can sell $4 million of roasted coffee, then you might want to consider a "buyout" by a larger company. It is one way to make a lot of money.

Tapping into Consumer Attitudes

Purchases of specialty foods have grown to more than $48 billion per year because of consumer demand for quality. Specialty foods represent affordable luxury. Even in recessions, purchases of many fancy foods tend to remain constant.

In the late 1970s, the United States experienced a consumer backlash to mediocrity. Notably, people had begun to take an interest in products with natural ingredients, no preservatives, and no artificial coloring. Purchases of fancy foods were based on considerations of quality and health.

The consumer backlash occasioned the remarkable growth of fine foods throughout the 1980s and 1990s. All of a sudden, everyone knew about brie. As more products were introduced and new entrées proliferated, consumers developed a preference for particular product brands or makes. In the specialty food industry, the concept of brand preference was just becoming a factor in understanding consumer behavior. There is still plenty of room for experimentation, and fortunately for new entrepreneurs, consumers appear disposed to continue in that vein.

With the exception of a handful of transition products, very few specialty food brand preferences have emerged. Those brands that are requested by name include Heublein's Grey Poupon mustard, Celestial Seasonings herbal beverages, Godiva chocolates, Ben & Jerry's ice cream, high-end natural cheeses, sports drinks (Traxx and Sqwincher are two), bottled waters (Earth Water is one), and many more.

The specialty food retail business thrives on appealing to the senses. This makes for considerable impulse buying. Some of the most successful products are those sold in retail outlets, where shopping can be an exciting adventure. There, consumers are surrounded by new aromas and different tastes from sampled products. Products with eye-catching displays and packaging further enhance this experience.

Once consumers become familiar with a specific product, they will experiment with other products from the same line. For example, one company's strawberry preserve will be tried. If it is liked, consumers will feel more disposed to try other types of preserves offered by the same company. Other producers' products will be tried only if the preferred brand is unavailable; if the company does not have a blueberry preserve, then consumers may try one from another firm.

Finally, consumer attitudes toward specialty foods are influenced by what appears to be exclusive, new, and different. Products offering something unique will attract consumer interest. As long as consumers want newer and better foods, there will be continuing growth potential for new products.

Specialty foods that make the transition often fail in the mass market and are eliminated by the chains. In turn, the eliminated lines, once the bulwark of gourmet food outlets, attempt to regain their foothold in those outlets, causing even further fallout in this widely over-assorted industry.

Consider olive oil, which is merchandised in too many versions by too many supermarkets. The specialty food market, acting like a contracting accordion, has insufficient room to accommodate these and many other competing products.

Meeting the Competition

With whom will you compete? Aside from every other food producer, you will find your direct competition from others with similar products. Competition from other makers of condiments, for example, will occur when the consumer chooses their product instead of yours.

You will be competing for shelf space, too. There is a finite amount of shelving and a growing number of products for the retailer to select. Fortunately, there is a lot of product movement. Product life cycles end, and products move to larger, down-market (grocery) distribution. As this occurs, specialty food stores demand products that will replace those that moved to supermarket shelves.

Consumer attitudes toward specialty foods are influenced by that which is exclusive, new, and different. You will be competing for the "scarce dollar." Consumers must want to spend more for your fancy sauce instead of a less-expensive, grocery-grade catsup. Consumers have differing perceptions of different products. Many decisions are impulsive—they like the packaging, for example. Choices as to how to spend limited discretionary income are difficult to make. Products that impart the most "sizzle" will attract the most scarce dollars (see figure 3.4).

In *The Business Planning Guide,* David Bangs considers the following questions in analyzing competition:

- Who are your five major competitors?
- How is their business—steady, increasing, or decreasing?
- How are their products similar and dissimilar to yours?
- What have you learned about their operation?
- How will your product be better than theirs?

A Word about "Green"

"Green" is a new option. It impacts everything you do, and it can be a sale maker or deal breaker. It involves many aspects of how you manage your business,

Figure 3.4: "Sizzle" Considerations for Your Product

- **Packaging:** Upscale (green)

- **Labeling:** Upscale, refined (green)

- **Ingredients:** The best (green)

- **Size:** Appropriate (no giant or economy size; green)

- **Price:** On the high side (due to cost of production)

- **Shape:** Upscale but practical (green)

including packaging, recycling, energy conservation, fuel conversion, and environmentally friendliness.

High Volume/Low Margin versus Low Volume/High Margin

A margin is the amount of money (profit) charged above the actual cost of the product. The specialty food trade consists of products that are characterized by low sales volumes and high profit margins. Profit percentages are higher in the specialty food industry than they are in the grocery industry.

The specialty food retailer will normally take a 40 to 50 percent profit margin, whereas the grocery store/supermarket uses markups of 3 to 20 percent on most staple groceries. In some cases, supermarkets will use 20 to 40 percent profit markups for certain fast-turnover items, such as bottled water, delicatessen products, and other products requiring service personnel. The reasoning behind this difference in profits is twofold:

1. Industry tradition suggests that specialty food marketers determine their profits by computing them as a percentage of product sales, rather than adding a percentage to product cost.

2. Product turnover. Retailers need to achieve a targeted contribution (sales × margins) from space used. The specialty food retailer is likely to move

ten jars of fancy preserves in a day. By comparison, the grocer may move several dozen jars of jam in the same period; therefore, because it costs more to carry the fancy preserves, the specialty food retailer must sell the product at a higher profit margin. A further explanation of the difference between *markups* and *margins* appears in chapter 4 under the heading "Pricing Your Product."

Producing Your Product

Because this is a marketing guide, little attempt is made to tell you how to produce your product. Your options are to produce it yourself—in an approved facility—or have it either copacked or licensed to some other food production company. However, some attention is devoted to product selection, packaging, and labeling, and you are encouraged to contact the NASFT for its listing of companies (copackers) that can package and help you produce your product. (See Appendix D.)

The food industry is notoriously product driven. You must make a clear connection between your product development efforts on the one hand and the market and consumer demand on the other. Just because you are convinced that your new product will take over the market is no assurance of success. You must keep listening to your customers to exceed their expectations.

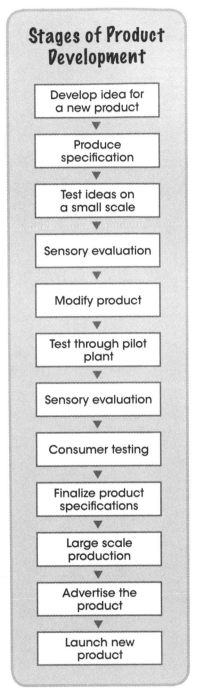

Stages of Product Development

- Develop idea for a new product
- Produce specification
- Test ideas on a small scale
- Sensory evaluation
- Modify product
- Test through pilot plant
- Sensory evaluation
- Consumer testing
- Finalize product specifications
- Large scale production
- Advertise the product
- Launch new product

GUIDELINES FOR SUCCESS

Product Development

With thanks to Daniel Best, technical director, Prepared Foods *magazine*

Network.
Contact others in the supplier community. Also, contact independent labs, universities, and reputable freelance product developers.

Know your customer.
Be "market oriented" rather than "product oriented." Region, ethnicity, and eating occasion can all affect perceptions of quality. Don't equate your taste preferences with those of your customers.

Identify product traits.
Begin by defining all consumer-relevant product features in advance of development. Engineer the desirable attributes into the product (packaging, color, flavor, etc.), rather than defining product attributes after product design. Consumer-test to determine how closely product variables match consumer needs and perception. Refine to reflect consumer reaction.

Manage your resources.
You must manage by focus and flexibility. New products require time, labor, and capital. Investing in highly specialized processing systems closely married to a single product or product line is risky and expensive. Think long-term. Apply processing systems that will be applicable beyond the immediate project requirements. However, by spreading your labor resources over a wide range of product development, you minimize the risk of generating both failures and superstars.

Maintain product quality.
A long series of minute cost reductions will not reduce perceptions of quality in consumer testing. But the end result will be compounded, and the overall quality of the product will suffer.

Product Development *(continued)*

Control your costs.	If your costs come in too high, then re-examine the basic factors. Are your ingredients priced too high, and are lower-cost sources available? Are alternative processing methods available? Can you find other market segments on which to capitalize and consequently increase volume projections? Was the projected price for the product too low?
Commit for the long term.	Failure to commit can result in constantly changing signals and erratic funding. Focus on your strategic objectives and tenaciously commit to their long-term achievement. However, know when to cut your losses and pursue alternatives.
Pay heed to the time factor.	Timing is critical. Too soon, and your product may not be ready. Too late, and someone else will be in the market with the same product.
Balance tactics and strategy.	Do not mistake tactics for strategy. Excessive focus on tactics can leave you struggling to find strategies to fit. Tactics are the processes employed to achieve your objectives. Your objectives are your marketing and financial goals. Strategies combine tactics to achieve objectives.
Manage by confrontation.	Risk avoidance can become the path of least resistance when there is no freedom to fail. In your case, management by avoidance will stop you dead in your tracks. You simply cannot avoid making the complex and success-threatening decisions associated with specialty food marketing.

Contract Packaging

Copackers are food processing companies that either have excess packing capacity or are specifically devoted to packing other people's products. Their capabilities vary, and some can only package dry, nonperishable products.

You may want to seek assistance in formulating and packing your product. See the comments that follow and check with industry sources in your state, especially your state's business development agency, for assistance.

The complexities of moving a product from conception to market can be overwhelming even to experienced entrepreneurs. Developing networking relationships with reliable copackers permits the small businessperson to achieve maximum utilization of physical and financial resources—and save time. Working with copackers allows the business owner to call the shots while drawing on various team members to perform, when needed, on a fee-for-service basis.

Copacking Drawbacks

Watch out for large run requirements (perhaps several thousand), where you may outstrip your assets through the preparation of the packages. Also beware of "true" versus "fake" copacking, where your label ends up on their salsa, for example. Check the integrity of the copacker.

When you approach copackers, be prepared to present your product and your needs clearly and concisely. You will be received best if you deal efficiently without wasting their time or yours. Be open in discussing your needs and their costs.

Copacker Services

The major areas of copacker operation include basic product development services, food processing services, and food packaging services. Each is described below (with thanks to John Darack, formerly with the Dirigo Spice Corporation, now Newly Weds Food).

Basic Product Development Services. These are often available from ingredient suppliers, such as seasoning manufacturers. Such service providers perform an important function by helping you convert at-home or menu recipes to a manufacturable form. Then dry ingredients and, often, several wet ingredients, such as fresh vegetables, liquid sauces, condiments, meats, fats, and so forth, can be formulated into one specialized ingredient package. The resulting product can either be sold as an easy prep-as-is item or sent to a processor to be converted into a canned or jarred finished product.

Using basic product development services brings several benefits:

- **Quality control:** The blender guarantees that agreed-upon specifications for the product will be met.

- **Inventory control:** Only one item needs to be tracked, rather than several.

- **Recipe protection:** The blender signs a contract in which your recipe is kept confidential. Finished-product producers know only to add the simple liquids to a preweighed unit of ingredients.

- **Uniformity of finished product:** All ingredients are preweighed and batched. Opportunities for errors in production are eliminated.

- **Price stabilization and purchasing power:** The blender has the ability to purchase in large quantities from reliable and established sources. Cost averaging and unitized pricing eliminate being at the mercy of market fluctuations. You will know your costs over longer periods.

- **Networking:** You will be plugged in to an existing array of related services, such as analytical laboratories, packagers, processors, marketers, and distributors, which may not be otherwise available to the public.

Food Processing Services. After having your recipe converted into manufacturable form, you can bring your ingredient package and conversion recipe to a food processor. Be prepared to discuss the preparation of your finished product to your specifications. Liquid ingredients, process parameters, packaging, labeling, shelf-life testing, and possibly even distribution are topics you should address.

Be ready to deal with some practical limitations, such as larger or smaller batch proportions, limited sizes or shapes of containers, production scheduling, and availability of ingredients (seasonally or otherwise).

Find the best fit—don't go to a large producer for small-batch production. Conversely, be sure the processor has the capacity to accommodate your growth.

Food Packaging Services. If yours is a dry product, find a packaging company that has the right equipment to make your ideal package. As with a processor, the right fit must be found. Some companies specialize only in contract packaging.

Opportunities may also be found at plants that package products in materials similar to yours and would like to utilize downtime profitably. Good deals can be made here.

Copacker Benefits

Successful copacking can provide you with significant benefits and cost savings, including the following:

- **Elimination of capital costs:** You have no plant to build or equipment to purchase.

- **Utilization of well-seasoned experts:** Solving problems that overwhelm you are a part of their daily routine.

- **Compliance:** Undergo the amazingly complex process of meeting federal, state, and local regulations.

- **Product uniformity**

- **Purchasing power**

- **Networking**

- **Technical services:** These are often provided at cost or at low cost.

- **Marketing assistance**

- **Distribution**

A Word about Licensing

Many food entrepreneurs do not want to get actively involved in the production and marketing of their product. They think that since their idea alone has merit, they can find a big food producer to whom they can license the formula and technology for their new product. Once again, this is an example of the product-oriented nature of the food industry. Not much attempt is made to find out what the customer needs.

There is very little to protect your formulation. If the big company sees your product as competitive, it will either copy (clone) it or make you an offer. Often, such offers are in the form of licensing or copacking agreements. If you are fortunate enough to receive such an offer, consult your attorney for advice about the nature of such contracts.

Food Safety and Sanitation Requirements

The U.S. Food, Drug, and Cosmetic Act is very specific as to sanitation requirements. You should ask the Food and Drug Administration to provide you with a copy of the current Good Manufacturing Practice Regulations. These regulations set forth the requirements for establishing and maintaining sanitary conditions.

Food and Drug Administration regulations are contained in the Code of Federal Regulations. You can review these online at *www.fda.gov/cdrh/aboutcfr. html*. There are nine volumes of Title 21, but only chapters 1 through 3 will apply to you. They cover general regulations, color regulations, food standards, good manufacturing practices, and food additives, among other subjects.

In addition to federal regulations, each state has special requirements for inspecting and certifying food-producing facilities. If your initial production effort will occur in your own kitchen facility (separate from your home kitchen), then have it inspected and certified by your local food-regulating agency.

Product Liability

Many distributors will ask you to provide them with a current certificate of product liability insurance coverage. They will request that the certificate name them as an additional insured, to be included under "Broad Form Vendor's" coverage.

GUIDELINES FOR SUCCESS

Government Regulations

Process	Responsible Agency
Business Organization	State and local departments of economic affairs. Application depends on the type of organization (corporation, proprietorship, etc.) you elect.
Production	State health agencies. Sanitary certification, inspection laws.
Labeling	U.S. Food and Drug Administration. U.S. Customs (if you are marketing an imported product). Title 21 of U.S. Code of Federal Regulations includes the labeling laws.
Labor	Internal Revenue Service and state and local revenue agencies. Payment of FICA, withholding tax, and workers' compensation.
Tax	Internal Revenue Service and state and local revenue agencies for quarterly and annual income tax payments and procedures.
Distribution	Some states require registration of certain products before they can be sold in that state.

Be prepared to pay a hefty premium. Lately, when courts in the United States have found in favor of plaintiffs, they have awarded sums that have exceeded existing levels of defendants' liability coverage. As a result, coverage can be difficult to find and expensive to maintain.

If you are setting up your own manufacturing facility, you will have to pay for workers' compensation insurance. To attract the employees you want to hire, you will probably also have to offer some sort of group medical insurance. Check with your insurance agent for guidance about the types of insurance coverage best suited to your operation.

Warehousing and Shipping Your Product

Public Warehouses

These are companies that provide storage and warehouse services. Some offer cooled and refrigerated environments. They charge either flat rates by the month or rates based on product stored, as well as in-and-out charges, charges for preparing shipping documents (bills of lading), charges for repacking damaged or broken products (coopering), and other related services. If you require public warehousing, you should shop around to find the best combination of location, services, and costs.

Many warehouses will take your orders over the telephone and ship according to your instructions. This is where a fax machine can come in handy.

Storage and warehousing will be an important factor in determining your ex-warehouse costs (ownership is transferred from seller to buyer at exit of seller's warehouse).

Common Carriers

Common carriers are trucking companies other than the United Parcel Service (UPS), Federal Express (FedEx) Ground, DHL, and Parcel Post that offer pickup and delivery service. You will have to use common carriers for shipping large orders. UPS, FedEx, and DHL will take any size order, but no one container may weigh over 150 pounds (70 pounds for home delivery). You can save money sometimes by delivering large orders in two or more shipments. Note that most common carrier charges are based on a minimum shipment rate of 500 pounds.

Your customer may request that you ship via a certain carrier. Most common carriers offer discount rates that are based on total shipment weight. UPS, FedEx, and DHL rates are based on the gross weight per case. Gross weight includes the product, outer carton, and shipping materials.

Rates are keyed to hundredweight, or per CWT (cost per hundred pounds). For example, if the quote is $4 CWT, you will pay $0.04 per pound. Ask your warehouse to find the least expensive and most reliable carrier to fill your requirements.

GUIDELINES FOR SUCCESS

Warehousing and Shipping

Establish warehouse arrangements. Shop around for the best deal. A nonunion warehouse offers greater leeway to remove samples, take inventory, etc. and is less expensive than union or "covered" warehouses.

Product Workflow

- **Inbound:** Your product is shipped from your production facility, or pier, to the public warehouse.

- **Stocked:** It is inventoried and stocked in the warehouse.

- **Paperwork/records:** You will receive (can be via e-mail) a monthly inventory statement and invoice for services provided, preparation of bills of lading (the shipping documents), storage, etc.

- **Select a carrier:** You may request the warehouse to select a common carrier to ship your products to your customers. If you have frequent shipments, you can also arrange for a carrier to make daily calls on the warehouse to pick up and deliver the shipments to your customer.

- **Take inventory:** Once a quarter, or more frequently, you should personally supervise a physical inventory in the warehouse. This gives you a good inventory figure to use in preparing your accounts and in controlling your business, and it helps resolve any issues of missing or damaged merchandise.

If your production facility and warehouse are in your home, then you may have trouble working with a common carrier. It will be pleased to pick up and deliver your product, but you will have to arrange for the sometimes difficult process of working without a standard loading dock. Getting the product from your basement or kitchen out the front door and onto the truck can be a trial.

GUIDELINES FOR SUCCESS

Warehouse Selection Flowchart

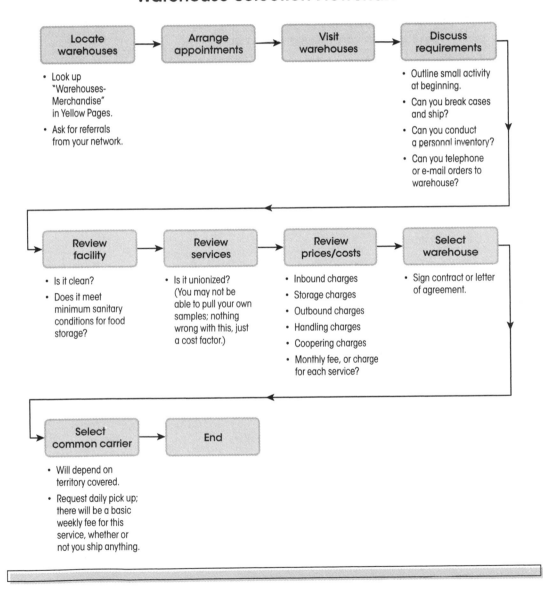

Locate warehouses
- Look up "Warehouses-Merchandise" in Yellow Pages.
- Ask for referrals from your network.

Arrange appointments

Visit warehouses

Discuss requirements
- Outline small activity at beginning.
- Can you break cases and ship?
- Can you conduct a personal inventory?
- Can you telephone or e-mail orders to warehouse?

Review facility
- Is it clean?
- Does it meet minimum sanitary conditions for food storage?

Review services
- Is it unionized? (You may not be able to pull your own samples; nothing wrong with this, just a cost factor.)

Review prices/costs
- Inbound charges
- Storage charges
- Outbound charges
- Handling charges
- Coopering charges
- Monthly fee, or charge for each service?

Select warehouse
- Sign contract or letter of agreement.

Select common carrier
- Will depend on territory covered.
- Request daily pick up; there will be a basic weekly fee for this service, whether or not you ship anything.

End

Private Pickup and Delivery Services

Call your local UPS, FedEx, or DHL office and request an information kit (or request one online). The shipping company will set up an account for you. It may require you to remit a deposit against which charges for shipping will be made. Generally, shipping companies charge a weekly fee for making daily calls at your pickup point. Shipments are charged by the pound, based on destination, and redelivery, next-day, second-day air, and COD services are offered. You can arrange for the shipment online and print complete shipping documents. Most carriers can also advise the shipper via e-mail when the shipment arrives at its destination

Chapter 4
Product Packaging, Labeling, and Pricing

To put the strongest foot forward in the market, it is important to be well versed in the issues of packaging, labeling, and pricing your product.

Packaging Your Product

Packaging is the single most important element in the consumer's decision to purchase a new specialty food product. Attractive packaging type and design are paramount to success in the specialty food trade. Nonetheless, appealing packaging is just one factor that prompts people to try new products. Other factors include the following:

- Coupons
- Price
- Reputation (the brand name is accepted widely)
- Convenience
- Newness
- Recipes included
- Influence of advertising
- Recyclable packaging

Ultimately, the purchasing decision is rarely based solely on packaging (except for gifts) but on a combination of the above factors.

Types of Packaging

The packaging you select will depend on the product. For example, different merchandising is required for bulk fancy foods, such as snacks and confections; however, if you have alternative packaging types to consider, then you should be aware of the impact some packages have over others. Witness the shape of the Perrier bottle. Packaging encompasses consumer perceptions, as well as practical considerations. Consider also the pyramid shaped tea "bag" now offered by a number of specialty tea providers. This is an example of great packaging, great product, and out-of-the-box thinking.

Glass containers are used because the product can be seen and there is no tin taste, whereas canned (tinned) products are generally restricted to soups, pâtés, caviar, and most loose teas. Most consumers tend to prefer products in jars rather than cans despite a can's practicality. Also, cans are slowly being overtaken by a new technology called *aseptic packaging*. This type of packaging is widely used by fruit juice producers, but it can be used wherever a carton, plastic cup, or metal can might be required. These include fruit juices, coffee creamers, puddings, and yogurt. Aseptic packaging saves shelf space and is less expensive to transport because it weighs less than other types of packaging. You may find using this a challenge because of the equipment costs, but its use is growing, and the market for aseptic packaging has exceeded $3 billion.

> ### Cost-Saving Hints
>
> Negotiate small initial production runs. Your unit costs might be higher, but you won't be saddled with a slow-moving inventory of thousands of units. Limit initial production costs by using readily available stock items.

Some of the fanciest packaging available is also the most expensive. At first, you will probably have minimal production runs, so you will not want to purchase thousands of empty jars, boxes, or other containers. The objective is to limit your initial costs, regardless of the economies of scale associated with large volume purchases. There is little point in ordering a thousand jars and a thousand labels if you are not sure of selling a thousand units of your product.

Packaging types for specialty food products are many and varied. You can select from among readily obtainable containers made of cardboard, plastic, wood, cellophane, glass, and metal. Try to find a good-looking and reasonably priced container. Try not to pack your product in an oddly shaped container. As a rule, your product must be able to fit and stack on standard store shelves. It is wise to start with stock items (such as jars and lids) rather than design special molds, etc.

RECIPE FOR SUCCESS

The King's Cupboard is a company started by a husband-and-wife team who are molecular biologists in Red Lodge, Montana. They loved Montana and wanted to start a business so they could stay there. The company produces very high-end chocolate sauces that retail for around $8.

In business for eight years and winner of six NASFT Outstanding Product Awards, The King's Cupboard became successful at the four-year mark.

Competitors' Packaging

It will serve your purpose to review products now on the shelves of specialty food stores. It stands to reason that, generally, you should package your product in a container type that is similar to those on the shelves. This comes under the heading of "you can't knock success."

It does not mean that your creative urges should be constrained, just that the consequent costs and requirements for educating consumers about your unique package may not be worth the expense.

Elements of Great Packaging

Aside from clearly conveying its contents, great packaging will cause your product to stand out from the others. It will command consumer attention and create interest in the product.

Visit several of your local gourmet food stores and attend the next Fancy Food Show to see examples of great packaging. The Fancy Food Show has a special display called "What's New, What's Hot!" It offers you the opportunity to see hundreds of new products, gift products, and food service products away from the producer's show booth. And it will provide you with a terrific chance to compare differing packaging styles.

Packaging for Warehouse Clubs

A growing market for specialty foods is the warehouse or club store (e.g., Costco and Sam's Club). They like to have the product delivered from truck to the shelf location all in one step. They don't require slotting fees (see "Arranging the Deals" in chapter 6). They do require, however, that you package your product either in large, nearly institutional-size containers or that you bind your products together into a two-, three-, or six-pack package. These outlets often invite local producers/vendors to display and sell their products, often on Saturdays. This is an option worth exploring.

Packaging Considerations

In selecting the container and the means of packaging, review government regulations that may apply. For example, the state of California has required that honey be sold in 8-ounce and 16-ounce containers. Any other size is viewed as potentially misleading to consumers.

Most big cities have glass suppliers, and it is worthwhile to visit their showrooms, obtain their catalogs, and try your product in sample containers before making any final decision.

Increasing use of tamper-resistant seals suggests that you should consider employing such a device on your product's container. Also, if you want to add a consumer information neck tag to help educate the specialty food consumer about the benefits of your product, then this should be planned before you make your final packaging decision.

If you plan to sell to supermarkets, consider such elements as supermarket shelf depth and height. If your product is packaged in a container that exceeds the shelf height, then it will be placed on the top shelf, out of direct eye range. This applies to the number of facings that can be accommodated. If the product is too wide, it will take up more than one facing per product, possibly limiting the amount of space that the store will authorize for your product or product line.

Outer Containers

The outer container is the shipping container. The most common outer container is a strong cardboard carton capable of holding one dozen units of your product. Because you will be making use of such pickup and delivery services as United Parcel Service (UPS), make certain that the outer container can withstand the rather substantial punishment shipments often encounter. A master pack capable of withstanding a 200-pound test with a size of 18 inches square will fit nicely on a pallet, for example, and make for easy and cost-effective shipping.

Retailers are asking for products in smaller outer packages. Generally, one dozen products per outer package will suffice; however, if you can break down the pack into two packs of six, for example, you will find retailers more willing to try your product. Also, your suppliers can provide glass jars in 12-pack cartons that you can reuse once the jars have been filled. Often these outer packs can be put into master cartons containing 2-by-12 by units (1 master carton with 2 inner cartons of 12 jars each) or 4-by-6 units (master carton with 4 inner cartons of 6 jars each).

You may want to purchase mailing containers that can be used for individual direct sales and for shipping samples to prospective buyers. These can be sold to retailers when your product has a gift potential, allowing the consumer to have the retailer mail it to the gift recipient.

> ## Size Points
>
> **Cost:** Select the best size for your budget.
>
> **Selling price:** The cost to consumer can influence container size selected.
>
> **Usage (repeat sales):** A 16-ounce jar may move once a month, whereas an 8-ounce jar may move three or more times in the same month.
>
> **Shipping containers:** These should hold no more than one dozen units.

GUIDELINES FOR SUCCESS

Packaging

- Describe the packaging type used by your competition (jar, can, plastic container, etc.).

- Describe your anticipated product package type (should be similar to that of the competition).

- Is the proposed package a stock item, or does it require a special order? (Check with suppliers.)

- What is the minimum order for stock item (supplier requirements)?

- What is the minimum production run for a special order (supplier requirements)?

- Is special handling required (e.g., cardboard to be lithographed or sticker labeled)?

- Are special shipping containers required (box, glass, etc.)?

- Are copackers available to package for you? (See Appendix D.)

- Does your package design conform to federal and local regulations? (Again as an example, honey in California cannot be put into 12-ounce jars; you need to use 8- or 16-ounce jars.)

- Is your package size consistent with consumer demand? (Price will have an impact.)

- Does the outer container hold no more than one dozen (unofficial industry standard) of your product?

Other packaging considerations include the use of corrugated cartons, bubble wrap, filler materials, and associated equipment such as wrapping tape and tape guns. Almost any manufacturer or copacker will be able to provide you with the name of a packing materials supplier.

Labeling Your Product

All labels must conform to government regulations. Even so, you will have a wide choice. Remember, your label is a crucial element in attracting consumers. It must convey the nature of your product, as well as the sense of affordable luxury.

At first, you should consider some type of pressure-sensitive adhesive label that can be designed and printed in small batches. Compare the costs of applying labels by hand and by machine. After you get the product up and running, you can have your labels printed in quantity. As with packaging, the color and style of your label will be important in attracting consumers.

Avoid the "supermarket look" with its reliance on bold lettering and lots of primary colors. The same company that packs your product can help you have it labeled. Otherwise, you can hire labor to hand-label the product until your volume warrants automated labeling.

Uniform Product Code (Bar Codes)

This is an optic-readable symbol that can be affixed to your product label. The UPC symbol allows use of automated checkout machines and conforms more readily to other products on the shelves. As items are presented to the checker, they are passed over an optical scanner that decodes the UPC symbol and transmits this information to a computer. The computer stores price and other information on all items carried in the store. It transmits back to the check stand the item's price and description, which are then displayed to the customer and printed on the customer receipt.

The UPC code is made up of 12 numbers called the Global Trade Item Number (GTIN). The code consists of a manufacturer identification number and an item code number. The last digit is a scanner-readable check digit. UPC codes are now generally required by all distributors, as food producers and distributors recognize the increasing influence of large grocery chains in specialty food distribution. These chains almost universally require UPC coding to save costs at checkout.

If you anticipate ever having your product on a supermarket shelf, it is less expensive and more efficient to have your initial label carry the UPC. In this manner, you will save labor by not having to affix it separately. UPC bar code software is available to assist you. Information regarding UPC allocation may be obtained from the Uniform Product Code Council, now called GS1 United States (see Appendix N).

FDA Labeling Requirements

Aside from your desire to impart ingredient information to the consumer, the U.S. Food and Drug Administration enforces label ingredient legislation. The laws require that

RECIPE FOR SUCCESS

Virgil's Root Beer was named Outstanding Beverage (English-style root beer). The firm was purchased by Original Beverage Company, where Principal Chris Reed, a friend of Virgil's Root Beer founder Ed Crowle, bought the company when Ed passed away. Chris is a big fan of ginger ale, a healthy beverage. Chris began by brewing ginger ale in his bathroom, putting trial bottles of various ginger ales in his refrigerator with lots of Post-It® notes. The company reports that it is the number-one ginger ale at Trader Joe's upscale grocery chain.

ingredients be displayed clearly and in accordance with regulations. A net weight statement is also required. In this connection, the American Technology Pre-eminence Act, which amends the Fair Packaging and Labeling Act, will require all packaging and labeling to use metric measurements of net quantity. The use of ounces and pounds will become optional. The law is very specific about the nutritional claims that can be made for any food product. Claims as to health, purity, low sodium, and the like must be made in precise accordance with the law, which specifies what wording is permitted and what wording is proscribed.

The FDA promulgated new labeling regulations in 1990 (Public Law 101-535), which require practically every food to have nutritional labeling. Regulations as to cholesterol content and serving sizes have also been issued.

Finally, there is some confusion as to which laws take precedence when federal and state requirements differ. It will be necessary for you to check Title 21 of the Code of Federal Regulations available online at *www.accessdata.fda.gov* (or from the Superintendent of Documents, Government Printing Office,

732 N. Capitol St. NW, Washington, DC 20001) to determine the requirements as they pertain to your ingredient statements.

Labeling Considerations

One of your greater setbacks can occur when you recognize that your beautiful labels might be "ruined" by the label requirements. You must have a net weight statement in the lower third of the principal display panel, for example. If you know of this requirement beforehand, then you can save time and money by designing your original labels to allow for the legal statements. There are many ways of retaining your artistic statement while complying with the law. Your labels should have eye appeal and be informative and legal. Remember that one of the key elements of a specialty food product is its presentation.

Labels offer more than practical and aesthetic forms of expression. They should convey your sales message. Consider including usage instructions, cooking directions, recipe tips, and the like.

The Nutritional Labeling and Education Act

Exceptions to the requirement for nutritional labeling include coffee, tea, and spices; containers too small to carry a nutritional label; and producers whose total annual revenues (food and nonfood) are less than $500,000. The Nutritional Labeling and Education Act (NLEA) of 1990 took effect in May 1994. A total workup on a single sample to determine compliance with the NLEA by a food laboratory can cost more than $600. For more information, see *www.fda.gov/ora/inspect_ref/default.htm.*

There are regulations governing the physical aspects of labeling as well. Certain information has to be placed on certain parts of the label, and the lettering size has to be in specific relation to the overall size of the label, or "principal display panel."

What if you goof? The Food and Drug Administration will not officially approve your label; however, your local compliance branch will provide comment on the manner in which the label does not conform to regulations. If you sell the product with incorrect labeling, expect the FDA to enforce the law at the store level, possibly causing the product to be removed from the store shelves.

GUIDELINES FOR SUCCESS

Product Labeling

- Will you do the labeling yourself?

- Can labeling be completed by a contract labeler?

- Can your initial label be produced in a limited quantity?

- Does your label conform to local and federal regulations (Code of Federal Regulations, Title 21)?

- Will your label contain a nutritional statement? (Not required if total annual sales will be under $500,000 or less than $50,000 of gross annual food sales will be to consumers.)

- Is your label consistent with that of an upscale product? Does it impart a sense of high quality?

- Does your label stand out from your competition? Or is it the same old, same old?

- Does your label give history of company, recipe tips, or other selling information?

- Describe how your label attracts consumer interest.

The front label (or principal display panel) is used for a different purpose than the side and rear labels. The front is the "tickler" that attracts consumer attention. The label immediately to the right of the principal display panel is used for the ingredients statement. The rear or left label may include a nutritional statement and additional messages regarding product use, such as those mentioned in the Guidelines for Success, or convey a message about other elements of your product.

Pricing Your Product

Rather than concentrating on beating the product leader for market share, I suggest positioning your product in a market niche with a goal of 1 to 2 percent market share and a 10 percent net profit margin. In striving for this goal, you should use margins instead of markups (cost plus profit). When using margins, profit is calculated on selling price. The specialty food industry uses margins instead of markups to develop prices. The following examples will illustrate the difference.

Markup

The unit cost of your peppercorn breadsticks is $1.00. If you use a 40 percent markup, your selling price is $1.40. To determine your selling price, multiply the $1.00 by 140 percent.

$$\$1.00 \times 1.4 = \$1.40$$

Margin

The unit cost of your peppercorn breadsticks is $1.00, and you decide to use a 40 percent gross profit margin. Your selling price will be $1.67. To determine your selling price, subtract $0.40 from $1.00 and divide the $1.00 cost by $.60.

$$\$1.00 - \$0.40 = \$0.60; \$1.00 \div \$0.60 = \$1.67$$

Using markup versus margin results in the different selling prices of $1.40 and $1.67, respectively. The markup is cost plus profit, whereas the margin is calculated on selling price less profit. Another example: Your honey mustard cost is $1.63. A 40 percent markup = $2.28 selling price. A 40 percent margin = $2.72 selling price.

Cost Accounting

This involves computing all your costs, then adding your profit and the profit margins taken by distributors and retailers to reach a consumer price (see figure 4.1).

Ingredients	**Cost of Contents of Your Product**
Packaging	Cost of outer package, the reinforced cardboard carton
Production	Labor and materials used in getting the ingredients into the containers
Containers	The jars, boxes, or cans used to hold your product
Labels	Design, artwork, electronic preparation, printing, and affixing costs
Selling	Cost of making sales calls
Promotion	Special events, trade shows, and in-store demonstrations
Advertising	Sales literature, trade journals, and related media costs
Administration	Cost of running your office (e.g., legal, accounting, etc.)
Overhead	Regular costs of running the business that you will incur whether or not anything is produced or sold (e.g., rent, utilities, upkeep, and taxes)
Draw	Your salary. Divide your annual gross salary requirements by 260 (average number of workdays per year) to get a realistic assessment of your daily pay. Divide that by 8 to get an hourly figure. Even though you probably will not take a draw, knowing this amount will be helpful in your breakeven analysis.

Figure 4.1: Selected Cost Factors

No matter what your costs, if your price to the consumer is greater than that of the competition, you will face substantial consumer resistance. For this reason, I recommend starting at your competitor's price and working backwards through the various profit margins to your product costs (unless you have that "one-in-a-million" product for which the world has been waiting; in that case, demand will be considered "elastic," and you will have more leeway).

You may use either a cost-plus or market-set pricing method. The former begins from the bottom up, while the latter works backwards from the consumer price to your product cost. My recommendation is to use the latter.

First, establish a consumer price (use your competitor's price as a reference). That will enable you to determine your gross profit after the retailer and distributor margins are deducted. Then determine if your costs and profit margin yield a price significantly different from that of your competition. Your strategic thinking can be assisted by applying a breakeven analysis, which will help you determine the price range available for your product. A breakeven analysis will let you know at what point your dollar or unit sales will meet your total dollar or unit costs. Any revenue generated above the breakeven point is profit—below it is loss.

Delivered Price versus Ex-warehouse Cost

Depending on the circumstances, some transactions will require that you include freight charges in your pricing for a "delivered price." Others will allow you to ship freight collect, or with the freight charges added to the invoice.

Ex-warehouse cost is the cost of the product (plus freight-in if you are importing) plus the cost of storage and handling. Your ex-warehouse cost plus profit margin yields your price to the retailer (see figure 4.2). In these examples, we will use a gross profit margin of 40 percent, which is consistent with profit margins used by many food processors. In our examples, prices do not include freight, and they are called FOB (Free On Board). Freight will be "collect," or added to your invoice to be paid by the buyer.

Figure 4.2 shows a pricing flow example, from consumer price back through retailer, through the distributor, and your ex-warehouse cost.

Your gross profit margin will include administration costs and sales and marketing costs (broker commissions, promotion, reserve for bad debts, advertising, and the like). Your gross profit margin will have to cover all of these costs. You should aim for a net profit of at least 10 percent. (See the suggested pricing formulas below.)

Figure 4.2: Pricing Flow Example		
Price to consumer		$6.25
Less 40%	×	0.60
Equals cost to retailer		$3.75
Price to retailer		$3.75
Less 25%	×	0.75
Equals cost to distributor		$2.81
Price to distributor		$2.81
Less 20%	×	0.80
Equals your ex-warehouse cost		$2.25

Customary broker commissions for sales direct to retailer = 10% ($0.38 in the above example). For sales to a distributor, the commission = 5% ($0.14 in the above example). You will use the same price to the retailer, regardless of whether you sell to a distributor. Sales to retailers will entail less volume, but you will make more in profit (40% gross profit before broker commission).

Suggested Pricing Formula for Sales to Distributors

Formula:

$$D = E \div (100\% - P)$$

where

D = Price to distributor

E = Ex-warehouse cost per unit

P = Gross profit margin

Example:

E = $2.25 (product cost of $2.20 plus $0.05 for storage and handling)

P = 20%

$$D = \$2.25 \div (100\% - 20\%)$$
$$D = \$2.25 \div 0.80$$
$$D = \$2.81 \text{ per unit}$$

Your gross profit would be \$0.56 (\$2.81 less \$2.25) for a 20 percent profit margin. Broker commission is 5 percent (\$0.14) and will be deducted from the profit margin.

Most retailers in the specialty food industry work on at least a 40 percent margin. They divide the cost to them from the distributor (or from you for a direct sale) by 60 percent (0.60) to arrive at the price to the consumer. In this example, the cost per unit to the consumer is \$2.81 ÷ 0.60 = \$4.68.

Suggested Pricing Formula for Sales to Retailers

Formula:

$$R = E \div (100\% - P)$$

where
R = Price to retailer
E = Ex-warehouse cost per unit
P = Gross profit margin

Example:

$E = \$2.25$ (product cost of \$2.20 plus \$0.05 for storage and handling)
$P = 40\%$
$R = \$2.25 \div (100\% - 40\%)$
$R = \$2.25 \div 0.60$
$R = \$3.75$ per unit

Your gross profit would be \$1.50 (\$3.75 less \$2.25) for a 40 percent profit margin. This is before broker commission (10%). In this example, the price to the consumer will be \$6.25: retailer price of \$3.75 ÷ 0.60 = \$6.25.

GUIDELINES FOR SUCCESS

Price Flow Worksheet

	Competitor's Product	Your Product
1. Price to consumer	$_____	$_____
2. Less 40% (retailer profit margin)	× 60%	× 60%
3. Equals cost to retailer	$_____	$_____
4. Price to retailer (same as Step 3)	$_____	$_____
5. Less 25% (distributor profit margin)	× 75%	× 75%
6. Equals cost to distributor	$_____	$_____
7. Price to distributor (same as Step 6)	$_____	$_____
8. Less 20% (your profit margin)	× 80%	× 80%
9. Equals ex-warehouse cost	$_____	$_____

Broker Commissions

Your gross profit margin should include, right from the beginning, the broker commission percentage. This will range from 5 to 15 percent, depending on the type of broker used. Brokers who sell to chain stores, independent wholesalers, and distributors will require a 5 percent commission. Sales via brokers to department stores, retailers, and gift shops will be commissioned at 10 percent. Brokers who have their own showrooms and who call on retail gift and food stores will require a 15 percent commission. A good policy is not to pay any commission to any broker until the referring order has been paid.

Distributor Margins

The distributor will add a profit margin to your distributor price, usually a minimum of 25 percent (divide the distributor cost by 75), to arrive at the distributor's price to the retailer.

Bear in mind the concept of price points, or thresholds, beyond which it would be imprudent to price your product. These price points are found usually just under the two, three, four, five, and up to ten-dollar figures. If your price is $4.09, for example, you may want to consider lowering it to $3.99 or $3.95 to overcome buyer objections.

The margins and discounts in the above examples are representative of specialty food trade margins and discounts. There are many variations on these, depending on the product, market, season, and so forth.

You should prepare two separate price sheets, one for the retailer and one for the distributor.

Key Question

How do the ex-warehouse costs compare?

You may find that the resulting consumer price of $6.25 in the "Sales to Retailers" example is competitive for your eight-ounce jar of cooking sauce. But if you are selling a one-ounce packet of dill dip mix, then the product will be above the price point for its category, and you will probably encounter stiff consumer resistance.

Breakeven Analysis

Applying a breakeven analysis to help determine the price range available for your product can assist some of your strategic thinking. A breakeven analysis will let you know at what point your dollar or unit sales will meet your total dollar or unit costs. Any revenue generated above the breakeven point is profit—below it is loss.

Detailed discussions of breakeven analyses appear in almost all of the business management books on the market. David Bangs's *The Business Planning Guide* is the source of the following explanation on the topic:

The breakeven point can be calculated by the following formula:

$$S = FC + VC$$

where

S = Breakeven level of sales in dollars

FC = Fixed costs in dollars

VC = Variable costs in dollars

Fixed costs remain constant regardless of sales volume (at least until your sales volume grows so much as to require capital improvements, such as new buildings, etc.). They are the costs that must be met even if you make no sales. Fixed costs include overhead (rent, administration, salaries, taxes, benefits, etc.) and depreciation, amortization, and interest.

Variable costs are connected to sales volume. They include cost of goods sold (beginning inventory plus freight-in, warehousing, variable labor, broker commissions, etc. less ending inventory).

To calculate the breakeven point in the absence of your total variable costs, use the following variation:

$$S = FC/GM$$

where

FC = Fixed costs in dollars

GM = Gross margin (profit) expressed as a percentage of sales and determined by adding gross sales to total costs (variable and fixed) and dividing the resulting total by gross sales.

Replace the dollar figures with unit figures if you want to determine the breakeven point in units produced instead of dollars earned.

Sample Breakeven Analysis

Total sales (TS):	$216,000
Cost of goods sold:	$158,320
Gross margin (GM):	$57,680

$GM\% = GM \div TS$

$GM\% = \$57,680 \div \$216,000$

$GM\% = 26.7\%$

Fixed costs (FC):	$60,570

Breakeven sales (S) = $FC \div GM\%$

$S = \$60,570 \div 0.267$

$S = \$226,854$ per year, or $18,905 per month

Understanding Payment Terms

Terms are the arrangements for shipping and payment that you establish with your customer. Include your terms on your price lists. An important element of your statement of terms is the establishment of a clear credit policy, from which you should try not to deviate. Among the forms of such a policy are the following:

- **Terms of payment.** Either FOB your warehouse, or delivered, with entire invoice amount due in 30 days.

- **Early payment discount.** Offer either a 1 or 2 percent discount for payment made within ten days.

- **Line of credit.** Inquire into customer's credit references to determine just how much you should allow. Consider withholding shipment if there is an open invoice, or no more than two open invoices within the credit limit.

- **FOB (free on board).** FOB warehouse, or delivered, establishes who pays the freight, and when title passes to the customer. If your terms are FOB, your warehouse, then the customer pays the freight and takes title to the merchandise when it leaves your warehouse. This means that the customer will be responsible for taking up the issue of any damaged or missing cases with the shipping company. He/she cannot deduct the missing or lost merchandise from your invoice.

  If your terms are FOB customer location, or prepaid, then you must seek recourse with the shipping company in the event that merchandise is missing on delivery or is damaged en route. Title passes to the customer when merchandise is delivered, signed for, and in good condition.

- **Suggested terms.** To distributors and large-volume purchasers: COD (cash on delivery) or credit card, until credit is approved, then 2%/10 days, net 30 days, delivered. (This means that the purchaser may deduct 2 percent from the net invoice amount if paid in full within 10 days. Otherwise, the total is due within 30 days.)

> ## Invoicing Hints
>
> Do not print up thousands of invoice forms! In fact, with the use of a computer, you can generate a different invoice each time you make a sale. Use your invoices as sales tools. From time to time, add a special deal on your invoices to retailers. Many of the retail buyers are also the payers. Offer them a special "reorder deal" that they can send in with their payments, with the deal to be billed later.

When selling to retailers use COD or credit card until credit is approved, then Net 30 days, FOB warehouse.

Include the comment: "Prices subject to change without notice," on price lists and invoices.

Credit

Your ability to assess effectively your buyers' integrity will influence the procedures you undertake to evaluate "credit worthiness." Do not become overly impressed by buyers from high visibility/high prestige outlets. Rarely do these companies pay according to your terms.

The process. Request prospective buyers to provide you with three trade references and one bank reference, or simply ask for payment via credit card. Ask for contact names and telephone numbers because some references will release this type of credit information over the telephone, and this will save time. You can expect that the credit-checking process will take about three to four weeks, which is why I recommend asking for credit card payment.

In the specialty food industry, most credit arrangements consist of the following, though credit card use is on the increase:

- **Open account.** This means that you are satisfied with the credit worthiness of your customer, and that you ship on receipt of orders on your usual terms, wherein payment is due at the end of the 30-day period.

Note that the specialty food industry tends to interpret payment terms of net 30 days, for example, as starting on the day the merchandise is received, rather than on the date of the invoice, or ship date.

- **COD.** Cash on delivery is generally used with first-time customers, until their credit is approved. COD terms may also be used on request by some small retailers who prefer it to the requirements for accounts payable bookkeeping. Note that you are not entirely protected with COD because the buyer can always refuse receipt of the shipment. You request the trucking company to collect a specified amount, usually the FOB invoice amount, plus freight, plus any special COD charges. This procedure will work only if you use specialized delivery services, such as U.S. Postal Service, United Parcel Service, Federal Express, etc.

- **Pro forma.** Used for prepayment. You prepare a standard invoice covering all costs agreed to (e.g., product and freight) and type on the front of the invoice the word "pro forma." Send the pro forma invoice to your customer, and ship product on receipt of payment. Pro forma invoices are rarely used for domestic shipments (and then only in circumstances in which credit cannot be established, or customer refuses COD). They are employed generally in those cases where buyer access to funds requires supporting papers, such as certificates of origin, etc.

- **Guarantees.** The only guarantee you will make will be against defects. If damage occurs during shipping, the buyer is usually called upon to pursue a claim with the freight company; however, it will be in your best interest to assist by offering to replace the damaged merchandise. Otherwise, some buyers will withhold payment of your invoice until the freight claim is resolved.

Chapter 5
The Role of the Internet

Internet sales of specialty foods have grown dramatically over the past five years. This chapter outlines what you need to do to capture your share of Internet sales.

The Role of the Internet

The global linkage offered by the Internet is driving everything in our economy. Some reports suggest that annual Internet grocery sales total more than $40 billion and at least 85 percent of consumers made an online purchase (including food) in 2007. The rules of economic intercourse are changing. What effect will this have on specialty food distribution? Will there be a continuing role for the broker, or will these middlemen become redundant? How will you respond to issues of business-to-business services, marketer-retailer partnerships, fulfillment operations, cybershopping, direct marketing techniques, electronic customer challenges, new online food trends, Web page design, customer retention challenges, and developing key alliances? It may be time to review your long-term vision. What if your dream included the ability to market your products direct to consumers?

These are just some of the opportunities confronting specialty food marketers who wish to take advantage of the Internet. The following pages address some of the more important issues associated with doing so.

A Website

You can create your own website by using page-creating software provided by online services. You do not have to be technically adept—though it helps. A basic working knowledge of computers will suffice.

The real concern is the effect your homepage has on attracting customers. Since the cost of preparing a simple page is minimal—your time and talent plus the access time charged by the online service—you might as well give it a try. However, given the increasing level of Internet homepage competition, a more sophisticated and complex website may be required. In this case, you would do well to retain the services of a professional Web page designer (see Appendix I).

Issues of privacy have been mostly resolved—how to protect your customers' use of a credit card, for example—and more consumers are researching and buying products online. A special thank you to SnapMonkey.com President Rita Wilhelm for providing the following information on websites.

How Much Should a Website Cost?

Websites can be anything you want them to be. There are many options, depending on your budget and your goals. You can hire a website developer to create a site for you; you can choose to create your own site and code it yourself; you can use open source technology; you can build your own website with easy-to-use templates, such as the ones found on SnapMonkey.com; or you can buy off-the-shelf software, such as Dreamweaver. Plan on budgeting $500–$10,000 or more, depending on the complexity of your site.

Goals for Your Webite

Your website is an integral part of your marketing campaign. Educating new and existing clients about your products and services is one of the primary functions of a website.

You can include sections such as "New" or "Featured Products." By adding a shopping cart to your website, you can transform your business into a 24/7 operation that makes it convenient for customers to do business with you. Your site should be a working product that changes and grows with you.

RECIPE FOR SUCCESS

As a business owner, it is imperative for your business to have an Internet presence. The Kelsey Group found that 70 percent of people do research online before buying a product or service. If you cannot be found by your target audience, you don't exist.

Website Design

Make your site a part of your image. Use your logo, your colors, your theme, and your images that make your business yours. A good design is set up in a professional manner and helps move the customer toward the ultimate goal—a purchase from you! You want to make sure that visitors immediately know what your site is about when they land on it. They should not have to read through too much text. Be concise and make sure you have a clear call to action.

Navigation

Good navigation is essential to a good website. Make it easy for your customers to move through your website and give them easy directions on how to get to the next step. A good site always provides customers with essential pages to motivate them to a purchase and always provides them with a way to get back to the homepage.

Clarity

Your homepage must be clear and to the point. Resist the temptation to put everything on your front page. Instead, stick with a couple of solid key facts and then lead your viewer through your site to gather information. Evaluate your site from your customer's point of view. Better yet, have your clients tell you what they think of your site. Listen to what they say—they are the users.

Content

Find ways to put rich and informative information on your site. Put product information, specifications, and instructions online. Information rules on the Internet.

Internet Marketing

Marketing online is the same as having your own storefront. The amount of traffic you receive depends on what you do to market your website. Share your Web address with everyone and include it on your business cards, brochures, product labels, and other marketing materials.

You also want to make sure that your website can be found in the search engines. As a businessperson, you would like to see your website show up high in search engine results for your kind of product. A search engine such as Google has over 100 factors that impact search engine ranking. Although we don't know everything about Google's secret algorithm, we know a few things for sure.

Google can only bring up your website as a search result if it knows what your site is about. Google needs clues. You can give Google these clues by using key phrases in your website and then optimizing pages in your website to your key words and phrases (or very similar key phrases). Make sure that these key words and phrases are also set up in your "meta tags," lines of code that describe what your site is about. Google ranks websites higher if the site is regularly updated. Google loves content. Content rules. Google will also rank your site higher in search results if other relevant quality sites link to you.

Social Networking

Another great way to drive traffic to your website is to participate in online social networking sites. According to iProspect.com, one in three Internet users is taking advantage of social networking sites to help decide whether to buy something or not. Social networking sites offer a great platform for people to share their experiences about products and services, to learn about potential opportunities for improvement, and to learn about new ways of doing things. A JupiterResearch report shows that 30 percent of frequent social networkers trust their peers' opinions when making a major purchase decision, but only 10 percent trust an advertisement.

There are many different types of online social networks. There are private groups with restricted membership and open groups that anyone can join. There are mom groups and dad groups. There are support groups. There are online business networking groups, industry networking groups, and volunteer communities. There are travel groups and hobby groups. Some social networking sites involve product or service reviews, while others allow members just to share their favorite bookmarks. Some online social networks are forums, while others are blog communities.

So which community do you pick? Find a group that you enjoy being a part of and one that makes sense to join. Take a moment to think about your ideal client. What does that ideal client look like? Where might that person go for information? What does your client do for fun? Also, consider where your referral sources go for information.

Once you have identified several groups that would be of benefit to you, first take some time to observe the community, the rules of the community, and the overall culture. In most groups, it's best to participate by being supportive and helpful. In most communities, it is *not* appropriate to advertise your business blatantly. Help a community member with your expertise and then use a short signature after your post, which may include your name, your website, and a short byline. This builds trust while, at the same time, allows you to show off your expertise (in a personable and professional way) on a particular subject. As with most any networking organization, one must participate in it to benefit from it. So find a group, observe the group, and if it feels right, participate in the group. It could bring new clients to you.

Email

Email marketing is the fastest growing form of marketing today. Unfortunately, it is also one of the most abused because if its ease and low cost. Your clients will gladly accept your emails if they benefit from them. When you get their email addresses, let them know you will be sending them periodic sales and information announcements. Do not abuse that trust.

Newsletters

As a transition from email, you can create an online newsletter. Determine your purpose first: Why are you sending a newsletter? What customer need will be met by your newsletter? Let your clients know why you are sending them the newsletter and stick with your original purpose. Always have opt-in/opt-out options on each newsletter, allowing your clients to remove themselves easily from your newsletter database. And then stay in contact with them! Give them what they want—useful information and sales promotions that help them grow their businesses!

Promote Your Site

Here are five tips to get your site in front of your target customer:

1. **Promote your site everywhere.** Include it in all of your brochures, ads, letterhead, business cards, voice mail messages, and order forms and invoices.

2. **Give customers a reason to visit your site.** Provide them with information. Information is what sells on the Internet. When people move from site to site, they are in search of someone who can help them answer their questions in ways that may never have occurred to them. Provide them with the information, and the sale will follow.

3. **Use your site to increase business.** There are only three ways to increase business: increase the number of customers, increase the initial order of each client, or increase the number of times each client purchases from you. Include ways in your website to accomplish each of these. Create "Refer a Friend" links from your popular pages. Create packages that include several of your top sellers and offer your clients a discount if they buy the packages instead of items one at a time. Generate recurring orders through programs similar to "fruit-of-the-month" programs. The key make getting the sale easy through your site.

4. **Create an email campaign.** Collect email addresses from every client. Gather email addresses from people who inquire about your products. Then send out email promotions regularly. Make sure you have direct links back to the products you promote and verify the links before you send the email. Put short deadlines on your offers; email is an instant function—make your clients take action quickly.

5. **Keep your website current.** This is the number-one turnoff of surfers. Changing your site shows its importance in your business structure. It tells potential clients you value their business and you want to provide them with the most up-to-date information. And by changing your website often, you can promote current events. Your site will become a relied-upon resource that many people look at and refer to. Provide the date each time you change your website and place the current year at the base of your homepage.

What Should I Do with My Website?

Begin by creating a site that contains information. Think about what content would benefit your client the most. Add your company background and history. Add directions, maps, office hours, contact names, and best ways of getting in touch with you. Include instructions and guidelines on using your product or service. Add articles, resource pages, and frequently asked questions (FAQ) pages.

When your site is complete and offers your clients the information they need, begin thinking of your site as a sales representative. What could be better than a sales rep who works for you 24/7 every day of the year? Put together a product catalog and include each of your products online with photographs, key descriptions, and customer testimonials. Then move clients from the description to a shopping cart, where they can confirm their purchases with just a few simple clicks.

Create an online community. How can you bring your clients together online and share ideas about your product and the way they can benefit from using your company? Use a message board to supply advice about happenings in the specialty food market and then lead discussions on current topics, especially as they may pertain to your product category (energy beverages foods, for example). This is a great reason for people to return to your site again and again.

Web Hosting Services

There is a huge variety of Website hosting services. For example, the "100 Best Web Hosting" website—*www.100best-web-hosting.com/top100/1.html*—lists 143 worldwide Web hosting services by rank, host name, and reviewer comments.

A website is just like any other marketing material you use in your business. For it to be effective, you must use it. A clever site entices people to return again and again. As with your brochures and advertisements, your site should be created to attract your target audience. Find out why people are visiting your site and give them as much of what they want as you can. One of the best things about a website is its ease of use and flexibility. Add daily tips, weekly specials, and monthly promotions on your front page. Keep building and keep trying. Give people what they are looking for!

Think about getting together with your state's business development or specialty foods group. Use the Internet to set up a combined sourcing site for supplies. You and your fellow marketers could take advantage of the economies of scale such larger orders offer.

The Internet and Cybershopping

Home shopping via the Internet will dramatically increase in this century. As specialty food marketers increasingly sell their products straight to consumers via the Internet, this will affect new product introductions. The large companies, of course, can't do the same. Their size makes it difficult for them to adopt an adaptive and flexible approach to quickly changing market conditions. What they do, instead, is find ways to convince those cybershoppers to go to the supermarket via samples, coupons, and refunds for debuting products.

Cybershopping has a long way to go before bricks-and-mortar stores become obsolete. Tech-savvy consumers are becoming aware of such sites but are wary that what might have been a private transaction at a local specialty food store is now part of a statistical abstract held in these companies' databases. With this practice, called "user profiling," the site owner attempts to collect information about the buyer's interests, habits, frequency of use, etc. The resulting profile aids the supplier in matching its products and services with the perceived consumer wants and needs.

Of all the factors influencing the specialty foods market, cybershopping has the most to gain and lose. As consumers become more comfortable with using the Internet to make purchases, there will be a greater likelihood that distribution patterns will change.

Table 5.1 shows the remarkable growth in the number of food-related websites since 2000. How does one get seen among so many? Take the Google search engine, for example. How realistic is it to expect that anyone would wade through 69,940,000 sites? Research reports that most viewers only look at the top 20 or so listings before either selecting one or leaving. A number of consulting organizations develop Web pages and know how to include words that give their clients top billing on these pages (see Appendix I).

| Table 5.1: Number of Food-Related Websites in 2008 Compared with 2004 and 2000 | | | | | | |

Search Engine	Number of Specialty Food Sites			Number of Gourmet Food Sites		
	2000	2004	2008	2000	2004	2008
Google	N/A	4,100,000	3,040,000	N/A	4,600,000	66,900,000
Yahoo	20	6,820,000	121,000,000	2,400	5,360,000	183,000,000
MSN	N/A	1,448,827	40,000,000	N/A	1,119,538	55,600,000
AOL/ Netscape	N/A	1,411,593/ 833	286,000	N/A	1,116,964/ 782	3,870,000
Alta Vista	71,134	3,245,904	No total	263,925	2,565,854	No Total
About	N/A	8,917	No total	N/A	233	No total
Ask	N/A	210	1,188,000	N/A	212	3,870,000
Web Crawler	38,577	1,540	86	110,957	2,680	81
Northern Light	498,826	N/A	3882	251,016	N/A	85

Blogging for Gourmet and Specialty Food Companies

The following is a commentary from specialty food industry colleague Ryan Montague whose firm, Gourmet Business Solutions LLC, provides extensive business and Web development services. Learn more by going to *www.gourmet businesssolutions.com.*

Everyone these days has a blog, or has at least thought about setting up one; however, for some reason, many gourmet and specialty food companies do not have a blog. This is amazing, given the many benefits of a blog. Blogging is nothing new, is easy to do, and it can help a small gourmet food company.

Blogging does not have to be expensive. In fact, it can be done for free. Some paid options can set up a really nice, custom, branded blog

GUIDELINES FOR SUCCESS

Use Your Website as Great Marketing Tool

By Rita Wilhelm, SnapMonkey.com

How do most of your clients find you? Is it by word of mouth or maybe some advertising media? Whatever means they use to find you, adding a website can have a huge impact on your sales. For example, a gift basket business is unique in the sense that your customers never really see the end product. What they receive is the goodwill of the recipient and an appreciative telephone call. So think about that. Naturally, your potential customers want make the best buying decision, and a website will help educate them as to their choices.

Visual information is a key component. Most of you probably distribute brochures for this purpose. And although a brochure can be an effective educational tool, potential customers will not always have one at their disposal when they are ready to make a purchase. A website, however, is easily accessible and affords your customer a leisurely opportunity to get an idea of your business' offerings and learn about the quality and type of service you provide. This, in turn, will help you become more efficient and save time on telephone orders.

Using Your Website Effectively

For your website to yield its potential, you must promote it. The goal is to broadcast your website address in every possible venue so that your existing and future clients will begin to recognize it, use it, and pass it on. A website address is simple to remember and makes it easier for your clients to share your wonderful service with the people around them. Word of mouth is always great in any business. The following suggestions will help you promote your website.

- Attach a label or tag with your business' name and Web address to every product you make. This is a free marketing opportunity for you.

- Include your Web address on all printed material including brochures, business cards, seasonal mailers, and advertisements.

- Invite customers to visit your website: "Visit our website to see our full selection." With the overwhelming number of choices your potential customers face, they will appreciate an opportunity to obtain more information to help them make their purchases.

(continued)

Use Your Website as Great Marketing Tool *(continued)*

- When you are selling, taking other calls, making more products, or otherwise unavailable and calls are being received by your voice mail, invite your caller to visit your website. For example, you might record: "Thank you for calling ABC Company. We will be back at three o'clock. In the meantime, feel free to visit our online studio at *www.ABCCompany.com.*"

- Remind your clients to add your site to their "Bookmarks" or "Favorites" so they can continue to visit your website as it is updated.

- Encourage visitors to your website to sign up for monthly emails on topics such as important gift-giving dates and special promotions.

- Having your products for sale online can also increase your productivity. During busy times, such as before the holidays, you will be able to take orders online as well as on the telephone.

Remember, using and promoting your website effectively can expand your business. Keep it updated with useful information and products. Broadcast your website address constantly.

but require an investment. Setting up a free blog is easy if you take a few minutes to register with either Wordpress.com or Blogger.com. Once created, you will get a domain such as *www.yourfoodcompany.wordpress.com.* Adding new posts is quite easy if you use Microsoft Word—no HTML experience is necessary.

The downside to having a free blog at sites such as Wordpress or Blogger is that it is hosted on their site, not on yours. Although the links from a free blog to your website are helpful, they do not add any depth and content to your site—a disadvantage from an search engine optimization (SEO) standpoint (more content on your website is advantageous). Also, the free blogs offer limited customization options, so you may end up with something that does not really reflect your brand image (and the blog's URL will have either the Wordpress or Blogger domain in it, not yours).

As an alternative, you may want to host a blog on your own site. All of the content you create on your blog will help build content and depth on your site, and the additional links will be helpful (remember to use key word-rich anchor text). If you go this route, you would tell people to go (or link) to *www.yourfoodcompany.com/blog/* or *www.blog.yourfood-company.com* instead of *www.yourfoodcompany.wordpress.com*. Additionally, when you host the blog software on your own site, you typically get much greater control over the look and feel of your blog. This way, your blog can have the same or similar branded look as your website instead of a generic-looking blog template. The only downside to this option (having the blog on your site) is that it requires some website development experience (FTP, HTML, CSS, PHP). You can always retain an experienced Web developer or marketing firm to design your blog.

Why are blogs important? Blogs give you the opportunity to talk about your products, new product launches, business experiences, opinions, and really anything you feel like writing about. Among other benefits, blogging can also allow you to connect and develop relationships with your customers (and potential customers). Blogs can be entertaining and educational. People like to connect on a personal level with companies, and the food industry is a great example due to the emotional nature of buying and consuming food products.

Now here is where blogging gets really good. The biggest advantage to business blogging is the online exposure and traffic. By creating regular blog posts, you are adding additional, key word-rich (and relevant) content to your website that will be indexed by the major search engines, Google, Yahoo, and MSN. Over time, your website will keep ranking better on those natural key word searches, such as "gourmet olive oil." This will help increase your Web traffic and hopefully sales, too.

In addition to the added search engine optimization benefits, having a blog is a great way to keep customers coming back to your website for updates, new products, specials, etc. You can set up an opt-in email signup form or an RSS feed subscription (that automatically notifies them when you write something new) to keep them up-to-date with your new posts. Most blog programs come with built-in RSS capabilities.

Marketing Specialty Foods over the Internet

Key topics associated with responding to the challenge and opportunity of online specialty food sales include the following:

- **Strategic planning:** Clarifying how Internet use can add value to your achieving your corporate long-range dream; understanding and developing useful tools for measuring your Internet performance and comparing it to your strategic goals and objectives; understanding the implications of Internet security (both for credit card transactions and around your computer)

- **Product development:** Using the Internet to conduct consumer and competitor research and find packaging, labeling, and production services

- **Marketing:** Understanding the impact Internet sales will have on the role of distributors, brokers, and retailers; establishing simple yet effective Internet relationships with retailers, brokers, and distributors; branding your product name on the Internet; using the Internet for market research; determining specific customer needs, trends, etc.

A Consumer Vision

You are the consumer. Using a hand-held scanner, you scan key ingredients that are in your cupboard and download that information to your home computer. The computer conducts a search of all the appropriate Internet sites. Missing ingredients are added to your shopping list, and the food is delivered to your home.

- **Merchandising:** Effectively matching the right product with the right customer at the right time; developing a community market where your products can be marketed along with complementary, noncompetitive products (called multistore architecture)

- **Customer relations:** Developing effective means of cultivating prospects and turning them into repeat customers; understanding the methods required for creating an outstanding customer experience; providing frequently asked questions (FAQ) sections in your website

- **Administration:** Developing easy and customer-friendly order entry and fulfillment processes

Another challenge of Internet marketing is that consumers tend to be wary of buying food sight unseen. Some of us would be happy to refill our larders with a half-dozen of that specialty mustard we like, but there are two problems with this. One is that the product is being offered to the consumer at the same, or even higher, price than offered by the nearby food store. An example: The eight-ounce crock of Kieller's Dundee Marmalade is sold at Trader Joe's for $3.79. The same product is available on the Internet for anywhere from $4.50 to $7.80. This is puzzling. The Internet seller can take a bigger profit than if it were sold to a distributor or retailer and still offer a really good deal to the consumer. The other problem is that not many specialty food marketers are actually using the Internet to sell their products to consumers. They fear negative reactions from distributor and retailers, who might view direct sales to consumers as competitive.

> **How Are You Using the Internet?**
>
> Have you developed an Internet strategy to turn your website visitors into customers?

Despite these challenges, it should be noted that a comScore Networks report states that there were nearly $26 billion in online sales during the 2007 holiday season. Also, the National Conference of State Legislatures reports that 32 million people have bought something online. If this behavior continues,

Table 5.2: Internet Food Sales Survey		

Sixty-five percent of food companies surveyed in 2008 sold specialty food via the Internet.

Internet Sales as Percent of Gross Sales	2007 Internet Sales as Percent of Total Sales	2008 Internet Sales as Percent of Total Sales
Less than 10%	40.0	37.5
11–20%	10.0	10.0
21–30%	1.0	10.0
31–40%	2.0	2.5
41–50%	0.0	0.0
51–60%	2.5	0.0
More than 60%	2.5	2.5
No response	22.5	27.5

it will naturally include growing Internet purchases of specialty foods.

The specialty food industry is viewing the Internet with great interest. Table 5.2 shows how Internet sales as a percentage of total sales went up from 2007 to 2008. While some agree to sell to an Internet retailer, such as GreatFood.com, they seem to be restricting use of the Internet to email and reorders from their existing trade clients. In addition, food entrepreneurs can use website directories, such as *www.specialtyfoodresource.com,* to locate suppliers, vendors, retailers, and distributors and to avail themselves of extensive Internet networking opportunities.

GreatFood.com

A techie started GreatFood.com in 1996. It was sold at the end of 1999 for a cool $18.5 million in cash to 1-800Flowers. GreatFood.com did what a lot of similar companies are trying to do: set up a virtual market that improves distribution efficiencies, collect fees for all of the goods traded, and create a highly valued company in the process.

Chapter 6

Taking Your Product to Market

To take your product to market, you will need a comprehensive review of the most fundamental aspects of specialty food marketing.

You've come a long way in developing your product, because you have done the following:

- Continued to listen to your customers.

- Developed partnerships with your suppliers.

- Tried and tested, packaged and priced your product.

- Identified your niche and are ready to affirm why you stayed with the enterprise: to promote, market, sell, and reap your rewards by exceeding your customers' expectations.

Now you want to do a first-class job of placing your product before the consumer.

Six Principles for Marketing Success

Before you begin this undertaking, you may want to review the following six principles of marketing that will underlie all your efforts:

1. **Focus:** Ground your business with the consumer, not the distributor or retailer. Know your market and be able to identify your consumer precisely. You will still have to meet the quality requirements of your distributors/retailers.

2. **Positioning:** Ensure that your product is not at a disadvantage with respect to the competition. Differentiate sufficiently to clinch consumer acceptance. How does it stand out? What is its unique selling point?

3. **Demonstrations:** Demos sell. Provide tasting opportunities as often as possible.

4. **Advertising:** Center your advertising on the one specific advantage or edge your product has over the competition. Employ proven advertising methods.

5. **Distribution:** Establish distribution sufficient to the needs of the market. Make sure enough product is in distribution to meet consumer demand, especially if you do any consumer advertising.

6. **Promotion:** Manage your promotions to increase in-store display to produce greater consumer sales.

Preparing Sales Literature

Product sales literature is essential to your sales effort. A sales kit may consist of a price list, catalog (product presentation) sheet, product information sheet, and point-of-purchase material.

Typically, a catalog sheet and a price sheet will suffice. The catalog sheet is generally an 8½ × 11 inch, four-color product photograph accompanied by

A Note on Consumers and Customers

Question: Who determines product quality? Is it the consumer? Or is it the retailer/distributor?

Answer: If your product does not appeal to the consumer (as in end user), no amount of retail orders will ensure your success. If your product does appeal to the consumer, *then* you must also know the quality wants of your customer—that is, the retailer/distributor.

approximately 50 words of copy that describe the product. Include company name, postal and website addresses, email address, and telephone and fax numbers.

In addition to price lists and catalog sheets, you may use a fact sheet to highlight promotable elements of your company and its products. Such elements as testimonials from famous people, historical anecdotes about your company, claims to fame, etc. can be included in the fact sheet.

Also, this is where you can amplify statements regarding recipes, applications, and health claims that relate to your product. These provide even more reinforcement of your sales message. Information that you include on your fact sheets may also be included on your price sheets. Lose no opportunity to impart your sales message!

Effective Sales Literature Can Help . . .

- improve distributor and broker knowledge of your product.
- convey preferred use.
- promote the product.
- make sales.

Much of your sales materials can be prepared with the aid of your PC. Several good software packages are both easy to master and cost-effective. Ask your local software reseller for advice. With digital imagery, one can capture product, download it, and add copy and print. The advantage of using your PC and a good color laser printer is that you can test a number of different promotional formats.

You can also prepare a color leaflet or mailer on your computer. Complete the design using your desktop software and burn it to a CD or save it to a USB flash drive. Take this to your local photocopy or stationery supply store. You can have

GUIDELINES FOR SUCCESS

Sales Literature

What to Include

Product description	Make it sizzle! Include the facts and figures (sizes, net contents, case lots, etc.) on the reverse of the catalog sheet. Use the front for the general presentation and the back for the details.
Photography/graphics	These should be top-notch, upscale.
Copy	Sell the product's benefits, not its features.
Contact information	Company name; mailing, email, and website addresses; and telephone number (don't forget area code)

What Not to Include

Prices

Dates

Any time-sensitive material (e.g., "just in time for Valentine's Day 2009")

the staff there print your color product using a PC and color printer. (Alternatively, you can buy your own laser color printer for under $300).

Selecting Point-of-Purchase Materials

Many retailers find point-of-purchase materials (also referred to as POP) useful in attracting attention to products they stock. POPs not only attract consumer attention, they also inform and educate the prospective buyer about the product's benefits. POPs may include tent cards (used primarily in restaurants), posters, shelf talkers, product information neck tags attached to bottles and other packages, and recipe handouts.

GUIDELINES FOR SUCCESS

Point-of-Purchase Materials

	Tent Cards	Posters	Shelf Talkers	Neck Tags
Size (approx.)	5" × 7"	18" × 36"	6" × 10"	2¾" × 2½"
Color	2-color	4-color	2-color	2- or 4-color
Number to prepare	1,000	500	1,000	One run's worth
Distribution	Food service/ retailers	Retailers	Distributors	With the product
When to use	Demos/ special events	New products/ new retailers	New products/ new retailers	During intro stage/ new products

Notes:

Size: Tent cards are used on tables, so the size is small and the message brief. I have used posters with cardboard backing that can stand alone or be placed on a wall. In both cases, the posters were 9 × 14 inches. The number of shelf facings available for your product may limit shelf talker size. You don't want your shelf talker to use space occupied by another product. Neck tags are small and can be unfolded to reveal several pages of product information.

Color: Two-color products are recommended, where possible, to save money. (You can produce some four-color media on your own color printer or one available at your local copy shop.)

Number to prepare: Go slowly; prepare as few as economically feasible.

Distribution: Tent cards, posters, and shelf talkers can be shipped either with the product or via your broker and/or distributor. Neck tags can be used all the time.

Tent Cards. These are small, tent-shaped cards that can be placed on counters, tables, and shelves. You have seen these used in restaurants to promote specials of the day, for example. Retailers use them to promote new products and to alert customers about items on sale.

Posters. Posters are used in store windows, on store walls, and, when properly mounted, on shelves and counters. Because of posters' relatively large size, many retailers are hesitant to use them, but they are especially useful during in-store promotions and in trade show exhibits.

Shelf Talkers. Used extensively in the grocery trade, these are small signs that are designed to protrude from underneath the product they describe. They can be effective for new product introductions and are more likely to be utilized than posters. Also, they are placed under the product, rather than nearby, making a clear connection between their message and the product.

Product Information Tags. These are most often used in the form of neck tags, which provide all kinds of promotional data. They may include recipes, company history, product uses, recommendations, ingredient descriptions, coupons, and free offers. You can ensure their use because they require no extra effort on the part of the retailer—they are already affixed to the product.

Promoting Your Product

One of the most important elements of niche marketing is product promotion. Product promotion often means the difference between success or failure. Getting your product before the consumer and having it recognized is the first step to making a sale. The most used means of promotion are trade show exhibitions, in-store demonstrations, giveaways, mailings, tie-ins, testimonials, show awards, and the Internet.

Trade Shows
Trade shows rate high on the list of important promotional vehicles. The benefits of food show participation include the following:

- Meet customers.
- Learn about the competition.

- Experiment with product ingredients.
- Evaluate product packaging.
- Test product pricing.
- Rate various promotion techniques.
- Identify important trends.
- Solicit customer reaction.
- Make sales.

Food show participation offers a cost-effective means of introducing a new product, gathering market research, learning about the competition, and making sales. There are numerous food shows, but few offer real value to most specialty food producers. See appendix C for a listing of some of the prominent food shows.

The major shows held in the United States attract buyers from most specialty food markets. The level of exposure at these shows can be met or improved on only by undertaking the time and cost of traveling to many of the leading specialty food markets.

Certain trade shows require exhibitors to be members of the sponsoring association, and some associations require you to be in business for at least two years to be accepted as a member. If a member distributor or broker takes on your product and thereby develops a client business relationship with you, then your products can be exhibited in that distributor's or broker's booth.

Before attending a trade show, you will have to consider the appropriateness of your sales literature for the target market, including the illustration and currency of information. You will have to consider booth design, layout, signs, demo equipment requirements (you will have to order display risers, electricity, and floodlighting). A standard booth order generally includes tables, chairs, and booth carpeting.

The estimated cost for a 100-square-foot booth, with minimum spot lighting, drayage, table covers, freight in and out, travel, and accommodations and meals for one person is *at least* $6,000.

As promotional tools, trade shows should be a part of a fully integrated and well-managed campaign.

GUIDELINES FOR SUCCESS

Trade Show Milestones

One year before show:

- Commit to attending the trade show.
- Begin work on total promotion campaign.
- Review booth design. Look for imaginative, inexpensive display schemes/materials.

Six months before show:

- Make plane reservations and hotel accommodations.
- Develop sales literature for show.

Three months before show:

- Check on sales literature produced by both your firm and the show sponsor.
- Review results in search for prospective brokers and distributors.
- Initiate contact and establish appointments with key prospects.

Two months before show:

- Arrange shipment of any display equipment and samples (all display materials must be fireproofed).
- Prepare press kits.
- Verify with freight forwarder that equipment has arrived. (Note: While you can hand carry samples/display materials from your car to the show booth, you generally cannot use any luggage carts or trolleys.)
- Confirm with show management that all arrangements have been made regarding shipping, electricity, extra tables/chairs, table drapes, signs, etc.
- Determine method for lead qualification following the show.
- Hand carry "just-in-case" package of samples, price sheets, and literature.

Upon arrival:

- Set up booth display (table covers, samples, signs, etc.).
- Become familiar with show layout, transportation, special events, etc.

Trade Show Milestones *(continued)*

- Deliver your press kits to the show Press Room.
- Survey competitors' products, booths, and product literature.

Upon returning home:
- Write thank-you notes to the appropriate people.
- Record recommendations for successive shows.
- Begin business follow-up with potential customers.

Trade shows should be incorporated into other promotional efforts for full effect. Aside from the all-important trade shows, specialty food promotion can take many forms; some of the most common are described in the next sections.

In-Store Demonstrations/Tastings

Consumers tend to buy products they have sampled, usually at sample tastings conducted at the point of purchase. These can involve a demonstrator, your product, and the means of sampling (crackers with cheese, for example). The demonstration is conducted during high-traffic periods over the course of three to six hours. Consumers have the opportunity to taste your product, to comment on it, to hear a pitch from the demonstrator, and to purchase. Often, demonstrations are accompanied by a special product price used to entice the consumer into making an immediate purchase.

A typical demonstration might be conducted from 10:00 AM to 3:00 PM on a Saturday. The idea is to get as much public attention as you can, so peak shopping hours are best.

Demonstrator costs are in the neighborhood of $15 to $25 per hour, with a $100 to $125 minimum fee per day.

GUIDELINES FOR SUCCESS

How to Reduce Trade Show Expenses

- Share booth with another food producer.

- Share booth with broker/distributor.

- Take your own (flameproof) table drapes, back drop, and riser covers. (Use a colorful oilcloth-type table cover for easy cleaning.)

- Use your own posters and signs.

- Order one double-neck floodlight per 100 square feet of exhibit space.

- Hand carry your samples (no luggage carts with freight are permitted through show doors, but you can carry boxes).

- Bring a handheld vacuum to clean your carpet (touch up).

- Take a Styrofoam cooler (for samples, cold drinks, snacks, etc.).

- Use ice from outside exhibit hall for your cooler.

- Take hot plate (if required for sample tasting).

- Take serving materials (plastic plates, bowls, spoons, forks, etc.).

- Consider a less expensive hotel and commute to the show.

- Survival gear:

____ Packaging tape/dispenser	____ Fishing line (to hang posters)
____ Cellophane tape	____ Paper napkins
____ Marking pens	____ Pliers
____ Stapler/staples	____ Ballpoint pens
____ Clipboard	____ Screwdriver
____ Business cards	____ Cell phone
____ Laptop computer	

Giveaways

One of the least expensive forms of advertising and promotion is a product give-away. A carefully managed program of free merchandise can place your product in front of the consumer, while attracting the attention of the retailer.

Usually, free merchandise is offered with in-store demonstrations, introductory deals, and sampling allowances. Free merchandise can also include specially packed sample containers for distribution at the point of purchase and during trade shows.

Mailings

A mailing can consist of a price list, a sample, and a catalog sheet sent to several retailers and/or distributors, or it can consist of a mass mailing with multiple inserts, full-color slick catalog sheets, and samples to thousands of prospective consumers. In entry-level niche marketing, mailings more than likely will be limited to selected retailers and distributors.

It is very difficult for a new supplier to sell a new and unseen food product via the mail. Mailings should be made to prospective distributors in accordance with a complete marketing promotion. In other words, generate more than just a mailing! Devise a follow-up program that will include telephone screening and sales calls. A mailing should sell as well as inform.

Mailings to retailers are slightly different than mailings to distributors. Usually, they do not include the follow-up telephone call or the sales call. You will be mailing to many retailers, instead of a couple of dozen distributors, so you design a different mail campaign. The inserts you use should include a postage-paid return order form for easy use by the retailer. Mailings to retailers are best used as information providers, invitations to visit your trade show booth, invitations to request free samples, or more information and inducements to reorder.

Tie-Ins

You can get more out of your promotion dollar by sharing the costs with another food producer. This is accomplished by "tying" your product with a complementary product (e.g., tea with pastries, cakes, or cookies; cheese with crackers; preserves with special muffins or breads).

Arrange to have a series of in-store demonstrations conducted where both products are being served. Share the costs of the demonstration with the other producer. Presenting the two products in a special promotional package can support the tie-in concept.

GUIDELINES FOR SUCCESS

Postal Mailings to Distributors

- Develop a mailing list. (This may be purchased through a mailing list broker.)
- Prepare the mailer. Include a cover letter, catalog/price sheet, and a sample (if possible). Cover letter should be brief, informative, and to the point. State that you will telephone the buyer "next week."
- Prepare the envelope.
- Mail the materials.
- Follow up by telephone in about seven days.
- Qualify the buyer (discern level of interest).
- Arrange an appointment.
- Send a brief note confirming appointment details and stressing a benefit of your product.
- Call on the prospect, stress the benefits, and make the sale!
- Follow up with a brief note about sale details.

Emailed Mailings to Distributors

Emails to distributors involve the same process as regular mail, except that you can mail to a larger audience less expensively. Large email address listings can be obtained from the same mailing list brokers as regular mail address listings. A number of new software programs can help you manage large email projects. Also, services provided for a fee by Constant Contact, for example, are worth exploring.

Testimonials and Show Awards

One of the most effective, and least expensive, promotional tools is to get someone who is in the public eye to say something nice about your product.

Send your samples and product information to all of the important food editors in your major markets, as well as food-preparing personalities who appear on radio and television. Include a press kit with press release, sample (if possible), company history/data, and a listing of where the product can be purchased. To assist you, if your budget permits, you may wish to have this accomplished by a professional public relations firm.

Submit your product to trade show managements that have product award committees. Your product will be evaluated against many others, but if you win "best new product for such-and-such year," you can use this in your product literature, trade show exhibits, and advertisements. Both the testimonials and show awards offer third-party endorsements that attest to the quality of your product.

Publicizing Your Product

A prominent public relations firm offers the following information about public relations.

Cost-Effective

Public relations is a cost-effective way to draw attention to your product from a group of people who influence consumers. The targets of a public relations campaign are the editors and writers of newspaper and magazine food sections and producers and hosts of radio and television shows that feature cooking and food products. A positive feature or mention in the press can be even better than advertising, because it carries the implied seal of approval of a respected source—the food journalist.

While consumer media reach the ultimate purchasers of food products, public relations can also be effective in expanding distribution by reaching retailers, brokers, and distributors through food industry publications.

Public relations should be a part of any total marketing plan, and because of its relatively low cost, it can be especially important when marketing funds are scarce. In some cases, public relations can even replace advertising.

Components of a Public Relations Campaign

There is no formula for a public relations campaign. It should be tailored to your needs, whether you are introducing a product in just one area or nationwide.

The critical elements are an informative, well-written press release and an up-to-date, targeted mailing list. Depending on your budget, include a photograph, tips on how to use the product, recipes, and a prewritten feature that ties your product to an emerging food trend. All of these elements, especially the photograph, can increase chances of pickup.

Many top editors want to try any product personally before writing about it; however, sending hundreds of samples can become prohibitive in terms of the postage alone. Consider sending samples to the top 100 prospects on your media list, return-addressed postcards requesting samples to the next 250 names, and a line on the release itself offering a sample to the remaining names who call for one.

Increase Your Visibility

While product announcements and endorsements can lead directly to sales, raising general visibility can be accomplished in other ways. A small ice cream company made the front page of a large metropolitan newspaper by handing out ice cream samples the night of April 15 to thousands of people waiting to mail their income taxes, and a small company importing sparkling waters gained the same sort of name recognition by giving T-shirts to runners in a race. Other public relations vehicles include recipe contests and production of recipe newsletters.

If you are introducing a product nationally, consider retaining a small public relations agency that specializes in food products. Such an agency already will have researched and organized the mailing lists you will need and can advise on the most effective materials to use in your press package.

How to Know If a Press Release Is Successful

Knowing where and when a story has appeared is important for several reasons—first, to know in which areas your potential customers are likely to have read about your product and, secondly, to see how the product is being received. This information can be used to fine-tune your sales messages.

Clipping services, such as BurrellesLuce, monitor the Internet, newspapers, magazines, and radio and television programs nationally. They provide their clients with an original copy of each story that mentions the product name—or

GUIDELINES FOR SUCCESS

Public Relations

How to get an editor's attention:

- Write a headline that tells the story in two lines or less.

- Include all information: company and product name, product benefits, size and/or weight, kind of package, where and when available, and price.

- Include a photo if possible, one in 5 x 7 inch color glossy (in digital format). Be sure to identify the photos—they can get separated from the release.

- Provide a separate fact sheet so the editor can get the basic information at a glance. Be aware of publication deadlines. Newspaper food sections work weeks in advance, and magazines need three to four months lead time prior to their publication date. When in doubt, call and ask.

- Send the information to the right person. If necessary, call the general office number and ask who covers food and/or new product at the media outlet.

- Follow your release with a phone call to ask if you can answer any questions. But don't make a pest of yourself; leaving one message is sufficient.

messages specified by the client—complete with the name of the publication, date the story appeared, and the circulation.

How to Write a Press Release

When writing your product announcement release, keep in mind the needs of the recipient. Food editors and writers want to know the "Five Ws"—who, what, where, when, and why—of your product so they can decide whether to pass the information along to their readers. You should also tell them about its advantages over competitive products and tips for using it, as well as any interesting facts about the development of the product.

The release can be printed on your letterhead. The general format should look something like the sample press releases in figures 6.1 and 6.2.

Figure 6.1: Sample Press Release: Distributor Named

FOR IMMEDIATE RELEASE:

Contact: [Your name, telephone number, and email address]
Date:

WILD RICE EXCHANGE APPOINTS ENCORE SPECIALTY FOODS

Gourmet Valley, a California-based producer of wild rice and specialty blended rice and dried heirloom beans, has named Encore Specialty Foods LLC as its U.S. master distributor. The joint announcement was made by The Wild Rice Exchange General Manager Carlos Zambello and Encore Specialty Foods President Ron Johnson. The appointment extends a 14-year collaboration between the two executives.

The Gourmet Valley line includes organic Giant Canadian and California extra fancy wild rice, plus blended rice for both retail and food service market sectors. Gourmet Valley recently introduced a line of heirloom beans and new three-pound stand-up jumbo packs of both beans and rice.

Johnson says the Gourmet Valley line is a good strategic fit with his company's lines of European imported specialty foods. "The healthful nature of this line and its attractive retail packaging and reasonable price points position it perfectly with our other products. The line appeals to the same creative cook and professional chef who are looking for healthful and cost-effective ingredients to use in the kitchen."

Encore will trim costs for the line by shipping to Midwestern and Western distributors from the packer's Sacramento-area warehouse. "We're lowering previous pricing by as much as 18 percent," said Johnson.

Advertising Your Product

We tend to think that consumer advertising is the easy way to draw attention to our product. However, it's not necessarily so easy. In the first place, your product has to be in the market before an advertisement directed at the consumer will work.

Occasionally, consumers will see inserts in the likes of *Gourmet, The New Yorker, Smithsonian,* and other magazines that advertise fancy foods; however, in

Figure 6.2: Sample Press Release: Name Change

FOR IMMEDIATE RELEASE:

Contact: [Your name, telephone number and email address]
Date:

WILD BLUEBERRY HARVESTOR ANNOUNCES NEW NAME
Food Firm Marks Tenth Anniversary with New Name and New Label

To celebrate its tenth anniversary and to better reflect nature of its business, Alaska Tribal Cache has changed its name to ALASKA PURE BERRY. Jams, vinaigrettes, and candy are but a few of the high-quality specialty food items that are produced by the women-managed firm.

The newly named firm is pleased to offer high-demand specialty foods that include wild blueberry and salmonberry vinaigrette, wild blueberry jam, low bush cranberry sauce, and fireweed pepper jelly. Please see details on our website: *www.alaskajamandjelly.com.*

Alaska Pure Berry's wild blueberries are rich in antioxidants. Antioxidants are molecules that can prevent oxidation—a chemical reaction that can damage human cells. Alaska Pure Berry's wild blueberries have an antioxidant value of 13,427 compared to green apples (3,900) and small red beans (13,727).

About Alaska Pure Berry
The firm, an operating entity of the Seldovia Village Tribe, harvests organic-like berries on Alaska's Kanai Peninsula—a wild natural habitat rich in berries containing among the highest antioxidants on earth. Alaska Pure Berry CEO Crystal Collier notes that "the Society for Neuroscience reports that exposure to wild blueberry extracts can reverse age-triggered ailments."

These wildest of wild berries grow on sunny, spruce-clad slopes overlooking pristine Seldovia Bay. Seldovia's wild berries are a natural treasure nourished by clean winter snows, fresh spring rains, and the long sunshine-filled days of Alaska's summer.

For thousands of years, Alaskan Natives have handpicked these plump, exceptionally sweet, wild berries. Today, local and tribal residents continue this tradition, bringing some of these wonderful berries to our modern kitchen.

(continued)

Figure 6.2: Sample Press Release: Name Change *(continued)*

Tribal members cook small batches of these choice berries using recipes handed down for generations. The resulting mixtures are hand poured into distinctive jars.

Collier reports that her firm "prides itself on a vision that calls for a self-sustaining, environmentally sensitive, Alaska Native enterprise that creates jobs, shares naturally abundant resources, and enhances lives."

According to Collier, "Our people have made the sheltered waters of Seldovia their home for thousands of years. The Seldovia area was the meeting and trading place for the Kodiak Koniags, the Aleuts from the Aleutians, the Chugach people of Prince William Sound, and the Tanaina Kenaitze people of Cook Inlet." This rich cultural heritage is evident in the quality and design of Alaska Pure Berry's products.

---

the specialty food industry, the only advertisements that seem to be directed to consumers with any regularity in those magazines are those that offer product via mail order instead of through retail stores. Successful consumer advertising requires ingenuity and deep pockets. According to the American Association of Advertising Agencies (*www.aaaa.org*), the average American is exposed to approximately 7,000 advertising stimuli a day.

You are well advised to tread lightly when it comes to consumer advertising, especially if you are considering television or radio. Stick with advertising inserts in specialty food trade journals. See Appendix A for a listing of trade journals devoted to this industry.

Media Selection

Several of the trade journals will work with you to save money in preparing your advertisement. Consider retaining a small and hungry advertising agency. It will cost a little more, but the result will be better than cutting and pasting on your own. Make sure that advertising costs are figured into your overall budget in an amount equal to 10 to 15 percent of sales or projected sales.

GUIDELINES FOR SUCCESS

Advertising Hints

- Use the advertisement over the course of 12 months, or longer, and in a number of issues of different trade journals.

- Make certain the artwork and design of the advertisement can be used in point-of-purchase posters and other promotional materials.

- Use the advertisement in combination with a well-planned and effectively managed advertising and promotion program.

- Coordinate advertising inserts with press releases, in-store promotions, show displays, mailings, and point-of-purchase posters.

- Don't waste money by running one fancy advertisement only once or twice in a single journal.

- Coordinate promotions with current and prospective retailer and distributor promotions.

Some advertising can be accomplished using local radio and newspapers, but this is best done in connection with larger retailer promotions, such as those conducted by department stores.

What you undertake in the form of advertising will be determined by available funds. You will depend more on your own resources if you have a $1,000 budget and more on outside help if you have a $10,000 budget.

Advertising Costs

- **Insert preparation ($2,000 to $4,000):** An insert is an advertisement you will have inserted in the magazine/newspaper. Many specialty food trade journals will take your camera-ready artwork and produce it as an advertisement. You can expect to pay upwards of $4,000 for a black-and-white ad with about 50 words of copy. Illustrations and photography will cost extra. Cost factors in a half-page, black-and-white insert include art work, copywriting, design, and layout.

- **Photography ($600 to $1,000):** If you have a photograph made of your product or product line, then arrange to use the same photograph in your catalog sheets and other promotional materials.

- **Insert space ($2,000 to $3,300—and up):** Media costs (the magazine or newspaper space) to insert a half-page (vertical or horizontal), black-and-white ad, for example, will range from $3,000 to $3,100, depending on the magazine or newspaper. Color ads will cost more. These costs can be discounted by running the ad more than once.

Finding Buyers

Now that you have had your product produced, packaged, and labeled, how do you find the specific buyers identified as a category during your initial market research? The type of customer you identify will depend on the type of product you have to sell. Whether the product is canned, fresh, frozen, or refrigerated will influence its distribution possibilities.

Identifying the Potential Customer

We have numbered approximately 23,000 retailer prospects as potential buyers of your product. This figure presumes a product not requiring special handling and display, such as frozen and refrigerated foods. About 15,000 of them will be able to stock refrigerated items, such as cheese and fresh pâté. The competition for that space will be keen. It presumes also an ability to get the product to all these prospects.

The number of retailer prospects swells substantially if your product can be sold in a gift store, of which there are approximately 74,000. Our 23,000 retailer figure includes only 10 percent of gift stores devoting any shelf space to specialty foods. More often than not, a gift store will carry a food product, notably candy, and will merchandise it as a gift, rather than food.

GUIDELINES FOR SUCCESS

Hints for Finding Buyers

- Exhibit at major (national and regional) specialty food trade shows.

- Arrange for one of the specialty food trade journals to conduct a mailing on your behalf.

- Contact the NASFT for information about its retailer and distributor members.

- Purchase a mailing list of gourmet food retailers from available business list consolidation services (appendix N).

Approximately five dozen distributors specialize in selling specialty food to retailers. In addition, full-line grocery distributors, of which there are hundreds, are carrying more specialty foods every year.

Qualifying Potential Buyers

Qualifying a buyer involves assessing the potential buyer's interest in and likelihood of making a purchase. In the case of distributors, you do this by reviewing the product lines currently carried, mailing information, sending samples, and following up by telephone. Once you have qualified your buyer, you can then make arrangements to set an appointment for a sales call.

You can rely on your broker to qualify retailers, or you can make the call yourself to determine the interest level and to make the sale.

Establishing Distribution Channels

You will employ various channels of distribution to get your product to the consumer. In fact, getting distribution will be one of your major challenges. Understanding these distribution options will enable you to refine your marketing plans. In the specialty food trade, you will use either distributors (also called store-door distributors, full-service distributors, jobbers, and wholesalers), retailers (including gourmet food stores, warehouse clubs, department stores, and mass merchandisers), direct mail, and/or catalog houses.

The exact type of distribution used will depend on a number of factors, some of which include the following:

- The market segment (by product type, geographic region, etc.)
- The expected sales volume (large volume may require different distribution capabilities)
- The nature of the product promotion

The profusion of specialty foods has made the process of obtaining distributor interest in carrying new products increasingly difficult. As a result, distribution often requires that you do all the pioneering yourself (selling direct to retailers) to attract the attention of a distributor. If you are lucky, however, your product may have sufficient appeal to attract a distributor as soon as you introduce it.

Before you approach a distributor, you should review certain aspects of the specialty foods business. The list below includes the topics you should understand (all of these are contained in this book; consult the table of contents or index for page numbers). Here are the negotiating details to know:

- Pricing/deals
- Length of contract
- Postsales support/training
- Performance measurements
- Territory
- Promotional activities—who pays?
- How specialty foods get to the consumer
- The role of the distributor in this process
- Required profit margin/promotion support
- The relevance of introductory deals

- Details of your competition
- Specialty food pricing strategies
- Specialty food promotion strategies
- Marketing elements specific to the territory

Distributor Options Vary by Your Annual Sales Volume

Your distribution options will be more sophisticated at higher levels of gross revenues. Also, higher revenues will mean a greater commitment to funding advertising and promotion programs. The following describes the approximate distinctions between varying levels of sales and distribution schemes:

- **High-volume sales (> $1 million):** Buyer has own warehouse and uses mass merchandising. Significant advertising dollars are required. This is not a major factor in specialty food distribution.

- **Medium-volume sales ($500,000 to $1 million):** Selling to supermarkets via rack jobbers (they do all the shelf work). Costs can include demos and free merchandise. Some specialty food distributors have established relationships with both independent and major supermarket chains.

- **Low-volume sales (generally < $500,000):** Selling to store's back door via wholesaler/distributor, who uses brokers and own salesforce, or direct to store via your broker. This is the primary distribution option used in the specialty food trade.

How Distribution Works

Distribution depends on the product; season; market segment; region; product stage of development; and consumer awareness, perception, and attitudes. As mentioned in the introduction to this guide, as soon as you find a profitable way to distribute your product, someone else will be doing just as well with a similar product but with an entirely different distribution strategy. A number of distribution avenues are open to you.

You can sell direct to the consumer by running your own retail operation, either in a permanent setting or at special holiday fairs, for example. You can also do this via mail order. Send a mailing to prospective customers or take out a mail order advertisement.

You can reach the consumer via a retailer. This approach will probably be your initial means of entering the specialty food industry. You put the samples in the trunk of your car and call on as many retailers as possible to make sales. Or make the sale and then ship to the customer.

Selling to a retailer through a broker is similar to the above approach, but instead of you doing it yourself, a commissioned broker takes your samples to the retailers in that broker's territory and makes the sales calls.

You may also reach your retail market through a distributor. The distributor buys your product and sells it to the retailer. Some products, especially heavy products in jars, generally require distribution in this manner. It tends to be too expensive to design the containers required to ship a dozen jars via UPS so they arrive undamaged at the retailer's door. (Nevertheless, direct-to-retailer sales are often necessary for the beginner to spark interest from the distributor.)

Sales are also made via a broker to a distributor to a retailer. Again, you employ a commissioned broker to take your samples and to make sales calls on distributors.

Your product may be sold via a catalog house, although very few catalogs have been successful selling retail packaged specialty foods. Those that are successful usually sell products that can be used as gifts. Some catalog companies will ask you to "drop ship." This means that they send you the order and a mailing label, and you ship the individual product directly to the consumer. The catalog company pays you. You can also use a broker to make sales to a catalog house.

Significance of Exclusivity

All brokers and many distributors will ask for an exclusive territory. With brokers, the exclusive arrangement is to your advantage. It makes little sense to have two brokers competing for the same buyer with the same products.

Distributors often request exclusivity, especially when introducing a new product. It makes some sense to work closely with a distributor in a given market on an exclusive basis. This helps focus your marketing and distribution strategy. You might want to limit the arrangement, depending on the distributor and on the market, to six months.

Some strategies work for some producers and not for others. Many successful specialty food producers have never offered any exclusive arrangements. Once again, it depends on the timing, territory, product, price, etc. One way to ascertain distributor interest in an exclusive arrangement is to ask what sort of volume is guaranteed.

Food Service

A growing segment of the specialty food trade consists of selling to hotels, restaurants, and institutions offering better food service. Distribution in this market segment requires the use of brokers and distributors who sell to food service accounts. Food service opportunities exist for specialty food producers who supply fancy jams, preserves, syrups, and the like in single servings for use on hotel restaurant tables, in room service, and other situations, such as takeout orders and picnic baskets.

Offering single-serving food products to food service outlets adds an opportunity to attain sampling and brand awareness, because single-serving packages will be labeled with your brand name.

Providing your product for use as a prepared food ingredient will meet increasing demand by restaurants, which are preparing more foods with specialty food ingredients. It is also a way to generate revenue during your start-up stage and to reduce product costs by arranging for larger production runs. On the other hand, there is little branding opportunity for your products sold in institutional containers, and you will be subject to the vagaries of food service trends.

The food service sector is extremely price-conscious. High-priced products are better served by creating demand first at the retail level instead of wasting too much time exploring the food service segment. The market is there, but you must be price-competitive to crack it.

GUIDELINES FOR SUCCESS

Specialty Food Distribution Channels
with Incremental Profit Margins/Commissions

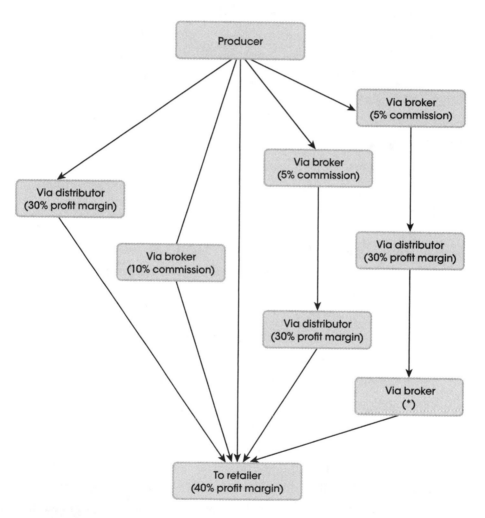

* Commission paid from distributor's share of profit margin.

Mail Order

According to *Direct Marketing* magazine, there are more than 800 mail order companies specializing in a wide range of food by mail, "each averaging about $1.5 million sales." As you may imagine, fruit, steaks, dairy, and alcoholic beverages account for most of the sales. Examples of these companies include Harry & David, Swiss Colony, Figi's, Wisconsin Cheeseman, and 800 Spirits. The "gourmet" portion of mail order sales comes mostly from companies that have retail operations. Companies such as Zabar's, Sutton Place Group's Balducci's, and Williams-Sonoma promote their products with seasonal catalogs.

A number of small specialty food companies have expanded their business and reached broader markets by mail. Among these are Cost Plus, Williams-Sonoma, and Zabar's. Notice that the these are primarily retailers that use mail order sales to increase business during holiday periods and to offer repeat customers the opportunity of ordering by mail. The New York-based communications firm Ehrlich Creative Communications Inc. (Ec Communications) provided the basis for the following advice to prospective mail order companies:

Begin by testing your market. Select a publication you think your customers read. If they are well off and live in small towns, for example, try something like *Country Living;* if you plan to sell to a professional market (chefs or librarians, etc.), buy an ad in one of the trade publications, and so on.

If you profit from the returns on the ad, then you may want to try it again. Advertising won't tell you much about the size of your market. If you get 100 responses to your ad and 12 people eventually buy, is that good? The only way to know is through experience over time. You will be able to compare ad results from different publications, at different times of the year, etc.

You could try a co-op mailing. This involves using a catalog that advertises other catalogs or a mailing that includes card packs and coupons. The advantage of co-op mailings is that you get to compare your results with others in the program. They can help you determine some aspects of the market for your product; however, it is not particularly scientific (you have very little control over who gets the mailing or whether or not they read it).

Another option is to get your products into someone else's catalog. This is one of the more cost-effective ways of getting into a new mail order market. Your advantages include no up-front costs; no requirement for a full product line (you can run with just one product); a reasonably accurate idea of the demand for your product; and, possibly, demographic and other information about the people who order your product.

Working with a Catalog House

Ask your catalog house to tell you its typical response rates. The catalog can't promise you a response rate, but it can give you a general indication of other companies' experiences. Determine what catalog fees include: Creation of the ad or catalog cover? How many issues will include your offer? How many issues are mailed each year?

Finally, you can conduct your own mailing. This is the most expensive option, but it is the most reliable. You will control all the variables—who receives your offer, when they receive it, how it is presented, etc.—and you will get all the results. If you elect to produce your own catalog, then you will want to purchase a mailing list of at least 50,000 names.

The list is the most crucial part of your mailing. Test the list first, then your prices, offer, and copy. The rule of thumb for your test should be to generate 50 responses, or a return of 1 percent. This means a list of at least 5,000 names. You can get these lists from other catalog companies that serve markets similar to the one you want to enter.

You can count on spending about $15,000 for a 50,000-piece mailing, plus costs for producing the catalog or mailing piece.

GUIDELINES FOR SUCCESS

Selling to Mail Order Catalogs

Adapted from an outline developed for the Roundtable for Women in Foodservice by Nina Dorsett, director of sales and marketing, Plaza Sweets Bakery.

The good news: Mail order buyers are accessible! Review catalogs and pursue those that seem a likely fit.

- Know your products well. Know their limitations. Understand what they will be put through. Do they require specialized shipping?

- Do you drop ship? What does this involve?

- Can you do business via email?

- Private label—yes or no?

- Properly price your product to cover all your costs and make a profit yet allow enough room for the catalog to make its margin.

- Sales projections: How accurate are they? How do you plan?

- Be prepared to come through at all times.

- After the selling season, review catalog sales with the buyer. Try to get a commitment to continue with the product and take the opportunity to introduce new items.

- When exhibiting in shows, set aside a separate area to feature your mail order products. Make sure your mail order items are clearly identified.

- Remember that catalog sales can mean volume orders and seem resistant to economic downturns. With more people having less time to shop, there is an increasing reliance on catalogs for gift giving and entertaining. The catalog market business is on the upswing, and you should do your best to become a part of it.

Arranging the Deals

Because of the risks involved, both in terms of wasted time and expended resources, few of your potential customers will be willing to carry a new product without some incentive.

Consequently, most retailers, and particularly distributors, require special deals to earn extra profit during start-up and to introduce your product successfully.

The most common is the introductory deal. This can involve some combination of those described below. With all deals, you can offer a "60-day buy-in" that allows the buyer to purchase up to a predetermined credit limit for 60 days and get the introductory deal.

Competition is so stiff in this industry that getting retailers and distributors even to try your product can be a major undertaking. The reasoning behind the deals is to help the buyer justify some of the costs and risks associated with introducing, or pioneering, the product. Most distributors, for example, would like to be assured of their normal profit at the outset of a product introduction in the event the product does not succeed. This way, they do not have to wait until the product takes off before they make a profit. The cost of deals is a cost to you, just like the cost of ingredients, and must be budgeted and controlled accordingly.

Deals offer extra profits to the buyer, lower selling prices to attract customers, sources of funding for advertising/promotion, and assistance in gaining attention over competing brands.

Note that many of the following deals/allowances should be offered only if the buyer asks for them and considered only if you feel the overall benefit is worth the expense. Weigh your decisions carefully. You will want to develop a long-term relationship with the buyer, which may not evolve if at first you give the product away and then later withdraw the deal.

The Overall Best Deal: Guaranteed Sales

As a rule, most food marketers only guarantee that their product is packed properly and will replace only broken or damaged merchandise. Now think about how much you appreciate your local appliance/electronics store policy that allows you to return almost any product within 30 days of purchase for an exchange, credit, or full refund—no questions asked. Such a policy develops tremendous store loyalty. Wouldn't it be terrific if the food industry did that? (Safeway does it.) What if you allowed your consumer to return the unused portion of your product for a full refund, no questions asked? If you did this, you could quickly carve out a niche that would appeal to almost any distributor or retailer. The offer would be for the consumer only.

Of course, the matter is tricky in that we are dealing with a consumable. The CD player you bought can be returned, no questions asked, and then sold at clearance, thereby offering the seller an option to recoup at least the cost of the product. On the other hand, you are stuck with the half-used jar of mustard that was returned by an unhappy consumer.

A twist on this would be to guarantee the sale, within a specific period, to both the distributor and the retailer. In other words, if your product fails to move, for whatever reason, either the distributor or the retailer could return it for a full refund or credit. In this case, it would be fair for the retailer or distributor who returns the product to pay the return freight.

Free Merchandise

"One free case with 10, the 11th case is free." The distributors or retailers may use the free product in any way they wish. The retailers may choose to pass the savings along to the consumer, or the distributors may pass it along to the retailer, or either may take the difference to defer the cost of introducing the product and to increase profits.

Note that this differs from the offer "one free case *in* ten." Offering the 11th case free is preferred because you ship more product, which is, after all, the point. One free case *with* ten amounts to a 9.1 percent discount; one free case *in* ten would be a 10 percent discount. Table 6.3 shows various discount percentages with free merchandise.

If you specify that the free goods are for the retailer, then obtain proof of delivery for free merchandise shipped from the distributor to the retailer. In this

Table 6.3: Discount Percentages on Free Merchandise

Here are some other free merchandise discount percentages:

1 free with 2	=	33.3%	1 free with 12	=	7.7%
1 free with 3	=	25.0%	1 free with 20	=	4.7%
1 free with 5	=	16.7%	1 free with 25	=	3.8%
1 free with 10	=	10.0%			

way, you have greater assurance that your product gets to the customer, and you get the names and addresses of the customers.

Sampling Allowance

Another free merchandise offer involves providing free product to the distributor (or retailer) so that free samples can be offered to consumers. This can also help the distributor get a retailer to purchase for the first time.

Demonstration Allowance

The demo allowance can combine free product along with a cash discount to cover the cost of a demonstrator. The demonstrator is retained either by you, the retailer, or the distributor to serve and promote your product in the retail store. Ascertain beforehand the demonstrator's abilities and the day and time of the intended demonstration. If possible, control and monitor the demonstration carefully, for experience shows that the absence of active producer involvement in control of demonstrations can waste time and money.

Prepare a standard demonstration kit that contains the procedures you want to be followed for the demonstrator to be paid. It should include detailed instructions and an evaluation form that must be sent to you after the completed demonstration.

Demonstration costs vary, depending on the store and on the nature and length of the demonstration. Please refer to the section on promotion earlier in this chapter for a discussion of demonstration costs.

Special Payment Terms

Many companies offer a discount for payment within ten days. This can be expressed as "2 percent, 10 days, NET 30 days, F.O.B warehouse." This means that the distributor and retailer will pay the freight (either freight collect or added to the invoice) and that you must receive their payment with a 2 percent discount on the 10th day or in the full amount by the 30th day after delivery.

As an introductory deal, you can offer special terms to the distributor, such as "2 percent, 30 days, delivered," which means that you pay the freight and the buyer takes a deduction of 2 percent from the F.O.B. invoice amount, which is due in 30 days.

You can offer any combination of these deals to either the distributor or the retailer. My recommendation is to stick to your original terms, unless it is a major purchase that would not work without special terms.

Freight Allowance

You can peg freight allowances to volume orders. For example, you might offer a 5 percent freight allowance for any order over 50 cases of assorted product. This means that the buyer may deduct 5 percent of the F.O.B. invoice amount from the payment. The idea is to encourage larger purchases by offering the benefit of economy to the buyer.

You can also calculate freight into your prices. Link these with three geographic zones—East, Central, and West—so that you will have three different delivered prices, depending on customer location.

Your terms of F.O.B. warehouse mean that the buyer is responsible for the freight costs from your loading dock to the buyer's warehouse or store. When selling to distributors, you may have occasion to ship freight collect. This means that the trucking company will pick up and deliver your merchandise and collect for the freight costs on delivery.

When shipping to a retailer, you can add the freight costs (usually a United Parcel Service-type shipper) to your invoice. Further discussion of shipping procedures and theory appears under "Warehousing and Shipping Your Product" in chapter 3.

Slotting Allowance

Many supermarket chains and specialty food distributors will require that you pay them a slotting allowance (also called push money and placement fees). This is a dollar amount, which may be paid in the form of cash, cash discounts, or free merchandise, to cover the cost of slotting the product in the distributor's warehouse. Depending on region, slotting allowances can range from $2,500 to $25,000 per product.

Ostensibly, the slotting allowance is exacted from the distributor by the supermarket chain to justify the costs, and risks, of taking on a new product. The result is that many new specialty food producers have had to seek other means of distribution, such as direct sales to small retailers, and thereby experience considerable difficulty in establishing full distribution.

Here's one way this works: your distributor will not even take your product to the selection committee unless you offer an appropriate slotting allowance.

> ### Industry Leader Comments on Slotting Allowances
>
> "Slotting allowances allow chains and distributors to make money on the buy versus the sell; therefore, success is being measured not by product performance but by product profit. This has lead to virtually flat growth for supermarkets as opposed to nearly double-digit growth within the specialty/gourmet food sector."

You can expect that the distributor will deduct up to 10 percent of the gross value of your invoice. Often, distributors will deduct an amount equal to their gross profit (your price plus their profit margin).

If you agree to a slotting fee, then you should demand proof from the distributor that the product has actually reached store shelves. The requirement for slotting allowances is a hotly debated, and it is not universally popular.

GUIDELINES FOR SUCCESS

Deals in Review

- **Advertising allowance:** Used for special promotions (e.g., ethnic foods); to be monitored carefully

- **Catalog allowance:** For catalog sales

- **Demonstration allowance:** A useful promotional tool requiring effective management

- **Free freight:** Used as a special arrangement (trade shows, seasonal specials, etc.)

- **Free merchandise:** A broadly employed and cost-effective means of getting new business

- **Freight allowance:** Used to encourage larger orders

- **Sampling allowance:** Similar to free merchandise

- **Slotting allowance:** Mostly required by supermarket chains and larger distributors; to be avoided

- **Special terms:** Not encouraged except in special circumstances (e.g., the buyer is planning a major promotion and requests an extended payment period)

Advertising and Catalog Allowances

Advertising allowances should be agreed to in advance with specific elements of proof requested. Such proof of performance can include copies of the advertising inserts or circulars.

Another form of advertising allowance is cooperative advertising, wherein you and the buyer agree to share the cost of an advertisement in a local newspaper or on a local radio station. You may be requested to provide copy and black-and-white slicks (camera-ready artwork on glossy stock) that depict your product and/or logo.

The use of advertising allowances (the buyer deducts the allowance from the invoice) and bill backs (you request the buyer to remit a bill to you at the end of the period) should be restricted to those opportunities that offer the best potential for sales.

Using catalog houses is a good way of promoting your product. To defray some of the cost of producing a catalog, catalog companies require an allowance, usually 10 percent. This is a promotional cost to you, because the catalogs generally carry your product only once, but you do get the residual benefit of putting your product before a large audience.

Appointing Brokers

Brokers are manufacturers' representatives. They do not buy your products. They take your product literature, samples, and pricing information and make sales for you in a given territory. Brokers receive a commission for sales made, based on your F.O.B. invoice value. They generally receive 10 percent commission for sales to retailers and 5 percent commission for sales to distributors. The arrangements and commissions can differ, depending on the product and the market.

Brokers obtain supermarket authorizations and monitor distributor activity on behalf of the principal. Often referred to as "food reps," food brokers also sell to individual retail accounts, small boutiques, specialty food shops, and gift shops. A food rep often maintains a showroom.

Note that most experienced brokers already have extensive lines to represent. On the one hand, a broker with several lines may not be able to devote much attention to your line; on the other hand, a new broker may not be able to make a living just selling your product alone. Nevertheless, the system works, and most brokers are interested in exploring new opportunities.

Brokers can exercise an important influence on developing sales for your products. They have access to buyers, knowledge of territories, and experience that you probably cannot afford to replace in the form of a full-time sales staff. Brokers carry a number of lines, and they often provide the only cost-effective way for you to get your product to stores in regions away from home base.

GUIDELINES FOR SUCCESS

Broker Evaluation

- **Years in business:** A well-established broker may not have room for your line.

- **Territory covered:** Is it adequate to your needs?

- **Major accounts called upon:** Do they include your prime targets?

- **Account requirements for deals, etc.:** Can you accommodate these?

- **Lines currently represented:** Do any compete with yours?

- **Number of sales staff:** Sufficient to meet your needs?

- **References:** Contact three of them for comments.

- **Success stories:** You especially want to know if the broker has been successful with lines similar to yours.

Because of this, there is a trade-off. Depending on the situation, you may have to take second place in a product lineup carried by a broker who is interested in your product. Unless the broker can see potential for high volume (read "high commission income"), then it will be unlikely that the broker will devote much attention to pioneering your product.

Brokers can help implement your promotion plans, including in-store demonstrations, and new product introductions. You will not require a broker if you can manage the territory yourself.

Locating Brokers

A general broker listing is available in appendix E. Broker listings can also be obtained from advertisements in various specialty food industry journals (appendix A). In addition, brokers regularly present themselves for consideration at the fancy food shows.

Specialty Food Broker Enigma

By Kirk Camoriano, president, Camoriano & Associates Inc.

With little or no fanfare within the trade and absolutely no identity recognition from the public, the specialty food broker plays an important role in bringing high-quality products to the American home. Misunderstood by customers and principals alike, the specialty food broker actually lowers the cost of food distribution. If there were no food broker in the chain, the manufacturer would have to field its own sales staff at a much higher cost. The broker is the efficient way to bring a product to the marketplace. Since brokers are independent business-people, they pay their own way—covering their office, payroll, insurance, telephone, and car expenses, as well as pension and taxes. They do not receive a penny unless a sale is made. Today's modern broker has become, in addition to a sales force, a full-service organization. Brokers provide cost-effective professional representation that most manufacturers could not afford on their own. Brokers must negotiate the best deal and promotion for the customer while protecting the integrity of the product they represent. The successful broker's inventory includes a code of ethics the broker's credibility and integrity, and the services the broker provides as well as product knowledge and salesmanship.

I do not recommend advertising for a broker in trade journals. It is more effective to ask other producers, retailers, and distributors for recommendations and leads than to take a shotgun approach through an industry trade journal. Make certain the prospective broker understands your product and knows how to sell it. You should meet with the broker to achieve a sense of how effectively you can do business together.

Managing Brokers

Once you have selected a broker, you will prepare a contractual agreement (appendix E) that stipulates the territory to be covered, conditions of sales, terms, commissions, payment procedures, and so on. Remember, brokers work for you in specific, designated territories. Send the broker whatever quantity of samples, catalog sheets, price sheets, press kits, and other descriptive literature the broker requests.

To some extent, you can rely on your broker to provide information regarding the credit history of new accounts. You should also be able to rely on the broker to make a personal attempt to collect any overdue invoices. (Make sure the broker is amenable to this before you retain that broker's services.)

Essentially, brokers are your representatives in the field. Treat them well, pay your commissions on time, and keep them informed. You will earn attention to your product directly proportional to the amount of time and effort you expend on maintaining the broker's interest. Make it easy for the broker to make money, and you, too, will be rewarded.

Generally, brokers are paid monthly or after the customer invoice has been paid. Payment terms are something you will negotiate when the broker is appointed.

Broker Management Hints

- Visit the broker and make joint calls on key customers at least twice a year.
- Send monthly or bimonthly product information notes.
- Inform your broker of new products, testimonials, and all success stories.
- Work with the broker on planning your product promotions.
- Ask the broker to visit and work your booths at the major trade shows.

Locating Distributors

Specialty food distributors (direct store distributors) buy your product for their own accounts and sell it to retailers, and to other distributors, using their own sales forces and independent brokers.

As a rule, they offer the specialty food producer a higher volume and profit-generating alternative to direct retailer sales. The grocery food distribution system is very efficient. Because of this, it leaves little room for the lower-volume specialty food product. Specialty food distributors fill this niche by carrying products that have not yet reached the level of consumption experienced by products in the grocery trade.

GUIDELINES FOR SUCCESS

Appointing Distributors

Consider the following elements before you appoint a distributor:

- **Length of appointment:** Your letter of appointment should stipulate the period covered (e.g., one year from signing, renewable annually thereafter).

- **Territory covered:** Stipulate which state, region, or large metropolitan area you are assigning to the distributor.

- **Promotional support:** Determine which combination of advertising allowances, special deals, free merchandise, etc. will be required by the distributor. Negotiate the details that are best suited to your mutual requirements and circumstances.

- **Frequency of contact:** You should attempt to be in regular contact with all your distributors. Use mail, telephone, and fax plus personal visits and combined sales calls.

- **Termination provisions:** Your appointment letter should provide the means for terminating the contract. Either party can effect this in writing with 60 days advance notice.

Note: In many instances, you will have to take what is available and proceed without any formal appointment. If a distributor wants to buy your product, you cannot refuse on the basis of other distributor arrangements. This can be considered restraint of trade and is against the law; however, you can always appoint your distributor in a given territory as master distributor. That distributor would then sell to other distributors. In fact, once the distributor buys your product, you have no legal control over what that distributor decides to do with it!

Many newer specialty food processors begin by selling direct to the retailer. A number of them retain this method of distributing their products even after they have gained a foothold in the market. With the increasing incidence of slotting allowances (see "Arranging the Deals" earlier in this chapter), most small companies are unable to afford the cost of introducing a new product through distributors.

Distributors will let you know what they require. To attract their attention, you will most likely have to develop some of their territory first. This means selling direct to retailers. You will have to assess your circumstances carefully and be prepared for the long haul if you wish to continue selling direct to the retailer.

Distributor Services

Specialty food distributors offer a variety of services to the producer and to the retailer. Many, but not all, specialty food distributors perform the following services:

- Make sales calls on retailers and chain buyers.
- Purchase, inventory, and deliver your product to the retailer.
- Stock retailer shelves (usually only at chains).
- Oversee in-store demos.
- Prepare shelf diagrams for optimal display of the product (usually done only at chains).
- Provide product sales and profit data to the retailer.
- Distribute point-of-purchase (POP) materials (obtained from you).
- Instruct store personnel in the benefits of your product.
- Rotate shelf stock and remove unsalable merchandise (usually done only at chains).

Making the Sale

Now that you have an appointment, remember to take product samples, price lists, catalog sheets, pens, and a handheld calculator. You will need the latter to verify your mental gymnastics. These will come about as you respond to fast questions about various discounts and quantity orders and other details from the buyer.

Use your price list as an order form. This will make it easier to process the order when you return to the office. Generally, you will not be required to give a copy of the order to the buyer. Many distributors will provide you with their own computer-generated order forms.

Examples of What Not to Say

Buyer: "My 42-inch flat screen isn't working."
You: "I've had one sent to you from Macy's."

Buyer: "This stuff's too expensive!"
You: "Oh, here's $1,000 in cash to help you pay for it."

Closing the Sale

The single greatest obstacle to closing a sale, aside from ignorance, is the fear of rejection! We all want friendly environments. We all want everybody to love our product, but we tend to avoid asking the most important question: "How many cases may I ship you?"

A great salesperson goes for the jugular! This salesperson never cries uncle, no matter how many rejections, insults, or refusals received. The process is constantly being improved. No salesperson rests on laurels. All salespeople love selling. Learn about the importance of stressing benefits to the buyers instead of simply pointing out product features.

Listen to the buyer and learn how to handle objections (most of which can be turned to your advantage, once you know what to say).

Do not impugn your competition, especially if the competing product is carried by the company to which you are trying to sell. This puts the buyer in an awkward position, for the buyer probably made the decision to carry the other product, and putting the buyer's judgment in question may impede your progress.

Your first goal has been achieved. You are in the company of a qualified buyer who has expressed an interest in hearing your pitch. Don't lose sight of your objective. It's not to make friends or to have an informal chat. Your sole objective is to make that sale!

Keep focused! So many of us go off on tangents. When you are stressing the benefits of purchasing your product, it is easy to react defensively when the buyer

GUIDELINES FOR SUCCESS

Handling Buyer Objections

Buyer: "I already have a dozen brands of mustard."
You: "Offering variety and choice is a specialty food trade strength. This is especially true in the mustard and condiment category."

Buyer: "Your competition offers a better deal."
You: "Let's compare the two deals, and I will consider meeting or bettering it."

Buyer: "Your product is just too expensive."
You: "Ours offers the highest quality of any product in its category. It is more than worth the money. Why not let your customers decide?"

Buyer: "I have no more room in my product assortment."
You: "You can purchase a smaller beginning order of the unique item(s) in my line." (For example, if your line consists of five different condiments, offer the one that is really different, not readily available from other suppliers, as the lead.)

Buyer: "Not now." (This is very common.)
You: "If not now, then when?" Or, "What would it take to make the offer of interest now?" (There may not be much you can do about this, except to offer to come back, call, or make contact by mail later.)

Buyer (a retailer): "I don't want to deal with another supplier."
You: "I can ship COD and save you the time and cost of setting up a new file/account."

Buyer (a retailer): "I don't want to deal with another supplier."
You: "Can you give me the name of a distributor with whom you like dealing and from whom you would consider buying my product?"

Buyer (a distributor): "I don't want to do the pioneering your product requires in my territory."
You (having made several successful sales calls in the distributor territory): "Here are a half dozen orders from retailers in your territory. All you have to do is deliver my product in your next shipment to them."

(continued)

Handling Buyer Objections *(continued)*

Buyer (distributor who doubts worth of product): "We don't have any call for
this product."

You: "People (retail customers) won't ask for products they know you don't have.
Why not poll your retailer customers by phone or mail to determine the product's
potential?"

Buyer (who already buys similar products): "Why should I change suppliers and give
you the business?"

You: "We're not asking you to abandon your current supplier—just let us supply you
with a few items and let us prove our service and value to you."

Buyer: "Will you guarantee the product?"

You: "We will guarantee the product against defects and will replace or refund.
We do not guarantee the sale of the product." (See earlier comments about
guaranteed sales).

---

asks something like: "What am I going to do with just another _____?"
The buyer is not tearing down your "baby." Instead, the buyer is looking for
ammunition to help make a favorable decision. Who else but you should know
why it is important to purchase your product? Remember that you are providing
a solution (benefit) to the buyer.

Sales ability is acquired. We do it in all walks of life. Make the call once you
are solidly prepared and practice beforehand. Don't let your pitch sound canned.
It does not take a lifetime to master the successful sales pitch.

Specialty food buyers are not interested, ostensibly, in product quality, variety, choice, or newness per se. They want the product line that offers them the
best deal—one with the most up-front profit.

The buyer/seller dialogues in the Guidelines for Success provide a small sampling of how you could respond to some of the more common objections.

Exporting:
Sales to Nontraditional Markets

Food exporting can be both profitable and challenging. You will encounter legal requirements for pull dates in the European Economic Community, for example, and you will have to provide labels in a number of languages.

Nevertheless, always be on the lookout for opportunities to sell your product overseas. For most specialty food products, this will mean sales opportunities generated by overseas visitors to your booth at U.S. trade shows.

This is especially the case with the shows sponsored by NASFT and the National Association of State Departments of Agriculture (NASDA). The latter organization focuses exclusively on promoting U.S.-made food products in overseas markets. The NASDA show, called U.S. Food Export Showcase, is held in concert with the new Global Food & Style Expo in Chicago (see appendix M). See *www.nasda.org* for show listings.

Your first point of contact should be the staff of your home state's department of agriculture. They will direct you to the local resource for export assistance. In Massachusetts, for example, the Executive Office of Environmental Affairs—Department of Food and Agriculture coordinates export assistance.

At the national level, the U.S. Department of Agriculture's Foreign Agricultural Service (FAS) is the best source of information and assistance for entering overseas markets. Be advised, though, that the FAS has focused most of its energies on agricultural commodities. Only recently has the service begun to offer aid to what it calls high-value food products. The FAS offers marketing assistance that includes trade leads, low-cost advertising in its weekly newsletter, buyer and supplier listings, and U.S. pavilions at major international trade shows. The FAS also provides market promotion, export enhancement, and credit guarantee programs. Finally, foreign market information is published in government publications and research documents.

A good point of contact is the Trade Assistance and Program Office, USDA/ FAS, 3101 Park Center Drive, Suite 1103, Alexandria, VA 22302; (703) 305-2772; *www.fas.usda.gov.*

Chapter 7
Running Your Business

Many new food producers spend too much of their time focusing on food production and marketing and not enough time on how to set up the business. There are a number of ways to organize the structure of your business; you just need take the time to define what works best for you.

Organizing Your Business

Before reading this, please review "Establishing a Strategic Network" in chapter 1.

Your organizational choices include a sole proprietorship; partnership; subchapter S corporation; limited liability corporation (LLC); and other, somewhat complicated arrangements. Most of the companies in the specialty food trade are proprietorships. If you want to form a corporation, you can do so by calling a corporation-forming service in Delaware. Costs run around $75. However, I recommend that you seek counsel from a qualified attorney before you proceed.

Partnerships: What Are They All About?

If you are producing and marketing a product with a colleague, then you may want to form a partnership.

Benefits

Along with sharing profits, you also share the workload, expenses, liability, and taxes. Doing this takes a great deal of thought. If you are considering forming a partnership, you should find answers to the following important questions.

Why Do I Need a Partner?

It may be as simple as needing additional money to invest in your business, or you might just want another person's expertise, experience, and industry contacts to help your business grow.

Each partner brings individual talents to the business. For example, one partner may bring sales and marketing skills, while the other brings design skills, development of new products, and warehouse management.

Is the Chemistry Right?

Partners have to be sure of compatibility. Each partner brings a different perspective. Similar guiding principles and moral philosophy will ensure respect for each other. Having the same philosophy is very important to a successful partnership.

One way to find out if the organizational fit is right before forming the partnership is to set up a trial period. Avoid committing yourself financially until you are sure you and your partner(s) are compatible.

Can You Trust Your Potential Partner?

A lot of your business activities will be based on trust. Trade is done in a straightforward manner. Partners who don't trust each other will suffer the consequences. Similar abilities and skill levels help, but understanding among the partners has to take place in an environment of trust.

Can Partners Be Friends?

Many a friendship has ended when friends live together or go into business together. Two or more people who get along as friends will not necessarily make good business partners. And when you are friends before you are partners, it may be more difficult to offer opposing opinions for fear of hurting each other's feelings. Dissolving a partnership can be messier than the messiest divorce.

Successful partnerships are based on professionalism and attitude, as well as a burning desire to succeed. This doesn't mean you have to sacrifice your friendship to profit; it just means you have to base your decisions on business needs, not the friendship.

Each partner must agree not to make business decisions unilaterally. This is where respect for each other's talents comes in.

> ### Focus
> Creating a business partnership takes work, especially since entrepreneurs tend to be very independent. People with such zeal find it difficult to fuse their efforts in one direction, which can be very costly.

Can You and Your Partners Reach Consensus?

Partners must be able to compromise and reach consensus in decision making. Once you are in agreement on your company vision, the direction you take will be clear to all concerned. Regular communication is essential to avoid the usual misunderstandings. Make time to talk about your business ideas only. Learn how to become an effective listener.

Financing the Venture: Who Invests What?

The amount of money you allot to the business can be determined by a clear understanding of who will be doing what. If the partnership work is not evenly distributed, will this mean a greater investment for one than the other? And how will profits be distributed?

Will You Need a Formal Agreement?

Ultimately, no amount of paper will replace the basic trust and understanding between you and your partners, the kind of understanding that is sealed with

---

Figure 7.1: Some Elements of a Partnership Agreement

- Date of agreement
- Names of all partners
- Business name
- Place of business
- Term of partnership
- Nature of the business

- Partner roles
- Finance and investment details
- Compensation details
- Who has authority to do what
- Termination provisions
- Special provisions

---

a handshake. However, drawing up a formal agreement with the advice of a lawyer will clarify the issues and settle any future disputes should one of the partners decide to quit. All parties should write down all the issues each thinks are important. See where the issues converge and where they diverge. Negotiate the details. Reach consensus.

Figure 7.1 lists some of the elements your partnership agreement should contain. It is advisable to consult with a lawyer once you have worked out the various articles of your agreement.

Processing Orders and Office Management

Order processing and office management are employed in preparing the paper-work associated with shipping and paying for orders. All of your order processing should be done with the use of a computer.

Accounts Receivable Bookkeeping

It will be important for you to understand some basic accounting, called double-entry accounting, which is easy to learn. Perhaps it will be easier for you to retain the services of an accountant or bookkeeper; however, many of you will not be able to afford this luxury in the early stages of your business development. Also, it will be necessary for you to understand the principles involved so you can communicate effectively with the bookkeeper.

Carl A. Lindblad, an associate with Rogers-Suleski & Associates LLC (specializing in small business service; *cal@rogers-suleski.com*) offers the following guidance:

From the very start, it is essential that you set up an accurate and informative bookkeeping system. An exhaustive study has revealed that of the eight primary causes of business failure, six are financial. They are insufficient capital, inventory mismanagement, overspending on fixed assets, too liberal a credit policy, taking too much out of the business, and too rapid growth. The other two are lack of experience and wrong location.

Furthermore, it should go without saying that your business should have a bank account separate from your personal account. Personal funds should not be comingled with business funds, and all transactions should go through the bank account and not through distant cash or other accounts.

If you do not have a good working knowledge of bookkeeping, you should hire the services of a competent professional to set up your books and teach you how best to use them. This applies even if you are unable to afford a bookkeeper or ongoing services in the early stages of your business.

In seeking professional help, check with friends and acquaintances to find a highly recommended accountant or bookkeeping professional. They may have designations all the way from Certified Public Accountant (CPA) to public accountant to bookkeeping service. If you have employees, payroll is always a complicated subject. Usually, fairly inexpensive payroll services (even some banks) can handle this for you.

In your discussions with these firms, you will want to ascertain what sort of financial programs each offers. The more important systems include income statements, balance sheets, the general ledger, and budget statements. A brief description of each follows:

- **The statement of activities** (the income statement) is an historical report showing how your business did during a certain period. It is a primary source for business planning and should contain such vital information as sales by product, cost by product, gross profit, expenses by type, and ratios used to monitor the financial health of the business.

- **The statement of financial position** (the balance sheet) is a snapshot of the financial condition of the business at the time stated. It not only shows the net worth or book value (assets minus liabilities) of your business but also provides the remaining figures needed to calculate the important ratios of business analysis. Such ratios include liquidity, safety, profitability, and asset management. The ratios are important for financial control and are used by bankers and other lenders when considering loans to the business. Your bookkeeping firm should be able to analyze the ratios of your business.

- **The general ledger**, commonly called the "books" of the company, records all of the day-to-day financial transactions. The more detail, for later understanding, the better. Supporting the general ledger are subsidiary ledgers and records, which may include the employee ledger, sales journal, purchase journal, and inventory report.

RECIPE FOR SUCCESS

Nantucket Off-Shore Seasonings, a start-up operation manufacturing a unique line of blended herbs and spices, relied solely on public relations via trade show sales and telephone/mail order to support its entry into the specialty food market. The product's benefits (as told by their public relations firm) were among the first of their kind and fit into current consumer desires for quality, taste, convenience, and low-fat cooking. The effort resulted in features in the *New York Times, Family Circle, Food & Wine, Parade,* and other publications. The favorable publicity convinced top retailer and catalog distributors that the product was worth carrying. This increased availability generated further publicity.

- **Budget statements** are estimates of future results. A carefully prepared budget will enable you to plan marketing strategy, production criteria, personnel needs, and financing requirements. A good budget not only supplies a reasoned road map for future operations but also yields essential information for potential lenders or investors. This is where you "plan your work, then work your plan."

The vital consideration in selecting a financial services professional is not the university degree or designation but the quality of training and the amount of experience such a person can bring to get your particular business headed in the right direction. Interview and compare the prices and experience of several such firms and don't necessarily pick the cheapest one.

Your system should include a complete set of books, monthly financial statements, required tax returns (which do require a professional), and an accurate and aged tracking of accounts receivable and accounts payable transactions. Anything less puts your business at risk.

Essentially, accounts receivable bookkeeping is simply keeping track of who owes you money during a period in time. Usually, you will work on a monthly basis. Using Quickbooks saves time. This allows you to keep track of sales and receivables and payables during the month, to budget, and to allocate the funds involved using the columns provided.

You make entries when transactions occur: sales (or debits) and receipts (or credits). Each account ledger card is filed alphabetically by customer name, which offers you an easy way of keeping track of each customer account. Much of the accounts receivable bookkeeping can be accomplished with the use of computer software programs.

Dunning

Dunning is what you do when the account you thought was going to pay on time doesn't. If your terms are net 30 days, then around the 35th day, mail or email the first of three dunning letters/notes.

About ten days after the final letter/telephone call, place the account into collection. A number of firms provide this service. At the level of your activity, these firms will charge as much as 40 percent of the invoice amount to make the collection. If they fail, they will recommend that you seek legal recourse. As a rule, this is only practical for amounts over $5,000, and it can be very costly, usually more than either the invoice amount or the amount that would be awarded in court. Consider writing the outstanding amount off as a bad debt (a factor that should be considered in your pricing under a "reserve for bad debts" category).

Forms Usage and Filing

Many of your basic supplies, including invoices, envelopes, price sheets, letter-head stationery, address labels, credit check forms, and dunning letters/forms, can be designed with the help of a personal computer.

Forget about running your business without a personal computer, because the 21st century is upon us and no business can be in the least way professional—or profitable—without computers. Figure 7.2 suggests some tips to get maximum mileage out of your invoice.

Figure 7.2: Tips to Get Maximum Mileage Out of Invoices

The invoice copies may be used for some or all of the following purposes:

Part 1: Customer via mail or email

Part 2: Broker via email

Part 3: Accounts receivable (There's no need to produce a hard copy; use your electronic file.)

Part 4: Warehouse copy via email

Part 5: Packing slip via email

Naturally, you will want to maintain files of all your business correspondence, accounts receivable, accounts payable, completed sales transactions, etc. Generally, hard copies of files are kept current for one year, then placed in a different drawer. Keep one current-year file drawer, plus two others for the past two years. Files from earlier years may be retired to boxes and should be stored for at least seven years (for tax purposes).

Filing should be set up in accordance with what makes life easier for you. Files should be organized according to some rationale that is easy to remember and easy to employ. A file set up for completed sales transactions alphabetically by geographic location is one of the easiest to use. (The actual filing of paper will not be necessary for most of the aforementioned, because the same thing can be achieved with your computer and accounting software. Just make sure to back up your computer files frequently.)

Notwithstanding my statement about the importance of computers, we still need some paper backup for our records. Make certain to back up your computer files. A number of software titles can do this. I recommend storing copies of all your files on a USB flash drive, for example, or a special zip drive and disk or a CD-ROM.

Order-Processing Flow

There are a number of good software packages that you can employ to keep track of your transactions. For example, QuickBooks and One-Write Plus Accounting offer full business accounting systems. Until you get the requisite software, you will need a "one-write" accounting system, consisting of binder, journal forms, and ledger cards.

The flowchart in "Guidelines for Success," can be applied to understanding and clarifying both manual and computer applications. The flow shows both hard copy and computer software processing. You will not have to place invoice copies in a hold file if you are using a software-generated invoice. Simply save the information in the customer's computer account. With the use of computers, there is no need for hard copies beyond those mailed to the customer (and one can also email these to customers).

GUIDELINES FOR SUCCESS

Order-Processing Flowchart

Much time can be saved if the processes described below are accomplished with the use of order-processing software (e.g., entering an order number, deducting from inventory, and invoice distribution).

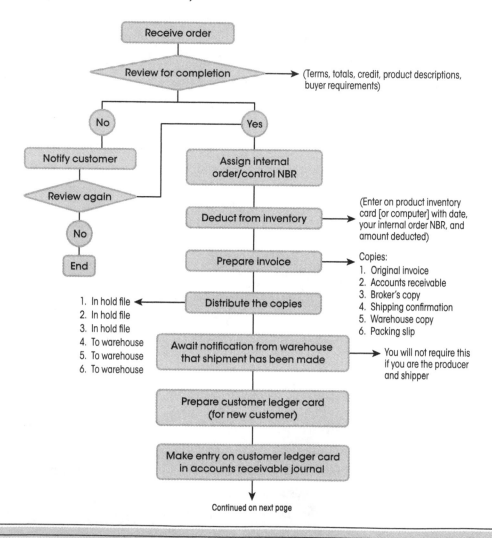

Continued on next page

Order-Processing Flowchart *(continued)*

```
                    ┌──────────────────────────┐        1. To customer
──────────────────▶│ Distribute the hold file copies │───▶   2. To accounts receivable
                    └──────────────────────────┘        3. To broker
                    ┌──────────────────────────┐
                    │ Review accounts receivable journal daily │
                    └──────────────────────────┘
                              (and)
                    ┌──────────────────────────┐
                    │  Depending on terms, begin  │
                    │ dunning process if payment is overdue │
                    └──────────────────────────┘
                        ┌─────────────────┐
                        │ Receive payment │
                        └─────────────────┘
         (No) ◀────────◀ Review for correctness ▶
    ┌──────────────────┐
    │ Contact customer │
    └──────────────────┘
         Correct now? ────────────────────────────▶ (Yes)
              (No)
                                    (Date paid, amount,   ◀─┌──────────────────────────┐
                                     check number, etc.)    │ Make entry on file copy of invoice │
                                                            └──────────────────────────┘
                                    (Credit accounts     ◀─┌──────────────────────────┐
                                     receivable)            │ Make entry on customer ledger card │
                                                            │ and accounts receivable journal │
                                                            └──────────────────────────┘
  (Recommendation: File drawer with hanging  ◀─┌─────────────┐
   folder files labeled by state, or territory, with │ File papers │
   papers filed alphabetically by customer name.     └─────────────┘
   Place in drawer marked by calendar year
   and retire to archive boxes after three years.   ┌──────────────────────────┐
   Or, you may file all of your data in your hard    │ At end of cycle (30 days) prepare │
   drive. Back this up at least once a week.)        │ broker statement and commission │
                                                     │ check; mail check and file papers │
                                                     └──────────────────────────┘
                                                              (End)
```

Notes to Order-Processing Flow

The flow shows both hard copy and computer software processing. You will not have to place invoice copies in a hold file if you are using a software-generated invoice. Simply file the information in the customer's computer account. No need for hardcopies beyond those mailed to the customer.

Risk Management

Poorly managed risk is often painful for individuals and small businesses and can become a dangerous obstacle to economic growth, discouraging the sort of entrepreneurial risk taking that has long fueled the specialty food market. Risk-related topics include disaster planning, insurance, product recalls, office crime, and risk/return analysis.

Food Product Liability Insurance

For your purposes, liability insurance springs to mind. Insurance industry expert Scott Mikkelson (*scott@mkkins.com*) offers the following on the topic:

RECIPE FOR SUCCESS

The organic fruit juice company Adina for Life was successful after 18 months and a $2 million investment. Owner Dominique Leveuf won the BEV NET Best Noncarbonated Drink in 2005 with the Organic Cooler line after only a five-month rollout. Adina for Life has since added an all-organic and fair trade line and a line of Miracle Fruit coolers.

The company philosophy "is based on the principle of sustainability, meaning bringing products to the market that are good for your health and your planet while being profitable. [We're also about] persistence and love of the work you do."

Insurance is an important safeguard for any business, and insurance coverage is available in a variety of options.

Specific requirements should be carefully evaluated with your insurance provider. Many specialty food entrepreneurs consider insurance coverage only when a buyer requests it or when circumstances suggest that it would be prudent (such as the possibility of a lawsuit).

Food product liability coverage is one form of insurance coverage that food entrepreneurs should consider. This type of coverage should provide some protection in the event that the insured food product injures the user. Most retail outlets "require" that a product have a minimum level (normally $1 million) of product liability coverage before they will carry it.

Policy-issuing firms can be contacted by "any" local or private insurance agency to discuss the writing of a food product liability policy;

however, they will require specific product information and business data (annual sales, annual payroll, etc.) to provide a premium quote. They may require that the request be made by an insurance agency rather than the business owner.

Product liability coverage cost is not easy to estimate. Most providers can quote for a $1 million policy but only when a series of business and product-specific questions are answered. A rule of thumb suggests that the annual premium for a $1 million policy is around $1,000, but such rules of thumb can be a long way from reality.

There is no standard rate for food product liability policies, because product liability insurance providers are reluctant to provide policy estimates. To get an actual quote, most companies require a completed application and the submission of the business' production, distribution, and marketing plans. The level of the applicant's gross sales and prior claims history are variables that can significantly contribute to the annual premium.

The following information, from an informal survey of insurance providers, provides a good place to start. The survey found a wide range of annual premium estimates for food product liability coverage.

> ## Food Entrepreneur eZine 2008 Survey
>
> At what point in your business development did you purchase product liability insurance? Responses in order of prevalence:
>
> - At start-up (70%)
> - I do not carry product liability insurance. (17.5%)
> - Within 1–3 years (7.5%)
> - Within 3–5 years (4%)
> - Other (4%)

- Annual premiums for food product liability insurance coverage range from $500 to $20,000.
- The average food product liability premium is estimated at $3,000.

GUIDELINES FOR SUCCESS

Insurance

Sweet Heat author Melissa T. Stock comments about food product liability insurance:

The bottom line is that to be a real company, you need to have insurance. That's the word from every hot shop, gourmet shop, and grocery store we talked to. In fact, most retailers want to see a certificate of insurance before they place their first order. Some want to see proof of coverage before they will even consider a product for placement. Just as your vendors have the right to ask for verification of sufficient insurance, it makes good business sense for you also to ask for certificates of insurance from suppliers who are part of your business, from bottlers, copackers, and distributors. There are coverages besides product liability that you may want to consider. Here is a list of a few additional endorsements to explore:

- Property coverage
  - Brands and labels
  - Property in transit
  - Property at fairs and exhibits
  - Spoilage

- Food industry-specific risks
  - Refrigeration equipment insurance
  - Rejection insurance to cover the cost of a shipment of imported food should it be rejected by the USDA
  - Coverage for internal "shrinkage" and theft
  - Ocean, cargo, and U.S. transit coverage

- The most significant factors contributing to an annual premium are as follows:
  - Level of gross sales or annual payroll
  - Prior claims/history
  - Level of coverage
  - Specialty or standard market

- Type of product
- Type of market
- Recall plan
- Batch system for production

Some agencies base the premium totally on estimated gross sales and charge a certain dollar premium per thousand dollars of estimated gross sales. For example, a premium for a product with an estimated $50,000 in annual gross sales might cost $500, or $10 per $1,000 worth of estimated sales. In general, the rate per $1,000 of sales tends to decrease as gross sales increase. Many small business policies are subject to a minimum premium, which can be around $500 per year.

Tax Considerations

Depending on the type of company you establish (proprietorship, partnership, corporation, limited liability, or subchapter S corporation), you may be required to file certain types of tax returns, both with the IRS and with your state revenue service. The important thing to remember is to keep accurate and complete records of all your business income and expenditures. You would be well advised to seek the advice of an accountant when you first set up your books. The process of meeting your tax obligations will be less cumbersome if you get the paperwork in order from the start.

Customer Service Management (CSM)

The basic premise of good customer service is to operate for the convenience of your customer. This means that you call the customer back instead of asking the customer to return your call. You accept the responsibility for getting answers to customers' questions. Don't ask them to telephone someone else to get an answer. The examples are endless. Suffice it to say that many food producers fail to get the point about customer service: it is service to the customer. Figure 7.3 illustrates this point.

Figure 7.3: Customer Service

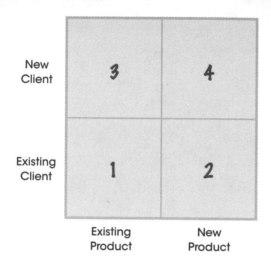

1. The easiest sale to make is to sell an existing product to an existing client.
2. The second-easiest sale is to sell a new product to an existing client.
3. Third is to sell an existing product to a new client.
4. And the hardest sale is a new product to a new client.

One often overlooked aspect of marketing is the after-order follow-up process. Sometimes this is simply an email, telephone call, or visit to see that all arrived in good order. This helps cement your professional relationship, and it creates goodwill. You impress the customer as someone who will stay around and not run off with the check.

Consider email marketing to ensure that customer contact is maintained. In those areas where you are not using a broker, you can generate continued sales via the Internet. You can use email to contact all your customers, regardless of broker use, regarding special promotions. Alert your broker of any subsequent interest so that a sales call can be made.

Earlier, we talked about the distinction between *customer* and *consumer*. The consumer consumes your product; the customer buys it for resale. The latter determines the quality of your service/product. Your success can be measured only by how you meet your customers' quality needs.

Customer Feedback Hint

After the order is shipped, invite your customer to comment on the condition of the product or the nature of any of your services via email. This can also be designed as a convenient and easy-to-use reorder form.

Creating Your Own Success Niche

This book began by testing your motivation. You learned that obtaining nationwide distribution—in every grocery on every corner in every city and town—costs the market leaders a fortune. More than 15,000 new food products are introduced every year, and there is a 96 percent failure rate over the first three years. Yet here you are, now versed in the methods and procedures for marketing your specialty food product. Or armed as you are with the knowledge, you have decided, or are about to decide, that it is just not for you. Perhaps you are going to give it a good think before proceeding.

In either case, you are ahead of the game. You now know the importance of developing a clear vision, how to become a focused niche player, and what is needed to get your product on the food store shelf.

How to Know If You Are Successful

Add up your revenues, deduct your costs, and if something is left over, you might be successful. This is the traditional means of determining success in business. A better and more long-term way is to measure the effect you and your company are having on your customers. Have you, in fact, delighted them?

There are tools you can use to measure your efforts at quality planning and exceeding your customers' quality needs.

The Malcolm Baldrige National Quality Award, administered by the U.S. Department of Commerce, incorporates criteria that you can use to evaluate your forward movement. The award was established in 1987 to promote awareness of the importance of quality improvement, to recognize organizations that made substantial improvements in competitive performance, and to foster sharing of best practices information among U.S. organizations. Only one food industry firm has won the award: Stay Fresh Foods, a manufacturer and distributor of more than 160 egg-based food products.

Whether or not you apply, a review of the award criteria may help in your search for excellence. Following is a brief summary of key elements of the award criteria.

Leadership

This category examines how you and your key managers create and sustain clear quality values and whether you have developed an appropriate supporting management system that promotes management excellence. An example of a quality value is your willingness to treat all customers equally. Another is to involve all members of your team in your product development and promotion planning. If you do it all alone, you risk the possibility of someone on whom you rely not having a stake in the outcome and, therefore, not giving a full share of the effort.

Describe your personal involvement in setting directions and in developing and maintaining a leadership system that fosters excellence. Here are some questions to ask yourself:

- Do you create and reinforce high expectations throughout your company?
- Do you set performance goals and measures through strategic planning?
- Do you maintain a climate conducive to continuous learning?

Strategic Planning

This category looks at how you set strategic direction and how you determine key planning requirements. Describe your strategic planning process and how this process determines and addresses key customer performance requirements (one might be a rapid turnaround of orders). Ask yourself: Do you translate these requirements into critical success factors (24-hour order processing, for example)?

Customer and Market Focus

Examines how you determine customer (both internal and external) satisfaction. Your primary customers (those without whom your company would not exist) are the food buyers. Other customers include companies that buy your products for resale (distributors and retailers), your employees, and any other entity for whom your company provides a product or service.

Ask yourself: How do you develop and maintain awareness of the needs and expectations of your current and future customers? Understanding the voice of the customer is essential to achieving customer satisfaction.

Measurement, Analysis, and Knowledge Management

This category examines how your organization selects, gathers, analyzes, manages, and improves its data, information, and knowledge assets and how it manages its information technology. This category also examines how your organization reviews and uses reviews to improve its performance.

Here are some questions to ask yourself:

- How do you select, collect, align, and integrate data and information for tracking daily operations and for tracking overall organizational performance, including progress relative to strategic objectives and action plans?

> **RECIPE FOR SUCCESS**
>
> New York Mutual Trading Inc. has been in business since October 2006 and has a spot in the NASFT "Best in Category" for its Benimosu with Honey. Ami Nakanishi believes that "true success is a never-ending voyage. For us, it has been a year now where we have seen noticeable improvement and advancement. We are far from where we would like to be and still continue to work at being even more successful."

- What are your key organizational performance measures, including key short-term and longer-term financial measures?
- How do you use data and information to support organizational decision making and innovation?
- How do you select and ensure the effective use of key comparative data and information to support operational and strategic decision making and innovation?
- How do you keep your performance measurement system current with business needs and directions?
- How do you ensure that your performance measurement system is sensitive to rapid or unexpected organizational or external changes?
- How do you review organizational performance and capabilities?
- What analyses do you perform to support these reviews and to ensure that conclusions are valid?
- How do you use these reviews to assess organizational success, competitive performance, and progress relative to strategic objectives and action plans?
- How do you use these reviews to assess your organization's ability to respond rapidly to changing organizational needs and challenges in your operating environment?

Workforce Focus

This category examines how your sales, operations, and administrative staff are aligned with your company's overall performance objectives. Also examined are your efforts to build and maintain a climate conducive to performance excellence, full participation, and personal growth.

Describe the training in quality concepts you provide for your sales, operations, and administrative staff. Here are some questions to ask yourself:

- Are your resource planning and evaluation aligned with your company's overall performance improvement plan?

- Do you evaluate your sales staff, for example, on how effectively it meets customer needs as opposed to just the number of sales made?
- Do you reward high-performing individuals or high-performing teams?
- Do you treat your employees as costs to be reduced or as assets to be developed?

Process Management

Key aspects of process management are examined, including design and delivery of services and business operations. Describe how you develop new products, or line extensions, in response to customer needs. Here are some questions to ask yourself:

- Is current information on customer requirements disseminated to the employees responsible for product development and improvement?
- Do you involve everyone in discussing possible alternatives?

Results

This category examines your company's results (outcomes) in terms of how you met your customer needs. Ask yourself: How do you measure your success (return on investment, stockholder equity, gross profit margin, gross revenues, trends, number of repeat orders, new customers, complimentary letters, low employee turnover, etc.)?

The Deming Chain Reaction

Dr. W. Edwards Deming—considered one of the first leaders in the global quality movement—noted that when we focus on quality, our operating costs are reduced and our productivity improves. The process he described is a very simple chain reaction shown in table 7.2.

When you focus on quality, you improve the quality of your product, reduce its price, expand your market, and reap the profits.

Table 7.2: The Deming Chain Reaction

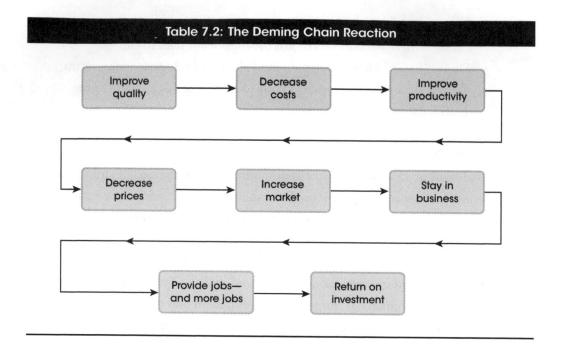

Cultivating Effective Habits

If you have decided to go ahead, then take a lead from Stephen Covey's book *The Seven Habits of Highly Effective People* and incorporate these habits into your repertoire.

- **Habit 1: Be proactive.** Proactive people develop the ability to choose their responses, making them more a product of their values and decisions than their moods and conditions.

- **Habit 2: Begin with the end in mind.** Effective people realize that things are created mentally before they are created physically. They write a vision or purpose statement and use it as a frame of reference for making future decisions. They clarify values and set priorities before selecting goals and going about the work.

- **Habit 3: Put first things first.** To leverage our time, we should devote less attention to activities that are urgent but unimportant and more time to those things that are important but not necessarily urgent. Use your business plan to help you keep on track.

- **Habit 4: Think win-win.** Effective people model the win-win principle in their relationships and agreements. The win-win performance agreement clarifies expectations by making the following five elements very explicit: desired results, guidelines, resources, accountability, and consequences.

- **Habit 5: Seek first to understand, then to be understood.** We see the world as we are, not as it is. Our perceptions come out of our experiences. Most credibility problems begin with perception differences. To resolve these differences and to restore credibility, one must exercise empathy, seeking first to understand the point of view of the other person. Remember to operate for the convenience of your customer.

- **Habit 6: Synergize.** This is the habit of creative cooperation or teamwork. For those who have a win-win abundance mentality and exercise empathy, differences in any relationship can produce synergy, where the whole is greater than the sum of its parts.

- **Habit 7: Sharpen the saw.** The habit of "sharpening the saw" regularly means having a balanced, systematic program for self-renewal in the four areas of our lives: physical, mental, emotional-social, and spiritual.

Take these seven habits to heart. They will be useful in everything you do.

Throughout this book, I have tried to make sense of some of the more complex issues of specialty food cost accounting, market research, pricing, sales, and distribution. The rest of it—production, packaging, and labeling, for example—are all pretty matter-of-fact, save the visceral issues of what is or is not aesthetically appealing (taste, packaging, labeling, etc.).

Ultimately, you will have to just put your foot in the water. To paraphrase a famous saying, "Gourmet food marketing, like the frog, can be dissected, but in the process, the beast dies." One can suffer death by analysis. If you have fire in your belly and if you have willpower, perseverance, motivation, focus, and self-discipline . . . and if you have the money, the health, the idea, the concept, the fever, the *vision* . . . then do it, and good profits to you!

I invite you to comment on this book and/or to make any recommendations for future editions. If you are a service provider, please submit your company name and description of your service to be considered for listing in the next edition of *Sell Your Specialty Food.* Please go to *www.specialtyfoodresource.com,* or send comments to Stephen Hall c/o Kaplan Publishing, 1 Liberty Plaza, 24th Floor, New York, NY 10006.

Appendix A
Trade Journals

∙∙

The following list is neither all-inclusive, nor does it mean to serve as an endorsement. Ask for sample copies and rate sheets. Please visit *www.specialty foodresource.com* for updates.

Direct Marketing Magazine
Penton Media Inc.
249 W. 17th Street
New York, NY 10011
(212) 204-4200

More than 800 mail order companies specialize in a wide range of food by mail, "each averaging about $1.5 million sales." As you may imagine, fruit, steaks, dairy, and alcoholic beverages account for most of the sales. Examples include Harry & David, Swiss Colony, Figi's, Wisconsin Cheeseman, and 800 Spirits. The "gourmet" portion of mail order sales comes mostly from companies that have retail operations. Companies such as Zabar's, Sutton Place Group's Balducci's, and Williams-Sonoma promote their products with seasonal catalogs.

Fancy Food & Culinary Products Magazine
20 W. Kenzie, Suite 1200, 12th Floor
Chicago, IL 60610
(312) 849-2220; Fax: (312) 849-2174
email: fancyfood@talcott.com

Primary focus: Specialty food and gourmet food products.

Festivities Publications Inc.
PO Box 636
Glen Saint Mary, FL 32040-0636
800-729-6338, (904) 634-1902
email: reader@festivities-pub.com
Website: *www.festivities-pub.com*

Food Entrepreneur eZine
Monthly ezine by and for food entrepreneurs. Timely topics of interest to anyone

interested in specialty food marketing, including

- specialty food website of the month;
- latest label requirements;
- mini case studies;
- pricing review; and
- strategic business and marketing planning.

Sign up for free subscription at *www.specialty foodresource.com*.

Food Product Design

Executive/Editorial Offices
3400 Dundee Road, Suite #100
Northbrook, IL 60062
(847) 559-0385; Fax: (847) 559-0389
email: contactus@foodproductdesign.com
Website: *www.foodproductdesign.com*

Primary focus: Business-to-business magazine for those individuals who design new and reformulated food products for the retail and food service markets.

Gift Basket Review Magazine

815 Haines Street
Jacksonville, FL 32206
(904) 634-1902; Fax: (904) 633-8764
Website: *www.festivities-pub.com*

Primary focus: Gift basket marketing and promotion. Design features, tips, industry news, and new products.

Gourmet News

PO Box 1056
106 Lafayette Street
Yarmouth, ME 04096
(207) 846-0600; Fax: (207) 846-0657
email: info@gourmetnews.com

Website: *www.gourmetnews.com*

Primary focus: "The business newspaper for the gourmet industry." Reports timely and newsworthy stories and events, issues, trends, and other happenings among the specialty food and natural food retailers, supermarkets and department stores, specialty distributors, and suppliers to the trade.

The Gourmet Retailer Magazine

Specialty Media Inc.
3301 Ponce de Leon Boulevard, #300
Coral Gables, FL 33134
(305) 446-3388, 800-397-1137;
Fax: (305) 446-2868
Website: *www.gourmetretailer.com*

Primary focus: A monthly trade publication that blends coverage of specialty food, kitchenware, coffee, and tea in a comprehensive source of news and information about the industry.

The Gourmet Retailer Online features all the latest industry news, access to online market research, editorial archives, comprehensive trade show information, and much more. Visit them at *www.gourmetretailer.com*.

Rave Reviews! Magazine/ Basket Connection

5045 Palm Valley Road
Ponte Vedra, FL 32082
888-RAVE101, (904) 273-0224; Fax: (904) 285-8025
email: cherie@ravereviewsmagazine
Website: *www.ravereviewsmagazine.com*

Primary focus: Rave Reviews! Magazine is the preeminent source for creative design ideas featuring gourmet products and gift baskets. In this national industry magazine published six times a year, the pages are filled with insightful articles to strengthen business awareness and beautiful designs to spark creativity. *Rave Reviews! Magazine* also sponsors an annual convention—Basket Connection—offering business, design, and marketing workshops to help retailers grow their businesses.

Specialty Food Magazine
120 Wall Street
New York, NY 10005
(212) 482-6440, 800-627-3869;
Fax: (212) 482-6459
email: info@nasft.org
Website: *www.nasft.org;*
  www.specialtyfoodmagazine.com

Primary focus: Specialty food. Strong retailer emphasis.

Prepared Foods
1050 Illinois Route 83, Suite 200
Bensenville, IL 60106
(630) 694-4353; Fax: (630) 227-0527
email: pfeditors@bnpmedia.com

Primary focus: Grocery trade, with a new products news section.

Appendix B
Trade Associations

· ·

This list is neither all-inclusive, nor does it mean to serve as an endorsement. Some references will be of minimal value to the food entrepreneur, but I have included them on the outside chance that you find one of interest. Please see *www.specialtyfoodresource.com* for updates.

General

American Association of Candy Technologists
175 Rock Road
Glen Rock, NJ 07452
(201) 652-2655; Fax: (201) 652-3419
Website: *www.aactcandy.org*

National Confectioners Association (NCA)
8320 Old Courthouse Road, Suite 300
Vienna, VA 22182
800-482-2962, (703) 790-5750;
Fax: (703) 790-5752
email: info@candyusa.org
Website: *www.ecandy.com*

National Food Brokers Association
3800 South Fremont, Suite 200
Springfield, MO 65804
877-329-1693; Fax: (417) 447-0738
email: cif@careersinfood.com
Website: *www.careersinfood.com*

American Culinary Federation
180 Center Place Way
St. Augustine, FL 32095
800-624-9458; Fax: (904) 825-4758
email: acp@acfchefs.net
Website: *www.acfchefs.org*

American Frozen Food Institute
2000 Corporate Ridge, Suite 1000
McLean, VA 22102
(703) 821-0770; Fax: (703) 821-1350
Website: *www.affi.com*

American Institute of Wine & Food (AIWF)

213-37 39th Avenue, Box 216

Bayside, NY 11361

800-274-2493; Fax: (718) 522-0204

email: info@aiwf.org

Website: *www.aiwf.org*

American Wholesale Marketers Association (AWMA)

2750 Prosperity Avenue, Suite 530

Fairfax, VA 22034

800-482-2962, (703) 208-3358;

Fax: (703) 573-5738

email: info@awmanet.org

Website: *www.awmanet.org*

The American Wholesale Marketers Association (AWMA) is the only international trade organization working on behalf of convenience distributors in the United States.

Association of Food Industries

3301 Route 66, Suite 205

Neptune, NJ 07753

(732) 922-3008; Fax: (732) 922-3590

email: info@ifus.org

Website: *http://afi.mytradeassociation.org*

The Food Institute

American Institute of Food Distribution Inc.

1 Broadway

Elmwood Park, NJ 07407

(201) 791-5570; Fax: (201) 791-5222

Website: *www.foodinstitute.com*

The Food Institute is a trade association and information-reporting organization that follows trends, changing legislation, and market statistics in the food industry. It publishes the weekly *Food Institute Report* and numerous

food-related reports, including *Food Retailing Review, Food Mergers & Acquisitions, Complying with the Nutritional Labeling & Education Act, Food Markets in Review, Supermarket Analysis Series,* and many more.

Food Marketing Institute (FMI)

2345 Crystal Drive, Suite 800

Arlington, VA 22202

(202) 452-8444; Fax: (202) 429-4519

Website: *www.fmi.org*

The Food Marketing Institute is a nonprofit association conducting programs in research, education, and public affairs on behalf of its 1,600 members, composed largely of multi-store chains, small regional firms, and independent supermarkets.

Global Market Development Center

1275 Lake Plaza Drive

Colorado Springs, CO 80906

(719) 576-4260; Fax: (719) 576-2661

Website: *www.gmdc.org*

Greater Midwest Foodways Alliance

280 Laurel Avenue

Highland Park, IL 60035-2620

(847) 432-8255

email: greatermidwestfoodways@gmail.com

Website: *www.greatermidwestfoodways.com*

The Grocery Manufacturers of America Inc. (GMA)

1350 I Street NW, Suite 300

Washington, DC 20005

(202) 639-5900; Fax: (202) 639-5932

email: info@gmaonline.com

Website: *www.gmabrands.com*

GMA is a trade association of the manufacturers and processors of food and nonfood products sold primarily in retail grocery stores in the United States. Readers may wish to request a copy of its 2007 report *E-commerce Opportunities in Direct Store Delivery*. There is no charge for this, and the report can be obtained online at the website's publications page.

Institute of Food Technologists

525 W. Van Buren, Suite 1000
Chicago, IL 60607
(312) 782-8424, Fax: (312) 782-8348
email: info@ift.org
Website: *www.ift.org*

International Association of Culinary Professionals (IACP)

455 S. Fourth Street, Suite 650
Louisville, KY 40202
800-928-4227, (502) 581-9786;
Fax: (502) 589-3602
email: info@iacp.com
Website: *www.iacp.com*

International Foodservice Manufacturers Association (IFMA)

180 N. Stetson Avenue, Suite 4400
Chicago, IL 60601-6710
(312) 540-4400; Fax: (312) 540-4401
email: ifma@ifmaworld.com
Website: *www.ifmaworld.com*

Retail Industry Leaders Association

1700 N. Moore Street, Suite 2250
Arlington, VA 22209
(703) 841-2300; Fax: (703) 841-1184
email: erin.byrne@rila.org
Website: *www.retail-leaders.org*

Kosherfest

121 Free Street
PO Box 7437
Portland, ME 04112-7437
(207) 842-5504; Fax: (207) 842-5505
Website: *www.kosherfest.com*

National Association for the Specialty Food Trade (NASFT)

120 Wall Street, 27th Floor
New York, NY 10005-4001
(212) 482-6440, 800-627-3869 (outside NY);
Fax: (212) 482-6459
email: custserv@fancyfoodshows.com
Website: *www.fancyfoodshows.com*

The NASFT is a nonprofit business trade organization that has been fostering trade, commerce, and interest in the specialty food industry since 1952. It has more than 1,800 U.S. and overseas members composed of food manufacturers, importers, distributors, and brokers involved in marketing specialty foods and beverages, fine confections, wine, cooking accessories, and publications. The association sponsors two major annual trade shows and an educational conference, and it publishes *Showcase* magazine, which tracks industry trends and presents processor and retailer profiles and pertinent government rules and regulations.

National Association of Concessionaires (NAC)

35 E. Wacker Drive, Suite 1816
Chicago, IL 60601
(312) 236-3858; Fax: (312) 236-7809
email: info@naconline.org
Website: *www.naconline.org*

National Food Processors Association
1350 I Street NW, Suite 300
Washington, DC 20005
(202) 639-5900; Fax: (202) 639-5932
Website: *www.gmaonline.org*

A primary scientific and technical association of the food industry, the National Food Processors Association (NFPA) has more than 90 years of experience and expertise in food issues. NFPA members manufacture the nation's processed/packaged fruits and vegetables, juices and drinks, meat and poultry, seafood, and specialty products.

The Food Processors Institute is the nonprofit education arm of the NFPA. Its primary educational goal is to provide curricula of workshops, seminars, materials, texts, and leadership training in support of the food-processing industry. Member dues in NFPA start at $3,000 per year and go up, depending on the member company's annual revenues.

National Frozen & Refrigerated Foods Association
4755 Linglestown Road, Suite 300
Harrisburg, PA 17112-0069
(717) 657-8601; Fax: (717) 657-9862
email: info@nfraweb.org
Website: *www.nffa.org*

National Grocers Association
1005 North Glebe Road, Suite 250
Arlington, VA 22201-5758
(703) 516-0700; Fax: (703) 812-1821
email: info@nationalgrocers.org
Website: *www.nationalgrocers.org*

National Restaurant Association (NRA)
Headquarters

1200 17th Street NW
Washington, DC 20036-3006
(202) 331-5900; Fax: (202) 347-331-2429
Website: *www.restaurant.org*

National Restaurant Association (NRA)
Convention Office
150 N. Michigan Avenue, Suite 2000
Chicago, IL 60601
(312) 853-2525; Fax: (312) 853-2548
Website: *www.restaurant.org*

Natural Products Association
1773 T Street NW
Washington, DC 20009
(202) 223-0101; Fax: (202) 223-0250
email: natural@naturalproductsassoc.org
Website: *www.naturalproductsassoc.org*

Organic Trade Association
PO Box 547
Greenfield, MA 01302
(413) 774-7511; Fax: (413) 774-6432
email: info@ota.com
Website: *www.ota.com*

The Organic Trade Association (OTA) presents *The Organic Pages Online* to provide users with a quick, easy way to find certified organic products, producers, ingredients, supplies, and services offered by OTA members, as well as items of interest to the entire organic community.

Private Label Manufacturers Association (PLMA)
369 Lexington Avenue
New York, NY 10017
(212) 972-3131; Fax: (212) 983-1382
Website: *www.plma.com*

Retail Confectioners International Inc. (RCI)
1807 Glenview Road, Suite 204
Glenview, IL 60025
(847) 724-6120; Fax: (847) 724-2719
Website: *www.retailconfectioners.org*

Southern Foodways Alliance
Center for the Study of Southern Culture
Barnard Observatory
University of Mississippi
Oxford, MS 38677
(662) 915-5993
email: sfamail@olemiss.edu
Website: *www.southernfoodways.com*

The Southern Foodways Alliance is an institution of the Center for the Study of Southern Culture at the University of Mississippi in Oxford.

Western Association of Food Chains
825 Colorado Boulevard, Suite 203
Los Angeles, CA 90041
(213) 254-7270
Website: *www.wafc.com*

Snack Food Association
1600 Wilson Blvd.,
Arlington, VA 22209
800-628-1334, (703) 836-4500;
Fax: (703) 836-8262
email: sfa@sfa.org
Website: *www.sfa.org*

Baking

American Bakers Association
1300 W. I Street NW, Suite 700
Washington, DC 20005-3305

(202) 789-0300; Fax: (202) 898-1164
email: info@americanbakers.org
Website: *www.americanbakers.org*

American Institute of Baking
1213 Baker's Way
Manhattan, KS 66502
(785) 537-4750; Fax: (785) 537-1493
Website: *www.aibonline.org*

Bakers' Association of the Carolinas
c/o Mother Murphy's Lab
PO Box 16846
Greensboro, NC 27416-0546
800-849-1277

Bakers Club of Chicago
c/o Flavorchem
1525 Brook Drive
Downers Grove, IL 60515
(630) 637-2212
Website: *www.chicagobakersclub.com*

Connecticut Bakers Association
c/o Thurston Foods
30 Thurston Drive
Wallingford, CT 06492
(203) 265-1525

Deep South Retail Bakers Association
c/o Atwood's Bakery
1125 MacArthur Drive
Alexandria, LA 71303-3123
(318) 445-9561; Fax: (318) 445-6679
Website: *www.deepsouthrba.com*

Greater Southwest Retail Bakers Association
3400 Hibiscus Drive

Wylie, TX 75098
(214) 564-7337
email: gswrba@verizon.net
Website: *www.gswrba.com*

Iowa Bakers Association
PO Box 85
Glenwood, MO 63541
(660) 457-2291; Fax: (660) 457-2291
email: mwilcox@nemr.net

Kentucky Bakers Association
3940 Shelbyville
Louisville, KY 40217
502-896-4438

Kentucky Retail Bakers Association
3911 Manner Dale Drive
Louisville, KY 40220
(502) 491-6444

Midwest Bakery & Deli Association
7030 E. 10th Street
Indianapolis, IN 46219
email: hartbakery1@juno.com

New England Bakers & Allied Association
15 Mill Pond Lane
Hampton, NH 03842
(603) 782-4888

New England Dairy-Deli-Bakery Association
20 Scanlon Drive
Randolph, MA 02368
(718) 963-9726

Pacific Northwest Baker's Association
2425 SW 322nd Street
Federal Way, WA 98023
(253) 874-9032
email: PNWBA@aol.com

Philadelphia Master Baker's Association
c/o Rilling's Bucks County Bakery
868 E. Street Road
Warminster, PA 18974
(215) 357-3860
email: volzbaker@comcast.net

Retailer's Bakery Association of New England
1209 Sumner Avenue
Springfield, MA 01118-2157
(413) 782-5710

Tennessee Bakers Association
c/o Chattanooga Bakery Inc.
PO Box 111
Chattanooga, TN 37401
800-251-3404

Retail Bakers of America (RBA)
8400 Westpark Drive, 2nd Floor
McLean, VA 22102
800-638-0924, (703) 610-9035;
Fax: (703) 810-9005
email: info@rbanet.com
Website: *www.rbanet.com*

Western Pennsylvania Bakers Association
620 Island Avenue
McKees Rocks, PA 15136
(412) 331-8900; Fax: (412) 331-8903
email: sbaker2424@aol.com
Website: *http://wpba.kbakery.com*

Wisconsin Bakers Association (WBA)
2514 S. 102nd Street, Suite 100
West Allis, WI 53227
800-542-2688, (414) 258-5552;
Fax: (414) 258-5582
email: info@wibakers.com
Website: *www.wibakers.com*

Beans/Legumes

Idaho Bean Commission
PO Box 2556
821 W. State Street
Boise, ID 83702
(208) 334-3520; Fax: (208) 334-2442
email: bean@bean.state.id.us
Website: *www2.state.id.us/bean/*

United States Dry Bean Council (NDBC)
PO Box 550
70 Robbins Road
Grapeview, WA 98546
(360) 277-0112; Fax: (360) 233=0621
email: info@usdrybeans.com
Website: *www.usdrybeans.com*

USA Dry Peas, Lentils & Chickpeas Council
2780 W. Pullman Road
Moscow, ID 83843
(208) 882-3023; Fax: (208) 882-6406
email: pulse@pea-lentil.com
Website: *www.pea-lentil.com*

Beverages

INTERBEV
1101 16th Street NW
Washington, DC 20036
(202) 463-6795; Fax: (202) 833-2484
email: interbev@cmgexpo.com
Website: *www.interbev.com*

International Bottled Water Association
1700 Diagonal Road, Suite 650
Alexandria, VA 22314
(703) 683-5213; Fax: (703) 683-4074
email: ibwaininfo@bottledwater.org
Website: *www.bottledwater.org*

American Beverage Association
1101 16th Street NW
Washington, DC 20036
(202) 463-6732; Fax: (202) 659-5349
email: info@ameribev.org
Website: *www.ameribev.org*

New York Wine & Grape Foundation
800 S. Main Street, Suite 200
Canandaigua, NY 14424
(585) 394-3620; Fax: (585) 394-3649
email: info@newyorkwines.org
Website: *www.newyorkwines.org*

Wine Institute
425 Market Street, Suite 1000
San Francisco, CA 94105
(415) 512-0151; Fax: (415) 442-0742
Website: *www.wineinstitute.org*

Cheese/Dairy

American Cheese Society
455 S. Fourth Street, Suite 650
Louisville, KY 40202
(502) 583-3783; Fax: (502) 589-3602
Website: *www.cheesesociety.org*

Dairy Processors Association of Canada
408 Queen Street, Suite 205
Ottawa, ON, Canada K1R 5A7
email: info@dpac-atlc.ca
Website: *www.dpac-atlc.ca*

Dairy Management Inc.
(American Dairy Assn., Nat. Dairy Council,
   and U.S. Dairy Export)
10255 W. Higgins Road, #900
Rosemont, IL 60018-5616
(847) 803-2000 x3205; Fax: (847) 803-2077
email: ilovecheese@resedmi.com
Website: *www.dairyinfo.com*

American Dairy Products Institute (ADPI)
116 N. York Street
Elmhurst, IL 60126
(630) 530-8700; Fax: (630) 530-8707
email: info@adpi.org
Website: *http://adpi.org*

California Milk Advisory Board
400 Oyster Point Boulevard, Suite 220
South San Francisco, CA 94080
(650) 871-6459; Fax: (650) 583-7328
email: askus@realcaliforniamilk.com
Website: *www.realcaliforniacheese.com*

**Cheese Importers Association of
America Inc.**
204 E. Street NW
Washington, DC 20002
(202) 547-0899; Fax: (202) 547-6348
email: info@theciaa.org
Website: *http://theciaa.org*

Dairy Management Inc.
10255 W. Higgins Road, Suite 900
Rosemont, IL 60018-5616
800-853-2479, (847) 803-2000
Website: *http://dairyinfo.com*

**Eastern Perishable Products
Association Inc.**
(Formerly: Eastern Dairy Deli Association)
17 Park Street
Wanaque, NJ 07465
(973) 831-4100; Fax: (973) 831-8100
email: eppa@eppainc.org
Website: *http://eppainc.org*

**International Dairy-Deli-Bakery
Association (IDDBA)**
313 Price Place, #202
PO Box 5528
Madison, WI 53705-0528
(608) 310-5000; Fax: (608) 238-6330
email: iddba@iddba.org
Website: *http://idda.org*

**International Dairy Foods Association
(IDFA)**
1250 H Street NW, Suite 900
Washington, DC 20005
(202) 737-4332; Fax: (202) 331-7820
Website: *http://idfa.org*

National Dairy Council
10255 W. Higgins Road, #900
Rosemont, IL 60018-5616
(708) 803-2000; Fax: (708) 803-2077
email: ndc@dairyinformation.com
Website: *http://nationaldairycouncil.org*

Every state has a dairy council, and if you visit the website listed above, the state's contact information will display.

New England Dairy-Deli-Bakery Association
20 Scanlon Drive
Randolph, MA 02368
(781) 963-9726

New England Dairy & Food Council
1034 Commonwealth Avenue
Boston, MA 02215
888-995-7600, (617) 734-6750;
Fax: (617) 232-0229
Website: *http://newenglanddairycouncil.org*

This organization serves Connecticut, Massachusetts, New Hampshire, Rhode Island, and Vermont.

Western Dairy Association
12000 N. Washington Street, Suite 200
Thornton, CO 80241
800-274-6455, (303) 451-7711;
Fax: (303) 451-0411
email: info@westerndairyassociation.org
Website: *www.westerndairyassociation.org*

Wisconsin Cheese Makers Association
8030 Excelsior Drive, Suite 305
Madison, WI 53719-1950
(608) 828-4550; Fax: (608) 828-4551
email: office@wischeesemakersassn.org
Website: *http://wischeesemakersassn.org*

Wisconsin Milk Marketing Board
8418 Excelsior Drive
Madison, WI 53717
(608) 836-8820; Fax: (608) 836-5822

email: feedback@wmmb.org
Website: *http://producer.wisdairy.com*

Cocoa

American Cocoa Research Institute (ACRI)
8320 Old Courthouse Road, Suite 300
Vienna, VA 22162
(703) 790-5750; Fax: (703) 790-5752

ACRI is part of the National Confectioners Association.

The Cocoa Merchants Association of America Inc.
World Financial Center
1 North End Avenue, 13th Floor
New York, NY 10282-1101
(212) 201-8819; Fax: (212) 785-5475
email: cmmaa@cocoamerchants.com
Website: *http://cocoamerchants.com*

Coffee

Hawaii Coffee Association
73-4327 Imo Place
Kaikua-Kona, HI 96740
(808) 325-0560; Fax: (808) 325-1083
email: rnpeters@aol.com
Website: *http://hawaiicoffeeassoc.org*

National Coffee Association of USA Inc. (NCA)
15 Maiden Lane, Suite 1405
New York, NY 10038
(212) 766-4007; Fax: (212) 766-5815
email: info@ncausa.org
Website: *http://ncausa.org*

Specialty Coffee Association of America (SCAA)

330 Golden Shore, Suite 50
Long Beach, CA 90802
(562) 624-4100; Fax: (562) 624-4101
email: coffee@scaa.org
Website: *http://scaa.org*

Confections

Chocolate USA

8320 Old Courthouse Road, Suite 300
Vienna, VA 22182
(703) 790-5750
Website: *www.chocolateusa.org*

National Confectioners Association (Chocolate USA)

8320 Old Courthouse Road, Suite 300
Vienna, VA 22182
(703) 790-5750; Fax: (703) 790-5752
email: carly.zoerb@chocolateusa.org
Website: *http://ecandy.com*

Pennsylvania Manufacturing Confectioners' Association (PMCA)

2980 Linden Street, Suite E3
Bethlehem, PA 18017
(610) 625-4655; Fax: (610) 625-4657
email: info@pmca.com
Website: *http://pmca.com*

Retail Confectioners International

1807 Glenview Road, Suite 204
Glenview, IL 60025
(847) 724-6120; Fax: (847) 724-2719
Website: *http://retailconfectioners.org*

Fish/Seafood

Alaska Seafood Marketing Institute (ASMI)

311 North Franklin Street, Suite 200
Juneau, AK 99801-1147
800-478-2903, (907) 465-5560;
Fax: (907) 465-5572
email: info@alaskaseafood.org
Website: *http://alaskaseafood.org*

Domestic Marketing Office

150 Nickerson, Suite 310
Seattle, WA 98109
800-806-2497, (206) 352-8920;
Fax: (206) 352-8930

American Shrimp Processors Association

PO Box 50774
New Orleans, LA 70150
(504) 368-1571; Fax: (504) 368-1573

National Fisheries Institute

Domestic Marketing Office
7918 Jones Beach Drive
McLean, VA 22102
(703) 752-8880; Fax: (703) 524-4619
email: contact@nfi.org
Website: *www.aboutseafood.com*

Flavors

Flavor & Extract Manufacturers Association (FEMA)

1620 I Street NW, #925
Washington, DC 20006
(202) 293-5800; Fax: (202) 463-8998
email: ccook@therobertsgroup.net
Website: *femaflavor.org*

Fruit

Apple Processors Association
1629 K Street NW, Suite 110,
Washington, DC 20006
(202) 785-6715; Fax: (202) 331-4212
email: agriwash@aol.com
Website: *www.appleprocessors.org*

American Cranberry Growers Association (ACGA)
126 Moores Meadow Road
Tabernacle, NJ 08019
(609) 268-0641

American Dehydrated Onion and Garlic Association (ADOGA)
221 Main Street, 16th Floor,
San Francisco, CA 94105
(415) 905-0200; Fax: (415) 543-4940

American Mushroom Institute (AMI)
1284 Gap Newport Pike, Suite 2
Avondale, PA 19311
(610) 268-7483; Fax: (610) 268-8015
email: mushroomnews@kennett.net
Website: *www.americanmushroom.org*
or
1 Massachusetts Avenue NW, Suite 800
Washington, DC 20001
(202) 842-4344; Fax: (202) 408-7763
email: ami@mwmlaw.com

Apricot Producers of California (APC)
2111 Geer Road, Suite 611
Turlock, CA 95382
(209) 632.9777; Fax: (209) 632.9779
email: apricots@apricotproducers.com
Website: *www.apricotproducers.com*

Calavo Growers Inc.
1141A Cummings Road
Santa Paula, CA 93060
(805) 525-1245; Fax: (714) 259-4810
Website: *http://calavo.com*

Calavo Growers of California
2530 Red Hill Avenue
Santa Ana, CA 92705
(714) 223-1111

California Apricot Advisory Board (CAAB)
1280 Boulevard Way, #107
Walnut Creek, CA 94595
(510) 937-3660; Fax: (510) 937-0118

California Artichoke Advisory Board (CAAB)
PO Box 747
Castroville, CA 95012
(831) 633-4411; Fax: (831) 633-0215
Website: *http://artichokes.org*

California Avocado Commission (CAC)
1251 E. Dyer Road, Suite 200
Santa Ana, CA 92705
(714) 558-6761; Fax: (714) 641-7024
Website: *www.avocados.org*

California Avocado Society (CAS)
PO Box 4816
Saticoy, CA 93007
(805) 644-1184
Website: *www.californiaavocadosociety.org*

California Cherry Advisory Board
33 E. Oak Street
Lodi, CA 95240

(209) 368-0685; Fax: (209) 368-4309
Website: *www.calcherry.com*

California Cling Peach Advisory Board (CCPAB)

531-D N. Alta Avenue
Dinuba, CA 93618
(559) 595-1425; Fax: (559) 591-5744
email: jim@tabcomp.org
Website: *http://calclingpeach.com*

California Date Administrative Committee (CDAC)

PO Box 1736
Indio, CA 92202
800-223-8748, (760) 347-4510;
Fax: (760) 347-6347
email: dates2000@earthlink.net
Website: *http://datesaregreat.com*

Specialty Crop Trade Council (CDFEA)

(formerly the California Dried Fruit
    Export Association)
710 Striker Avenue
Sacramento, CA 95834
916-561-5900; Fax 916-561-5910
email: merlej@dfaofca.com
Website: *http://cdfea.org*

California Fig Advisory Board (CFAB)

7395 N. Palm Bluffs, Suite 106
Fresno, CA 93711
800-588-2344, (559) 440-5400; Fax: (559)
    438-5405
email: info@californiafigs.com
Website: *http://californiafigs.com*

California Kiwifruit Commission (CKC)

770 E. Shaw, Suite 220

Fresno, CA 93710
(559) 229-4780; Fax: (559) 226-6721
email: kiwifruit@kiwifruit.com
Website: *http://kiwifruit.org*

California Strawberry Commission (CSAM)

PO Box 269
Watsonville, CA 95077
(831) 724-1301; Fax: (831) 724-5973
email: info@calstrawberry.com
Website: *http://calstrawberry.com*

California Table Grape Commission

392 W. Fallbrook, #101
Fresno, CA 93711
(559) 447-8350; Fax: (559) 447-9184
email: info@freshcaliforniagrapes.com
Website: *http://freshcaliforniagrapes.com*

California Tree Fruit Agreement

975 I Street
PO Box 968
Reedley, CA 93654
(559) 638-8260; Fax: (559) 638-8842
email: info@caltreefruit.com
Website: *www.eatcaliforniafruit.com*

Cherry Marketing Institute Inc.

PO Box 30285
Lansing, MI 48909
(517) 347-0010; Fax: (517) 347-0605
email: info@choosecherries.com
Website: *http://choosecherries.com*

Cape Cod Cranberry Growers Association

(Cranberry Institute, Cranberry
    Marketing Committee)
3203-B Cranberry Highway

East Wareham, MA 02538
(508) 759-1041; Fax: (508) 759-6294
email: info@cranberries.org
Website: *http://cranberries.org*

California Dried Plum Board
3840 Rosin Court, Suite 170
Sacramento, CA 95834
(916) 565-6232; Fax: (916) 565-6237
Website: *www.californiadriedplums.org*

Dried Fruit Association of California
710 Striker Avenue
Sacramento, CA 95834
(916) 561-5900; Fax: (916) 561-5910
email: info@dfaofca.com
Website: *http://agfoodsafety.org*

North America ZESPRI Kiwifruit
2001 W. Garfield, Pier 90
Seattle, WA 98119
(604) 284-1705; Fax: (604) 282-0533
email: zespri@oppy.com
Website: *www.zesprikiwi.com*

North American Blueberry Council (NABC)
PO Box 1036
Folsom, CA 95763
(916) 933-9399; Fax: (916) 933-9777
email: info@nabcblues.org
Website: *http://nabcblues.org*

Oregon Cherry Growers
PO Box 7357
Salem, OR 97303
(503) 296-5487; Fax: (503) 296-2509
email: mrm@orcherry.com
Website: *http://orcherry.com*

Cherry Central Cooperative
PO Box 988
Traverse City, MI 49685-0988
(231) 946-1860; Fax: (231) 941-4167
email: info@cherrycentral.com
Website: *http://cherrycentral.com*

U.S. Highbush Blueberry Council
PO Box 3366
Salem, OR 97302-0366
503-364-2944; Fax: 503-581-6819
Website: *http://blueberry.org*

National Peach Council (NPC)
12 Nicklaus Lane, Suite 101
Columbia, SC 29211
(803) 788-7101; Fax: (803) 865-8090
email: peachcouncil@att.net
Website: *http://nationalpeach.org*

National Watermelon Promotion Board
3501 Quadrangle Boulevard, Suite 321
Orlando, FL 32814-0065
877-599-9595, (407) 657-0261;
Fax: (407) 657-2213
email: info@watermelon.org
Website: *http://watermelon.org*

Pineapple Growers Association of Hawaii (PGAH)
1116 Whitmore Avenue
Wahiawa, HI 96786
(808) 877-3855; Fax: (808) 871-0953
email: dschenk@maui.net

Apple Products Research & Education Council
5775 Peachtree-Dunwoody Road, Building G,
    Suite 500

Atlanta, GA 30342
(404) 252-3663; Fax: (404) 252-0774
email: info@appleproducts.org
Website: *http://appleproducts.org*

Raisin Administrative Committee
3445 N. First Street, Suite 101
Fresno, CA 93755
(559) 225-0520; Fax: (559) 225-0652
email: info@raisins.org
Website: *http://raisins.org*

Sun-Maid Growers of California
13525 S. Bethel Avenue
Kingburg, CA 93631
(559) 896-8000; Fax: (559) 897-6209
email: info@sunmaid.com
Website: *www.sun-maid.com*

Sunkist Growers Inc.
14130 Riverside Drive
Sherman Oaks, CA 91423
Website: *www.sunkist.com*

Texas Fruit Growers Association
PO Drawer CC
College Station, TX 77841
(979) 846-3285; Fax: (979) 846-1752
email: orchard@wf.net
Website: *http://texasfruitgrowers.org*

Washington Red Raspberry Commission
1796 Front Street
Lynden, WA 98261
(360) 354-8767
email: info@red-raspberry.org
Website: *http://red-raspberry.org*

Washington State Apple Commission
2900 Euclid Avenue
PO Box 18
Wenatchee, WA 98807
(509) 663-9600; Fax: (509) 662-5824
email: info@waapple.org
Website: *www.bestapples.com*

Western Growers Association (WGA)
PO Box 2130
Newport Beach, CA 92658
949-863-1000; Fax: 949-863-9029
Website: *http://wga.com*

Wild Blueberry Association of North America (WBANA)
PO Box 100
Old Town, ME 04468
(207) 570-3535; Fax: (207) 581-3499
email: info@wildblueberriesqwi.net.com
Website: *http://wildblueberries.com*

Grain

California Wild Rice Advisory Board
4125 Temescal Street, Suite D
Fair Oaks, CA 95628
(916) 863-0312; Fax: (916) 863-0304
email: info@cawildrice.com
Website: *www.cawildrice.com*

California Rice Commission
8801 Folsom Boulevard, Suite 172
Sacramento, CA 95826-3249
(916) 387-2264; Fax: (916) 387-2265
Website: *www.calrice.org*

Flax Council of Canada
465-167 Lombard Avenue

Winnipeg, Manitoba R3B 0T6
Canada
(204) 982-2115; Fax: (204) 942-1841
email: flax@flaxcouncil.ca
Website: *www.flaxcouncil.ca*

Kansas Wheat Commission
217 Southwind Place
Manhattan, KS 66503
866-7WHEAT, (785) 539-0255;
Fax: (785) 539-8946
email: kswheat@kswheat.com
Website: *http://kswheat.com*

Minnesota Cultivated Wild Rice Council
4630 Churchill Street, Suite 1
St. Paul, MN 55126
(651) 638-1955; Fax: (651) 638-0756
email: mnwildrice@comcast.net
Website: *www.mnwildrice.org*

USA Rice Federation
4301 N. Fairfax Drive, Suite 425
Arlington, VA 22203
(703) 236-2300; Fax: (703) 236-2301
email: riceinfo@usarice.com
Website: *http://usarice.com*

Wheat Foods Council
10841 S. Crossroads Drive, Suite 105
Parker, CO 80134
(303) 840-8787; Fax: (303) 840-6877
email: wfc@wheatfoods.org
Website: *http://wheatfoods.org*

Hot and Spicy

The Chile Pepper Institute
New Mexico State University

Box 30003, MSC 3Q
Las Cruces, NM 88003-8003
(505) 646-3028; Fax: (505) 646-6041
email: hotchile@nmsu.edu
Website: *http://chilepepperinstitute.org*

Jams/Jellies/Preserves

International Jelly & Preserve Association
5775 Peachtree-Dunwoody Road
Atlanta, GA 30342
(404) 252-3663; Fax: (404) 252-0774
Website: *http://jelly.org*

Nuts

Sun-Diamond Growers of California (SDGC)
5568 Gibralter Drive, POB 9024
Pleasanton, CA 94588
(510) 463-8200; Fax: (510) 463-7492

Nutrition/Organic/Health

American Council on Science and Health (ACSH)
1995 Broadway, 2nd Floor
New York, NY 10023-5860
(212) 362-7044; Fax: (212) 362-4919
email: acsh@acsh.org
Website: *http://acsh.org*

American Dietetic Association (ADA)
120 S. Riverside Plaza, Suite 200
Chicago, IL 60606-6995
800-877-1600 (Weekday Consumer
    Nutrition Hotline); Fax: (312) 899-4899
email: exhibit@eatright.org
Website: *http://eatright.org*

Human Nutrition Program
The Rockefeller University
1230 Park Avenue, Box 246
New York, NY 10021
(212) 746-1617; Fax: (212) 746-8310
email: miller@rockefeller.edu
Website: *http://fnic.nal.usda.gov*

Pasta

National Pasta Association
1156 15th Street NW, Suite 900
Washington, DC 20005
(202) 637-5888; Fax: (202) 223-9741
email: info@ilovepasta.org
Website: *http://ilovepasta.org*

Produce

Produce Marketing Association
1500 Casho Mill Road
Newark, DE 19711
(302) 738-7100; Fax: (302) 731-2409
Website: *http://pma.com*

National Onion Association (NOA)
822 Seventh Street, #510
Greeley, CO 80631
(303) 353-5895; Fax: (303) 353-5897
Website: *http://onions-usa.org*

Salad Dressings

Association for Dressings and Sauces
1100 Johnson Ferry Road, Suite 300
Atlanta, GA 30342
(404) 252-3663; Fax: (404) 252-0774
email: ads@kellecompany.com
Website: *http://dressings-sauces.org*

Snacks

Snack Food Association
1600 Wilson Boulevard, Suite 650
Arlington, VA 22209
800-628-1334, (703) 836-4500;
Fax: (703) 836-8262
email: sfa@sfa.org
Website: *www.sfa.org*

**Snack Food Association—Western
Association of Food Chains**
825 Colorado Boulevard, Suite 203
Los Angeles, CA 90041
(213) 254-7270

Tea

**Tea Association of the USA Inc./
Tea Council/Specialty Tea Institute**
362 Fifth Avenue, Suite 801
New York, NY 10001
(212) 986-9415; Fax: (212) 697-8658
email: info@teausa.com
Website: *http://teausa.com*

International

Canadian Association of Specialty Food
PO Box 96509
Maple, Ontario L6A 1WS
Canada
888-726-9598, (905)-761-9951; Fax: (905)
761-9952

Appendix C
Trade Shows and Services

· ·

The following list is neither all-inclusive, nor does it mean to serve as an endorsement. Ask for sample copies and rate sheets. Please visit *www.specialtyfoodresource.com* for updates.

ANUGA (American Foods Pavilion)
World Food Market—Cologne, Germany
USDA, Room 4939
Washington, DC 20250-1000
(202) 720-7420
Website: *www.anuga.com; www.fas.usda.gov*
Show held in October in odd-numbered years.

Boston Gift Show
Boston Convention and Exhibition Center
George Little Management Inc.
10 Bank Street
White Plains, NY 10606-1954
800-272-7469; Fax: (914) 948-6180
Website: *http://glmshows.com*

Shows are in April and September. The Boston Gift Show features New England

specialty food products that can also be successfully merchandised via the gift trade. Attendees include retailers with strong purchasing power from a variety of gift, stationery, and department stores, as well as representatives from mail order catalogs, specialty stores, craft shops, college stores, museum shops, garden centers, and gourmet stores.

International Dairy Deli Bake Association Seminar & Expo
(608) 310-5000
Website: *http://iddba.org*

International Gift Basket, Floral and Balloon Jubilee!
Festivities Publications Inc.
815 Haines Street
Jacksonville, FL 32206

(904) 634-1903
Website: *http://festivities-pub.com*

International Fancy Food and Confection Show

NASFT
120 Wall Street
New York, NY 10018
(212) 482-6440, 800-627-3869;
Fax: (212) 482-6459
Website: *www.specialtyfood.com*

Owned and sponsored by NASFT. This organization sponsors three very important annual food shows for its members, which attract buyers and decision makers from all segments of the specialty food industry. The association also sponsors food processor seminars devoted to food marketing, retailing, and distribution issues.

International Bottled Water Association Trade Show (IMWA)

Mark Miller at InterBev
(703) 934-4700
email: interbev@cmqexpo.com

This show is held in Las Vegas, Nevada, annually in October. Members can exhibit for $27 per square foot, nonmembers for $37 per square foot.

International Restaurant and Foodservice Show of New York

Contact: Reed Exhibitions
383 Main Avenue
Norwalk, CT 06851
800-840-5612, (203) 840-4800;
Fax: (203) 840-5805
Website: *www.internationalrestaurantny.com*

Heavy emphasis on food service with over 900 exhibitors of food, freezers, utensils, uniforms, beverages, baked goods, etc. Sponsored by the New York State Restaurant Association and produced and managed by Reed Exhibitions.

NASDA—U.S. Food Export Showcase

Convention Management Group
National Association of State Departments
    of Agriculture
1156 15th Street NW, Suite 1020
Washington, DC 20005
(703) 876-0900, (202) 296-9680
email: ammccormick@cmgexpo.com

The Showcase is held each year at Chicago's McCormick Place in conjunction with the Food Marketing Institute's Supermarket Industry Exposition, the NASFT International Fancy Food and Confection Show, and All Things Organic. It attracts supermarket industry executives from around the world.

National Gourmet Food Show

800-DAL-MKTS
Website: *http://dallasmarketcenter.com*

This annual spring show is held at the Dallas Market Center.

National Restaurant, Hotel & Motel Show

National Restaurant Association (NRA)
150 N. Michigan Avenue, Suite 2000
Chicago, IL 60601
(312) 853-2525; Fax: (312) 853-2548
Website: *http://restaurant.org/show/*

Natural Products Expo

New Hope Natural Media Group
1401 Pearl Street
Boulder, CO 80302

(303) 939-8440; Fax: (303) 998-9020
email: info@newhope.com
Website: *http://newhope.com*

More than 52,000 retailers, manufacturers, functional ingredient suppliers, and industry professionals attended the country's largest natural, organic, and healthy products trade show, Natural Products Expo West/Supply Expo 2008 (*www.expowest.com*), an increase of 11 percent over last year's attendance. In its 28th year, this show attracted a record 3,392 exhibits to the Anaheim Convention Center in California.

New York International Gift Fair

George Little Management LLC (GLM)
10 Bank Street
White Plains, NY 10606-1954
800-272-SHOW, (914) 421-3200;
Fax: (914) 948-6180
Website: *http://glmshows.com*

This is a trade-only show held twice a year in January and August at the Jacob Javits Center and surrounding venues with 2,700 exhibitors offering 9 divisions featuring current and trendy home furnishings and specialty food gift items. Exhibit pricing depends on which category your product falls into and the physical location of your booth on the exhibit floor. Prices range from $34.75–$44.00 per square foot.

NGA Annual Convention

National Grocers Association (NGA)
1825 Samuel Morse Drive
Reston, VA 22090-5317
(703) 437-5300; Fax: (703) 437-7768
Website: *http://nationalgrocers.org*

The NGA is the national trade association exclusively representing the retail and wholesale grocers who comprise the independent sector of the food distribution industry.

Philadelphia National Candy, Gift, and Gourmet Show

651 Allendale Road
King of Prussia, PA 19406
(610) 265-4688 or (610) 369-1044
email: rcap@rcaphila.org
Website: *http://phillycandyshow.com*

Sponsored by the Retail Confectioners Association of Philadelphia, this show is held in September in Atlantic City, New Jersey.

Private Label Trade Show (PLMA)

Private Label Manufacturers Association
630 Third Avenue
New York, NY 10017
(212) 972-3131; Fax: (212) 983-1382
email: info@plma.com
Website: *http://plma.com*

This trade show will be held in November 2008 in Chicago, Illinois. It showcases fresh, frozen, and refrigerated items, snacks, beverages, and ethnic specialties sold under private label. It attracts major supermarket and drug chains as well as mass merchandisers.

SIAL (American Foods Pavilion)

39, Rue de la Bienfaisance 75008, Paris, France
IMEX Management Inc.
4524 Park Road, Suite B-103
Charlotte, NC 28209
(704) 356-0041
Website: *www.sial.fr*
or
Foreign Agricultural Service—USDA
South Building, Room 4647
Washington, DC 20250-1000

(202) 690-1182; Fax: (202) 690-4374
Website: *www.fas.usda.gov*

Show held in October in even-numbered years. SIAL and ANUGA are biannual food shows that are particularly beneficial to European producers desiring to introduce products to the United States and for U.S. producers wishing to export products to European markets. Average cost for a booth in the American Pavilion at SIAL, for example, is $13,495 (€8541). Use the website for initial contact. USDA employs one of those wonderfully convoluted telephone answering systems that generally requires making a long-distance call, listening to a listing of options, and then getting a voice messaging system.

In addition to SIAL and ANUGA, noted above, numerous other international trade promotion events may be of some value to food producers ready to explore international markets. SIAL China has been announced as an additional international trade show at the Shanghai New International Expo Center in the spring of 2008. Website: *www.sialchina.com.*

There is also the SIAL Montreal Show serving the markets of North America annually at the Palais des Congres de Montreal Exhibition Center April of every year.

SIAL Montreal
PO Box 159, Place du Parc
Montreal, Quebec H2X 4A4
Canada
(514) 289-9669; Fax: (514) 289-1034
email: info@sialmontreal.ca
Website: *www.sialmontreal.com*

SNAXPO
Talley Management Group
19 Mantua Road
Mt. Royal, NJ 08061
email: wsteven@talley.com
Website: *www.snaxpo.com*

This show is sponsored by the Snack Food Association in Orlando, Florida. Members pay $7,800–$11,500 for a 10 × 10 foot booth, depending on exhibit hall location, and nonmembers may exhibit for an additional $1,250 fee.

Specialty Coffee Association Annual Conference & Exhibition
http://conference.scaa.org

This annual conference and exhibition is held every spring, and attendance averages 8,000. The trade show is geared toward the coffee retailer and addresses issues of competition and profitability.

Western Foodservice & Hospitality Expo
Reed Exhibition
383 Main Avenue
Norwalk, CT 06851
800-840-5612, (203) 840-4800;
Fax: (203) 840-5805
Website: *www.westernfoodexpola.com*

This annual show, held at the Los Angeles Convention Center, is sponsored by the California Restaurant Association, Multi-Cultural Foodservice & Hospitality Alliance (MFHA) from Rhode Island, and the Multiple Unit Operator Alliance (MUOA). The show is geared to restaurant professionals with a focus on enhancing their businesses and informed themof the latest industry trends.

Appendix D
Product and Process Development/Copackers

··

The following list is neither all-inclusive, nor does it mean to serve as an endorsement. Ask for sample copies and rate sheets. Please visit *www. specialtyfoodresource.com* for updates.

The National Association for the Specialty Food Trade (NASFT) has a listing of nearly 700 contract packaging companies (copackers). Far too many people feel that a copacker is a copacker and that any copacker can do everything. In fact, copackers have a variety of specific functional areas in which they excel.

Readers may wish to request a copacker listing from NASFT:

Ms. Heather Paul
NASFT
120 Wall Street
New York, NY 10005
800-627-3869, x 102, (212) 482-6440; Fax: (212) 482-6459
email: hpaul@nasft.org

The listing consists only of NASFT members who have indicated to NASFT that they are copackers. It includes the copacker contact information, products that they copack, plant locations, types of packaging they use, and specialized packing equipment (such as enrobers, form-fill and seal, smokers, vacuum packaging, etc.).

Few copackers can provide all of the following range of services:

- Liquid products
- Dry products
- Ingredient preblends
- Labeling
- Packaging service only
- Product development/recipe conversion

Using a qualified contract packer will enable you to devote your time to management and marketing, while eliminating the enormous expense and responsibility of operating a production facility. Some will provide only the packaging, while others will help you with the entire formulation, production, packaging, and labeling process. Most offer no-cost initial consultation. Some even have marketing capability. See chapter 3 for a detailed discussion of copacker services. Many of the companies are just food processors that have extra production capacity.

Alabama

Cloverland Sweets
208 Old Fort Road E.
Fort Deposit, AL 36032
800-523-3505, (334) 227-8355; Fax:
    334-227-4294
email: info@giftbasketsupplier.com
Website: *http://giftbasketsupplier.com*

Product: Gift basket supplies and kosher capabilities

Jerrell Packaging LLC
802 Labarge Drive
Birmingham, AL 35022
(205) 426-8930, (205) 515-0681;
Fax: (205) 426-8989
email: john@jerrellpackaging.com

Website: *http://jerrellpackaging.com*

Product: Packaging dry food products

Kyleigh Farms
261 Wilson Jones Road
Geneva, AL 36340-6135
(334) 684-1404; Fax: (334) 684-9993

Product: Food processor of sauces, dressings, and specialty recipes

Arizona

Cahill Desert Products
Ray Broderick and Dave Simpson
3400 W. Osborn Road
Phoenix, AZ 85017
877-224-4557, (602) 627-0402;

Fax: (602) 627-0404
email: champagnesauces@aol.com
Website: *http://champagnesauces.com*

Product: Prickly pear fruit products are their specialty. Private label also available.

Cerreta Candy Company
5345 W. Glendale Avenue
Glendale, AZ 85301
(623) 930-1000; Fax: (623) 930-9085
email: orders@cerreta.com
Website: *www.cerreta.com*

Product: Almond toffee and various sugar-free confections

Cheri's Desert Harvest
1840 E. Winsett Street
Tucson, AZ 85719
800-743-1141; Fax: (520) 623-7741
email: help@cherisdesertharvest.com
Website: *http://cherisdesertharvest.com*

Product: Jellies, syrups, candies, and bread mixes

Cinnabar Specialty Foods
1134 W. Haining Street
Prescott, AZ 86305
866-293-6433, (928) 778-3687;
Fax: (928) 778-4289
email: sales@cinnabarfoods.com
Website: *http://cinnabarfoods.com*

Product: Chutneys, salsas, simmering sauces and marinades, rice and dal mixes

California

Adrienne's Gourmet Foods
849 Ward Street

Santa Barbara, CA 93111
(805) 964-6848; Fax: (805) 964-8698
email: crackers@adriennes.com
Website: *http://adriennesgourmetfoods.com*

Product: Cookies and crackers

Bakehouse Foods
2270 Camino Vida Roble, #U
Carlsbad, CA 92009
877-228-6385; Fax: (760) 607-6704
email: info@bakehousefoods.com
Website: *http://bakehousefoods.com*

Product: Meringue cookies

Bee International
211 Boswell Road, Suite 5
Chula Vista, CA 91914
800-421-6465, (619) 710-1822;
Fax: (619) 710-1822
Website: *http://beeinc.com*

Product: Seasonal candy offerings in tins and display

Belfiore Cheese Company
2031A Second Street
Berkeley, CA 94710
(510) 540-5500; Fax: (510) 540-5594
email: info@belfiorecheese.com
Website: *http://belfiorecheese.com*

Product: All varieties of fresh cheeses with no additives or preservatives and Indian paneer

Bella Viva Orchards
3019 Quincy Road
Denair, CA 95316
800-552-8218, (209) 883-4146
email: customercare@bellaviva.com
Website: *http://bellaviva.com*

Product: Dried fruits and nuts, trail mix, and chocolate-covered fruits and nuts

Bell-Carter Packaging
2200 Lapham Drive
Modesto, CA 95354
(209) 549-5939; Fax: (209) 549-5944
email: sales@bcpackaging.com
Website: *http://bcpackaging.com*

Product: Complete range of station-packaging and assembly line services

Biscotti Nucci
2310 Laurel, Suite 4
PO Box 1443
520 California Boulevard
Napa, CA 94559
866-858-5842, (707) 224-2360;
Fax: (707) 224-5342
email: info@nvfinefoods.com
Website: *http://nvfinefoods.com*

Product: Toffee, biscotti, and kitchen rental

Blossom Valley Foods
20 Casey Street
Gilroy, CA 95020-4539
(408) 848-5520; Fax: (408) 848-1249
email: info@blossomvalleyfarms.com
Website: *http://blossomvalleyfoods.com*

Product: Nonalcoholic cocktail mixers; vinegars; organic and all-natural sauces, dressings, and hot sauces

Busetto Foods
1090 W. Church Street
Fresno, CA 93706
(209) 237-9591
Product: Salami and meats

Capay Canyon Ranch
Leslie or Stan Barth
PO Box 508
Esparto, CA 95627
(530) 662-2372; Fax: (530) 662-2306
email: capaycanyon@msn.com
Website: *www.localharvest.org/farms/M3787/*

Product: Tomatoes (dried), table grapes, almonds, walnuts

Carol Hall's Hot Pepper Jelly Company
890 Franklin Street
Fort Bragg, CA 95437
866-737-7379, (707) 961-1899;
Fax: (707) 961-0879
email: hall@mcn.org
Website: *http://hotpepperjelly.com*

Product: Jams and jellies

Cascade Continental Foods
1089 Essex Avenue
Richmond, CA 94801
(510) 232-3103; Fax: (510) 232-5009

Product: Packaging lines for liquid and dry food products

Ceylon Teas Inc.
310 N. Palm Avenue, Suite B
Brea, CA 92821
(562) 690-2576
email: ceylonteas@aol.com
Website: *http://store.ceylonteas.com*

Product: Premium teas

Charlotte's Confections
1395 El Camino Real
Milbrae, CA 94030
800-798-2427, (650) 589-1417;

Fax: (650) 589-1923
email: jim@charlettesconfections.com
Website: *http://charlottesconfections.com*

Product: Premium quality confections

E. Waldo Ward & Son
Richard and Jeff Ward
273 E. Highland Avenue
Sierra Madre, CA 91024
800-355-9273
email: jelly@waldoward.com
Website: *http://waldoward.com*

Product: Jams, jellies, marmalades, sauces

Esco Foods Inc.
Marc Bosschart
1035 Howard Street
San Francisco, CA 94103
(415) 864-2147
Website: *www.escofoods.com*

Food packer: Syrups, toppings, salad dressings, marinades, BBQ sauce, flavors; extracts in glass, plastic, paper

Moon Shine Trading Company
Ishai Zeldner
1250A Harter Avenue
Woodland, CA 95776
800-678-1226
email: mstco@moonshinetrading.com
Website: *http://moonshinetrading.com*

Product: Varietal honeys, honey fruit spreads, select nut butters, Honey in the Straw; copacking (cold pack only); private label

Santini Foods Inc.
Roger Tan, PhD
16505 Worthley Drive

San Lorenzo, CA 94580
800-835-6888
email: roger@santinifoodsinc.com
Website: *www.santinifoods.com*

Product: Only West Coast sweetened condensed milk producer. Manufactures syrups and dressings; packs varieties of vegetable oils.

Sona & Hollen
3712 Cerritos Avenue
Los Alamitos, CA 90720
(310) 431-1379; Fax: (314) 598-6207
Website: *http://seedquest.com*

Product: Tomatoes and other wet food products

Sonoma Gourmet
21787 8th Street E.
Sonoma, CA 95476
(707) 939-3700; Fax: (707) 939-3730
email: sauceboy@sonomagourmet.com
Website: *http://sonomagourmet.com*

Product: Wet food products; minimum run 300 to 400 cases. FDA-certified for pH- and non-pH-controlled products. Nutritional labeling, product development.

Timber Crest Farms
4791 Dry Creek Road
Healdsburg, CA 95448
888-374-9325, (707) 433-8251;
Fax: (707) 433-8255
email: tcf@timbercrest.com
Website: *http://timbercrest.com*

Product: Licensed FDA high-acid and low-acid cannery canning in glass. Also form and fill machines and lines to pack 3 ounces to 5 pounds in flex packaging. Food technicians on staff for product development.

Triple H Food Processors
Tom Harris
5821 Wilderness
Riverside, CA 92504
(909) 352-5700; Fax: (951) 352-5710
email: tharris@triplehfoods.com
Website: *www.triplehfoods.com*

Product: Multiuse copacker

Wine Country Kitchens
Brian Witbracht and John McIntosh
511 Alexis Court
Napa, CA 94558
866-767-9463, (707) 252-9463
email: wck@winecountrykitchens
Website: *http://winecountrykitchens.com*

Product: Dipping oils and vinegars. Hot and cold fill copacker, specializing in private label, product development from recipe to market, storage, and distribution. Fully licensed and insured. Small minimum runs.

Colorado

Art Coco Chocolate Company
2660 Walnut Street
Denver, CO 80205
(303) 292-6364; Fax: (303) 292-6365
Website: *http://artcoco.com*

Product: Premium custom-molded chocolate

Connecticut

Lynard Company
15 Maple Tree Avenue
Stamford, CT 06906
(203) 323-0231; Fax: (203) 323-0231

Product: Packaged foods, popcorn, pretzels, candy

Florida

Paca Foods
5212 Cone Road
Tampa, FL 33610
800-338-7419, (813) 628-8228;
Fax: (813) 628-8426
Website: *http://pacafoods.com*

Product: Dry blended food products

Georgia

Blackberry Patch
PO Box 1639
Thomasville, GA 31799
(229) 558-9996
Website: *http://blackberrypatch.com*

Product: Jams, jellies, maple praline, and apple pie syrups

Hawaii

Big Island Candies
585 Hinano Street
Hilo, HI 96720
(808) 961-2199
email: contactus@bigislandcandies.com
Website: *http://bigislandcandies.com*

Product: Chocolate-dipped shortbread cookies

Idaho

Sandstone Farms
1888 E. Rodeo Lane
Kuna, ID 83634

866-203-2844
email: customerservice@sandstonefarms.com
Website: *http://sandstonefarms.com*

Product: Pickled vegetables and wine jelly

Illinois

Food Blends
1208 N. Swift Road
Addison, IL 60101
(630) 678-5300; Fax: (630) 678-5311
email: info@foodblends.com
Website: *http://oxydryfoodblends.com*

Product: Dry ingredients blending

Iowa

Palmer Candy Company
311 Bluff Street
Sioux City, IA 51106
(712) 258-5543
Website: *http://palmercandy.com*

Product: Full line of confections and nutmeats

Kansas

The Pantry Shelf
PO Box 613
Hutchison, KS 67504
800-968-3346, (620) 662-9342
Website: *www.pantryshelfco.com*

Product: Cake mix, muffin mix, brownie mix

Kentucky

Broadbent's B&B
6321 Hopkinsville Road
Cadiz, KY 42211

800-841-2202
Website: *http://broadbenthams.com*

Product: Country ham, bacon, sausages

Louisiana

Louisiana Gourmet Enterprises
222 S. Hollywood Road
Houma, LA 70360
800-328-5586

Product: Spices, spice blends, soups, sauces, cakes, and frosting mixes

Maine

Longmeadow Foods
32 Lewiston Road, Building 1B
Gray, ME 04039-7536
(207) 657-6446
Website: *http://pembertonsgourmet.com*

Product: Desserts, sauces, toppings, and treats

Maryland

Sea Watch International
8978 Glebe Park Drive
Easton, MD 21601-7004
(410) 822-7500; Fax: (410) 822-1266
email: sales@seaclam.com
Website: *http://mafi.com*

Product: Meat and poultry products

Massachusetts

Ashley Food Company Inc.
PO Box 912
Sudbury, MA 01776
800-61-SAUCE, (978) 579-8989;

Fax: (978) 579-8989
email: maddog@ashleyfood.com
Website: *www.ashleyfood.com*

Product: Sauces and condiments

Michigan

American Spoon Foods
PO Box 566
1668 Clarion Avenue
Petoskey, MI 49770-0556
(616) 347-9030, (231) 347-9030;
Fax: 800-647-2512
Website: *http://spoon.com*

Product: Preserves, salsa, sauces, condiments

Minnesota

G. E. F. Gourmet Foods
35584 Country Road 8
Mountain Lake, MN 56159
800-692-6762, (507) 427-2631;
Fax: (507) 427-2631
email: greatsnack@frontiernet.net
Website: *http://gladcorn.com*

Product: Organic flour, cereal, and mixes

Mississippi

Mississippi Gourmet
222 Crystal Creek
Hattiesburg, MS 39402
(601) 268-7698

Product: Cheese straws, cookies

Missouri

The Chocolate Lady
860 Louisiana
St. Louis, MO 63118
800-242-5283

Product: Chocolate snack food, candy, popcorn

Montana

The King's Cupboard
PO Box 27
1401 S. Broadway
Red Lodge, MT 59068
(406) 446-3060
Website: *http://kingscupboard.com*

Product: Chocolate sauces

Nebraska

Wanda's Nature Farm Foods
1700 Cushman Drive
Lincoln, NE 68512
800-735-6828, (402) 423-1234;
Fax: (402) 423-4586
Website: *www.superbakes.com*

Product: Bakery mixes

Nevada

Mrs. Auld's Gourmet Foods
572 Reactor Way, B-4
Reno, NV 89502
(775) 856-3350
Website: *http://mrs-aulds.com*

Product: Pickles, salsa, jams, jellies

New Hampshire

The Lollipop Tree

319 Vaughan Street
Portsmouth, NH 03801
800-842-6691, (603) 436-8196;
Fax: (603) 436-0282
Website: *http://lollipoptree.com*

Product: Pepper jellies, artisan bread mixes, condiments, salad dressings

New York

Accord Foods Inc.

961 Lyell Avenue, Building 4
Rochester, NY 14606
(585) 436-3668; Fax: (585) 436-1737
Website: *www.accordfoods.com*

Product: Acid, acidified and water activity-controlled sauces

Battenkill Kitchen

PO Box 784
58 E. Broadway
Salem, NY 12865
(518) 854-3032
email: manager@battnkillkitchen.org
Website: *http://battenkillkitchen.org*

Casa Visco Finer Foods

819 Kings Road
Schenectady, NY
(518) 377-8814; Fax: (518) 377-8269
Website: *www.casavisco.com*

North Carolina

Forge Mountain Foods

PO Box 1055
Flat Rock, NC 28731
(828) 692-9470
Website: *http://forgemountain.com*

Product: Jams, jellies, butters, relishes

For other copackers and programs, please contact

North Carolina State University

Raleigh, NC 27695
(919) 515-2011
Website: *www.ces.ncsu.edu/depts/foodsci/ext/pubs/
copackers.html*

Ohio

Martinez Food Products LLC

1220 Belmont Avenue
Toledo, OH 43607
866-293-5477, (419) 720-6973
email: info@martinezfood.com
Website: *www.martinezfood.com*

Pennsylvania

Wertz Candies

718 Cumberland Street
Lebanon, PA 17042
(717) 273-0511
email: questions@wertzcandy.com
Website: *http://wertzcandy.com*

Beanie's of Lancaster Inc.
2316 Norman Road
Lancaster, PA 17601
800-335-6663, (717) 397-9578;
Fax: (717) 397-0941
email: info@beaniesoflancaster.com
Website: *www.beaniesoflancaster.com*

Product: Quality jams, spreads, and sauces

South Carolina

The Sweetery
1814 E. Greenville Street
Anderson, SC 29621
800-752-1188, (864) 224-8394
Website: *http://thesweetery.com*

Product: Cakes, candies

Appendix E
Broker Information

The following list is neither all-inclusive, nor is it meant to serve as an endorsement. Please visit our website *www.specialtyfoodresource.com* for updates. The list is based on open source material and was accurate as of August 2008.

Alabama

Associated Food Brokers of Alabama
3720 River Bend Lane
Birmingham, AL 35223
(205) 967-9444
Website: *http://gourmetfoodbrokers.com*

D & T Sales and Marketing
1820 First Avenue S., Suite Q
Irondale, AL 35210
(205) 951-7788
Website: *www.dandtsales.com*

Intersouth Foodservice Group
100 Oxmoor Boulevard, Suite A
Brimingham, AL 35209
(205) 942-8243

Headquarters
868 Lagood Commercial Boulevard
Montgomery, AL 36117
(334) 277-4708

Alaska

Pierce Cartwright Company
1205 E. International Airport Road,
 Suite 204
Anchorage, AK 99518
(907) 563-3032 Fax: (907) 562-3473
Website: *www.piercecartwright.com*

Arizona

Amalgamated Foodservice Brokerage
6945 E. Second Street, Apt. 5
Scottsdale, AZ 85251
(480) 452-5850; Fax: (480) 247-9385

Cahill Desert Products
Ray Broderick
3400 W. Osborn
Phoenix, AZ 85017
(877) 224-4557
website: *http://cahilldesertproducts.com*

California

ACB/Richard Watson
Mr. Richard Watson
501 Via Casitas, #321
Greenbrae, CA 94904-1958
(415) 461-9255
email: rgwatson@pacbell.net

Burgess, Bradstreet, Leland & Associates
Mr. Ken Leland
PO Box 550
Millbrae, CA 94030
(650) 692-1585; Fax: (650) 692-1654
email: bbleland@aol.com

Byer Connection Brokerage Company
Steve Goldschlag and Linda Byer
1966 Tice Valley Boulevard, #420
Walnut Creek, CA 94595
866-531-2468, (925) 943-6653;
Fax: (925) 945-7471
email: byerconnection@aol.com

HSR Associates Inc.
Mr. Steve Goodman
18829 Paseo Nuevo Drive
Tarzana, CA 91356
(818) 757-7152; Fax: (818) 757-7141
email: steve@hsrassoc.com
Website: *http://hsrassociates.net*

Gorman Confections LLC
2076 W. 235th Street
Torrance, CA 90501
800-421-2297, (310) 548-6087;
Fax: (310) 548-0016
email: info@gormanconfections.com
Website: *http://gormanconfections.com*

Herspring-Gibbs Inc.
PO Box 1367
15 Crow Canyon Court, Suite 100
San Ramon, CA 94583-1640
800-871-4446; Fax: (925) 552-5205
email: jwollenweber@herspringgibbs.com
Website: *http://herspring.com*

Market Connections Group
Kate Flores
1212 S. Fifth Avenue, Suite H
Monrovia, CA 91016-3853
(626) 574-1600; Fax: (626) 574-1605
email: info@marketconnectionsgroup.com
Website: *http://marketconnectionsgroup.com*

Pinski-Portugal & Associates Inc.
Ms. Lynn Portugal
1933 S. Broadway, Suite 311
Los Angeles, CA 90007
213-763-5722; Fax: 213-763-5747
email: lynn.portugal@pinski-portugal.com
Website: *http://pinski-portugal.com*

Remington Sales & Marketing LLC
550 N. Park Center Drive, Suite 202
Santa Ana, CA 92705
(714) 547-6847; Fax: (714) 547-6848

Tomales Bay Foods
Ms. Carol Waxman

80 Fourth Street
PO Box 594
Point Reyes Station, CA 94956-0594
(415) 663-9335; Fax: (415) 663-5418
email: carol@cowgirlcreamery.com
Website: *http://cowgirlcreamery.com*

Colorado

Gourmet Marketing

1710 Glen Dale Drive
Lakewood, CO 80215
(303) 234-1137

FamilyQuest Marketing

Kimborough Johns
PO Box 212
790 Cumberland Drive
Jefferson, CO 80456-9727
888-836-3461; Fax: Same
email: hkjcofqm@yahoo.com

This broker serves seven states: Texas, Oklahoma, Louisiana, Arkansas, Mississippi, Colorado, and Wyoming.

Green Mountain Specialty Foods Inc.

Mr. Kregg Flowers
770 W. Hampden Avenue, Suite 250
Englewood, CO 80110
800-530-8511, (303) 530-3861;
Fax: (303) 530-3909
email: finefoods@gmsf.biz
Website: *http://gmsf.biz*

Wild Rose Marketing Inc.

Ms. Rose Pierro
1320 Pearl Street, Suite 107
Boulder, CO 80301
888-448-9556, (303) 448-9556;

Fax: (303) 448-9762
email: rose@wildrosemarketing.com
Website: *http://wildrosemarketing.com*

Connecticut

CS Brokers

Mr. Cyrus Settineri
53 River Street
Milford, CT 06460-2057
(203) 878-7788; Fax: (203) 877-6649
email: cyrus@csbrokers.com
Website: *http://csbrokers.com*

O'Leary and Company

Mr. Daniel T. O'Leary
31 Shepard Hill
Danielson, CT 06239
(860) 774-8384; Fax: (860) 779-1135
email: dolearycoffe@sbcglobal.net

Florida

Action Brokerage Consultants

2215 Tradeport Drive
Orlando, FL 32824
(407) 447-7500; Fax: (407) 447-7501
email: office@abc-fl.com
Website: *www.abc-fl.com*

Annie Hall Inc.

Ms. Annie Hall
5116 Coronado Ridge
Boca Raton, FL 33486
(561) 391-7636; Fax: (561) 391-3368
email: annie@anniehallinc.com
Website: *http://anniehallinc.com*

Coastal Gourmet Sales Inc.
Mr. Kenneth Pease
5048 Golf Club Lane
Brooksville, FL 34609
(352) 796-0539; Fax: (352) 796-4189
email: coastalgs@msn.com

The Cristol Group Inc.
Mr. Sam Cristol
4600 W. Commercial Boulevard
Fort Lauderdale, FL 33319
(954) 486-4129; Fax: (954) 486-4133
email: sam@cristolgroup.com
Website: *www.cristolgroup.com*

Maximum Marketing Inc.
Mr. Brad Magaro
7710 NW 56th Way
Pompano Beach, FL 33073-3509
(954) 725-3700; Fax: (954) 725-3400
email: brad@maximummarketing.com
Website: *http://maximummarketing.com*

Milmark Sales
Mr. Allen Rosenberg
1223 Ligurian Road
Palm Beach Gardens, FL 33410-2130
(561) 624-1422; Fax: (561) 624-7155
email: milmarksales@adelphia.net

Montague Gourmet Brands
129 N. Garden Avenue
Clearwater, FL 33755
800-975-7068

Seidman Hudson Food Brokerage Inc.
Mr. Gary Seidman
7684 Wiles Road
Coral Springs, FL 33067-2069

(954) 345-6622; Fax: (954) 345-8384
email: info@seidmanhudson.com
Website: *www.seidmanhudon.com*

Georgia

Fine & Fancy Foods
Mr. Tom P. Smith
349 Knots Circle
Woodstock, GA 30188
(770) 924-1760; Fax: (770) 924-9634
email: fineandfancyfood@bellwouth.net

S & S Sales
Ms. Alda Stephens
118 Caracas Drive
Woodstock, GA 30188
(770) 926-4770; Fax: (770) 926-4972
email: alsa@ssspecialtyfoods.com
Website: *http://ssspecialtyfoods.com*

Susan Frierson and Staff
Ms. Susan B. Frierson
3848 Ivy Road NE
Atlanta, GA 30342
(404) 261-0375; Fax: (404) 814-0385
email: pnstsu@aol.com

Taste Bud's, Etc. Inc.
Ms. Gennie Hampton
3052 Greyfield Place, Suite 100
Marietta, GA 30067
800-922-9435, (770) 951-9435;
Fax: 888-922-9435, (770) 951-0258
email: info@tastebudsetc.com
Website: *http://tastebudsetc.com*

Illinois

Bell Marketing Inc.
9800 S. Roberts Road, #203
Palos Hills, IL 60465
800-426-6113, (708) 598-8873;
Fax: (708) 598-8968
email: products @bellmarketing.com
Website: *http://bellmarketing.com*

Hanson Faso Sales & Marketing
Mr. Stewart H. Reich
246 E. Janata Boulevard, Suite 340
Lombard, IL 60148
800-264-8122, (630) 953-9800;
Fax: (630) 953-9889
email: genoffice@hansofaso.com

Master Food Brokers Inc.
10740-B Grand Avenue
Franklin Park, IL 60131-2212
(847) 451-9702; Fax: (847) 451-9716
Website: *www.masterfoodbrokers.com*

Mid-America Sales Co.
Mr. William Antognoli
1750 Dewes Street
Glenview, IL 60025
(847) 729-4500; Fax: (847) 729-4503
email: info@midamericasales.com

E. F. Reimann Company
1304 E. Cooper Drive
Palantine, IL 60074
(847) 991-1366

Exclusively Gourmet Ltd.
Ms. Beth Bitzegaio
1350 N. Wells Street, Unit G408
Chicago, IL 60610

(312) 397-9494; Fax: (312) 264-2550
email: beth@egsales.biz
Website: *www.egsales.biz*

Signature Specialty Sales & Marketing Inc.
Mr. Andrew J. Paul
510 Oakmont Lane
Westmont, IL 60559-6144
(630) 654-2100; Fax: (630) 654-2130
email: andy@signaturessm.com
Website: *www.signaturessm.com*

Wallish Association
Mr. Charles Patton
227 W. Grand Avenue
Bensenville, IL 60106
(630) 860-0770; Fax: (630) 860-0832
email: cpatton@wallish.com

Indiana

R. J. Muccillo & Associates
Mr. Robert J. Muccillo
1307 Touchstone Drive
Indianapolis, IN 46239
(317) 894-2352; Fax: (317) 894-2422
email: rjmuccillo@comcast.net

Kentucky

J. Seibert Company
Mr. Bob Kupper
200 W. York Street
Louisville, KY 40203
(502) 582-1654
email: bk@ajseibert.com

Maryland

Chesapeake Sales
Mr. Jack M. Epstein
11044 Wood Elves Way
Columbia, MD 21044
(301) 596-4859; Fax: (410) 740-2958
email: jechesapeakesales@comcast.net

Massachusetts

Acosta Sales and Marketing Company
Lake Williams Corporate Center
130 Lizotte Drive
Marlborough, MA 01752
(508) 486-8366; Fax: (508) 486-8695
email: mmcgoldrick@nssales.com
Website: *www.acosta.com*

Baron Associates Inc.
Mr. William Baron
15 Locksley Road
Lynnfield, MA 01940
(781) 334-2978; Fax: (781) 334-3622
email: ewbaron@comcast.net

Benchmark Sales & Marketing Inc.
1400 Providence Highway, Building 3,
   Suite 3200
Norwood, MA 02062-2626
(781) 746-0000; Fax: (781) 746-0099
Website: *http://benchmarksales.com*

This company also has sales offices in Buffalo, Albany, and Rochester, New York.

Peter Blatchford Company
Peter Blatchford
28 Middle Street
South Dartmouth, MA 02748-3414
(508) 994-5557; Fax: (508) 994-5579

Alfred H. Gledhill & Sons
Mr. Alfred H. Gledhill Jr.
133 Winsor Avenue
Watertown, MA 02478-3557
(617) 924-6213; Fax: (617) 249-1951
email: algledhill@att.net

Arnold H. Gitter Associates Inc.
Mr. Arnold H. Gitter
PO Box 30
Marblehead, MA 01945
888-773-7527, (781) 631-7527;
Fax: (781) 631-3852
email: gitter.assoc@verizon.net

Condimental.com
(a division of Housewaresdirect Inc.)
20 Myles Standish Road
Weston, MA 02493
877-438-4932; Fax: 877-438-4932
email: sales@condimental.com
Website: *http://condimental.com*

De Michele Associates/Fontana E. De Michele
Mr. James De Michele
12 Algonquin Road
Worcester, MA 01609-1702
(508) 755-9854; Fax: (508) 755-9298
email: demicheleassociates@charter.net

ESM-New England
411 Waverly Oaks Road, Suite 330
Waltham, MA 02452
(781) 314-7100; Fax: (781) 453-4448
Website: *http://esmne.com*

North Eastern Sales Solutions
27 Curve Street, Box 920473
Needham, MA 02492
(781) 444-7604; Fax: (781) 444-7607
email: office@salessolutions.com

Fresh Food Sales & Marketing
(Acosta Sales)
1001 Worcester Road
Framingham, MA 01701-5237
(508) 620-1515
Website: *www.acosta.com*

JBM Distinctive Fine Foods
Mr. Jerry Mintz
125 Washington Street
Foxboro, MA 02035
(508) 543-3611; Fax: (508) 543-8178
email: info@jbmsales.com
Website: *www.jbmsales.com*

J. J. Sloane & Associates Inc.
146 W. Boylston Drive, #203
Worcester, MA 01606
(508) 852-4444; Fax: (508) 852-6077
Website: *www.jjsloaneassociates.com*

Johnson, O'Hare Company Inc.
1 Progress Road
Billerica, MA 01821
(978) 663-9000; Fax: (978) 262-2200
Website: *www.johare.com*

Woolf Associates
Ms. Maureen Woolf
41 Milk Porridge Circle
Northborough, MA 01532-2308
(508) 393-8173; Fax: (508) 393-2496
email: maureenwoolf@charter.net

Michigan

B & B Specialty Foods Inc.
Ms. Mary Ann Greenawalt
4050 Stoneleigh Road
Bloomfield Hills, MI 48302-2018
(248) 645-2096; Fax: (248) 645-6725
email: bbspecialtyfoods@hotmail.com
Website: *www.bbspecialtyfoods.com*

Minnesota

A. P. Marketing Services
Mr. Brian W. Gilbertson
4904 Lincoln Drive
Edina, MN 55436-1071
(952) 931-9761; Fax: (952) 936-9690
email: briang@pclink.com
Website: *www.apmarketingservices.com*

R. L. Cooperman & Associates LLC
8834 7th Avenue N.
Minneapolis, MN 55427
800-237-6993, (763) 544-8613;
Fax: (763) 544-9280

The Gourmet Network
1859 Simpson Street
Falcon Heights, MN 55113
(651) 646-4750; Fax: (651) 646-5541
Website: *http://thegourmetnetwork.com*

Missouri

A. R. & Associates
Mr. Richard E. Redohl
4548 S. Square Drive
High Ridge, MO 63049
800-356-5956; (636) 677-4104;

Fax: (636) 376-9909
email: arassoc1@nuvox.net

Camoriano & Associates
Mr. Kirk Camoriano
14724 NW Tiffany Park Road
Parkville, MO 64153-1069
(816) 891-7755; Fax: (816) 891-6474
email: kirkc@camoriano.com
Website: *www.camoriano.com*

New Jersey

Advantage Sales & Marketing
Mr. Randy Allen
535 E. Crescent Avenue
Ramsey, NJ 07446-1208
(201) 825-9400; Fax: (201) 825-8556
email: rdallen456@aol.com
Website: *www.asmnet.com*

E. A. Berg & Sons Inc.
9 Brook Avenue
PO Box 1187
Maywood, NJ 07607
(201) 845-8200; Fax: (201) 845-8201
Website: *http://eaberg.com*

The Brauner Group LLC
Ms. Bonnie M. Brauner
32 Heron Road
Livingston, NJ 07039
(973) 535-3143; Fax: (973) 535-3142
email: bmbrauner@aol.com

Cappetta Associates Sales & Marketing
Mr. Frank Cappetta
1814 E. Route 70, Suite 406
Cherry Hill, NJ 08003

(856) 795-4541; Fax: (856) 795-9262
email: cappettasales@aol.com

ESM/Metro New York
Mr. Barry Rowen
2 Van Riper Road
PO Box 409
Montvale, NJ 07645-0409
(201) 307-9100; Fax: (201) 782-5153
email: browen@esm-ny.com

Golden Sales Associates Inc.
283 Stuart Street
Howell, NJ 07731
(732) 462-6004; Fax: (732) 462-1964

Golick Martins Inc.
Mr. Manny Martins
140 Sylvan Avenue
Englewood Cliffs, NJ 07632-2502
(201) 592-8800; Fax: (201) 592-9196
email: mmartins@golickmartins.com
Website: *http://golickmartinsinc.com*

Grant Hanson Metro
46 Jackson Drive
Cranford, NJ 07016
(908) 497-3000; Fax: (908) 497-3010

Michael Azurak Brokerage
Mr. Mike Azurak
17 Domino Road
Somerset, NJ 08873
(732) 356-3826; Fax: (732) 356-6057

Nancy's Fancy Foods
Ms. Nancy K. Waterhouse
166 Crescent Avenue
Waldwick, NJ 07463

(201) 670-1000; Fax: (201) 670-1811
email: nffds@aol.com

Schnakenberg Associates Inc.
Mr. John H. Schnakenberg
133 E. Broad Street
Westfield, NJ 07090
(908) 654-1133; Fax: (908) 654-3737

Strand Specialty Sales
Mr. John Strand
551 Monroe Court
River Edge, NJ 07661
(201) 261-6347; Fax: (201) 261-6638
email: strand1@aol.com

Tom Manning Associates
Mr. Thomas R. Manning
220 Pascack Avenue
Emerson, NJ 07630
(201) 262-3578; Fax: (201) 634-1298

World Finer Foods Inc.
300 Broadacres Drive
Bloomfield, NJ 07003
(973) 338-0300; Fax: (973) 338-0382
email: nkasket@worldfiner.com
Website: *www.worldfiner.com*

New York

A & D Sales Associates Inc.
550 Smithtown By-Pass, Suite 204
Smithtown, NY 11787-5013
(631) 979-4000

Acosta Sales & Marketing
4 Executive Park Drive, Suite 103
Clifton Park, NY 12065-5630

(518) 373-7100; Fax: (518) 373-7111
email: ddelong@acostasales
or
405 N. French Road, #114
Amherst, NY 14228-2010
Fax: (716) 636-0487
Website: *www.acosta.com*

Benchmark Sales & Marketing
4240 Ridge Lea Road, #101
Amherst, NY 14226
(716) 446-0800
Website: *www.benchmarksales.com*

R. J. Bickert Associates Inc.
10205 Main Street
Clarence, NY 14031-2011
(716) 739-8876; Fax: (716) 759-2823
email: rbickert@msn.com

DKB Sales & Marketing Inc.
Dianne Keeler Bruce
109 W. 70th Street
New York, NY 10023-4453
(212) 877-9676; Fax: (212) 787-9522
email: dkeelerbruce@earthlink.net

Di Meo-Gale Brokerage Co.
457 Wilson Road
Frankfort, NY 13340

F.O.S. Sales & Marketing Inc.
Doreen Faulhaber
PO Box 353
Atlantic Beach, NY 11509
(516) 239-0963; Fax: (516) 239-6130
email: fosfoods@optonline.net

Feenix Brokerage Ltd.
Frank Pensabene Jr.
6283 Johnson Road
Albany, NY 12203-4323
(518) 456-7664; Fax: (518) 456-0869
email: info@feenix.net
Website: *http://feenix.net*

Food Associates of Syracuse Inc.
Nick Petrosillo
71714 State Fair Boulevard
Syracuse, NY 13209
(315) 635-6338; Fax: (315) 635-1798
email: fasco1@dreamscape

Frazier Foods Ltd.
3841 S. Park Avenue
Bladsdell, NY 14219-1813
(716) 332-0988

G. A. Davis Food Service
325 E. Sunrise Highway
Lindenhurst, NY 11757
800-437-6322, (516) 364-0910;
Fax: (516) 364-0917
Website: *www.gadavis.com*

GEM Food Brokers Inc.
1260 Scottsville Road
Rochester, NY 14624
800-724-1475, (585) 436-0960;
Fax: (585) 436-3514
Website: *www.gemfoodbrokers.com*

Grant Hanson Metro
46 Jackson Drive
Cranford, NJ 07016
(908) 497-3000; Fax: (908) 497-3010

Herb Barber & Sons Food Brokers
7193 E. Main Street
Westfield, NY 14787
(716) 326-4692
email: herb@herb-barber-sons.com
Website: *http://herb-barber-sons.com*

Hudson Valley Food Brokers
3 Wembley Court, #102
Albany, NY 12205-3836
(518) 786-9174; Fax: (518) 786-9176
email: hudsonvalleyfood@aol.com

J'Ai Besoin Ltd.
Ms. Conni Kalman
20 Ridge Drive
Melville, NY 11747
(631) 424-5353; Fax: (631) 424-0130
email: c.kalman@juno.com

Lomac & May Associates
17 Wather Way
Albany, NY 12205-4945
(518) 452-7041; Fax: (518) 452-2826

Karam Foods
Ms. Lorrie B. Karam
17 Magnolia Drive
Dobbs Ferry, NY 10522-3508
(914) 693-6338; Fax: (914) 479-0067
email: karam.food@verizon.net

Mid-State Food Brokers Inc.
7489 Henry Clay
Liverpool, NY 13088-3545
(315) 451-2080
Website: *www.midstatefood.com*

M & Y Sales Associates Inc.
Mr. John W. Yates
1 Central Avenue
Tarrytown, NY 10591
(914) 332-1414; Fax: (914) 332-4882
email: mysalesassoc@aol.com

New Horizons Foods & Marketing
306 Lakeside Road
Syracuse, NY 13209-9729
(315) 488-3101

Reichenbach & Associates Inc.
1005 Glen Cove Avenue
Glen Head, NY 11545-1585
(516) 674-9200
Website: *www.reichenbach-assoc.com*

Ross Upstate Sales & Marketing Inc.
6501C Basile Rowe
East Syracuse, NY 13057

R. J. Bickert Associates Inc.
Mr. Roger J. Bickert
10205 Main Street
Clarence, NY 14031
(716) 759-8876; Fax: (716) 759-2823
email: rbickert@msn.com

RJM Trading
Mr. Ron Maiorino
374 N. Greeley Avenue
Chappaqua, NY 10514
(914) 238-6902; Fax: (914) 238-0498
email: rjmtrade@bestweb.net

Ross Upstate Sales & Marketing Inc.
480 Broadway, Suite LL-23
Saratoga Springs, NY 12866-2230

(518) 583-6633; Fax: (518) 583-6635
Website: *www.upstateconfectionery.com*

Valley Food Specialties LLC
Mr. Steve Auerbach
40 River Road
Chatham, NY 12037
(518) 392-6851; Fax: (914) 992-7278
email: office@valleyfoodspecialties.com
Website: *http://valleyfoodspecialties.com*

North Carolina

Blue Ridge Food Brokers & Consultants Inc.
Mr. Tim O'Rourke
2401 Wall Meadow Lane
Summerfield, NC 27358
(336) 643-8175; Fax: (336) 643-6690
Website: *http://blueridgefoodbrokers.com*

Gourmet Food Inc.
Mr. Garry M. Derrick
420 Bywood Drive
Durham, NC 27712
(919) 477-1917; Fax: (919) 479-5966
email: derrickgm@aol.com

Pioneer Food Brokers Inc.
4201 I Stuart Andrew Boulevard
Charlotte, NC 28217
(704) 527-5295

Ohio

Dunn Specialties
Mr. Michael B. Dunn
4188 Weathered Oaks Lane
Fairfield Township, OH 45011

(513) 844-2892; Fax: (513) 844-6575
email: dspec@aol.com

Harlow-HRK Sales & Marketing Inc.
Mr. Steve Harlamat
2620 Keenan Avenue
Dayton, OH 45414-4910
(937) 274-1905; Fax: (937) 274-5213

Kenyon & Kenyon Inc.
Mr. Michael C. Kenyon
7055 Engle Road, Suite 3-301
Cleveland, OH 44130
(330) 722-8008; Fax: (973) 273-5854
email: mckenyon1@aol.com

Martinez Food Products LLC
1220 Belmont Avenue
Toledo, OH 43607
866-293-5477, (419) 720-6973
email: info@martinezfood.com
Website: *www.martinezfood.com*

James V. Sidari and Associates Inc.
Mr. James V. Sidari
19291 Lorain Road
Fairview Park, OH 44126
(440) 356-4858; Fax: (440) 356-4857
email: jvsidari@aol.com
Website: *http://jvsidari.com*

Specialty Food Service
1370 Sanders Avenue SW
Massillon, OH 44647
(303) 837-0018

Pennsylvania

Associated Food Services
600 N. Bell Avenue, Suite 210
Carnegie, PA 15106
(412) 429-1433

Bell Export Foods Group
Mr. Ron Davis
2701 Red Lion Road
Philadelphia, PA 19114
(215) 965-3338

Louise Ceccarelli & Associates
8808 W. Chester Pike
Upper Darby, PA 19082
(610) 789-3565; Fax: (610) 789-3573

Gail Kramer Associates
Ms. Gail Kramer
19 Bala Avenue
Bala Cynwyd, PA 19004
(610) 667-0584; Fax: (610) 667-9476

Morton Schweitzer Sales
Mr. Morton F. Schweitzer
5582 Pocusset Street
Pittsburgh, PA 15217-1913
(412) 521-3674; Fax: (412) 421-2595
email: schweitzersales@aol.com

Santucci Associates Inc.
Mr. Stephen Delco
1010 Mill Creek Drive
PO Box 326
Feasterville, PA 19053-7321
(215) 676-2300; Fax: (215) 355-0986
email: main@santucciassoc.com

Tennessee

South Group Marketing
PO Box 40226
Nashville, TN 37204
(615) 244-2728
Website: *http://twwilsonandson.com*

Texas

Arnett Brokerage
5607 S. Avenue Q
Lubbock, TX 79412
(806) 744-1477
Website: *www.arnettbrokerage.com*

The Carroll Group
Ms. Mimi Carroll
2844 Dallas Trade Mart
Dallas, TX 75207
(214) 698-1172; Fax: (214) 748-3225
email: carrollgroup@aol.com

Chandler Food Sales
601 NW 10th Street
PO Box 532607
Grand Prairie, TX 75050-5415
(972) 642-5700

D. C. Scott and Associates Food Brokerage Inc.
Mr. David Scott
24830 Shining Arrow
San Antonio, TX 78258-2743
(210) 497-3589
Website: *www.dcscott.net*

Gourmetexas Inc.
Mr. Jason Polser
569 Barcus Street, Suite 100
Seguin, TX 78155
(830) 379-0033; Fax: (830) 379-6617
email: jason@gourmetexas.com
Website: *http://gourmetexas.com*

Kayser Sales and Marketing Inc.
8500 N. MOPAC Expressway
Austin, TX 78759-8375
(512) 454-4407
Website: *www.kayser-sales.com*

Wright Choice Gourmet
Mr. Chris Wright
5921 Locke Avenue
Fort Worth, TX 76107
(817) 626-1462; Fax: (817) 624-1411
email: chris@wrightchoicegourmet.com
Website: *http://wrightchoicegourmet.com*

Washington

Evergreen Fancy Foods
923 E. 34th Avenue
Spokane, WA 99203
800-767-5211, (509) 838-1977;
Fax: (509) 624-3375
Website: *www.evergreenfancyfoods.com*

Market 2 Market Sales & Marketing Group
Ms. Cheryl Hofer
6180 4th Avenue, Suite 372
Seattle, WA 98108
800-228-2159, (206) 365-4124;
Fax: (206) 365-0651
email: chm2m@comcast.net
Website: *http://market2marketllc.com*

Murdock & White
Ms. Charlene Murdock
6100 Fourth Avenue S., Suite 437
Seattle, WA 98108-3234
800-477-3262, (206) 767-9175;
Fax: (206) 767-3755
email: info@murdockandwhite.com
Website: *http://murdockandwhite.com*

Wisconsin

B.L.V. Marketing Inc.
3695 N. 126th Street, Suite 333
Brookfield, WI 53005-2424
(262) 790-0900
Website: *www.blvmarketing.com*

Shaw Specialty Foods
Ms. Susan Shaw
5227 N. Shoreland Avenue
Milwaukee, WI 53217
866-867-1658, (414) 332-5950;
Fax: (414) 332-5958
email: shawandassoc@cs.com
Website: *http://shawspecialtyfoods.com*

Specialty Products Inc.
Mr. Jose D. Teigeiro
PO Box 320123
Franklin, WI 53132
(414) 425-6225; Fax: (414) 425-4560
email: jose@candyspi.com

Sample Broker Appointment Letter

This is a very formal version. You may use a simpler form to suit your needs.

AGREEMENT between [your company], a [corporation, proprietorship, partnership] ("Company"), whose principal office is located at [your address], and [broker name], a [corporation, proprietorship, partnership] of [state] with principal office located at [address].

In consideration of the mutual covenants contained herein, the parties agree as follows:

Article I

APPOINTMENT Company hereby appoints [broker name] its exclusive representative for sales of all the Company's [indicate product types, if necessary] throughout the Territory, as designated below, on the following terms and conditions.

Article II

TERRITORY Territory means the [insert territory]. [Indicate any variations, accounts not included, etc.].

Article III

AUTHORITY [Broker name] shall promote the sale of the Company's products according to its best judgment, including carrying out the following activities:

A. Establishing and supervising all field sales;
B. Contracting and servicing dealers, suppliers, retailers, wholesalers, and other users and purchasers for resale;
C. Assessing marketing strengths and weaknesses prices, competition, and other contractual terms;
D. Recommending and implementing, if requested, advertising and promotional strategies and activities; and
E. Receiving and transmitting orders and other requests from customers.

Article IV

RIGHT TO SOLICIT AND ACCEPT ORDERS [Broker name]'s authority includes the exclusive right to solicit and accept orders, either directly or through its sales agents in the Territory, for all products of the Company. Company agrees to transmit regularly to [broker name] all information concerning orders and sales that the Company receives or obtains directly, whether from existing customers or from third parties. [Broker name] will supply the Company its best field information on credibility for any new account and will maintain field surveillance on established accounts in terms of stability/credibility. Company has the responsibility and authority to control credit line and terms to the customer.

Article V

COMMISSION ON SALES Unless specified otherwise:

A. [Broker name] shall be entitled on all orders shipped by the Company to a commission of 10 percent for sales to retailers and 5 percent for sales to distributors.

B. The commission will be calculated on the total dollar amount of the order FOB [your warehouse location].

Article VI

DEVOTION OF TIME AND SKILL

A. [Broker name] agrees to use its best efforts to promote the sales and use of, and to solicit and secure orders for, the products of the Company within the Territory.

B. [Broker name] shall observe Company policies, as provided in writing by the Company, as regards the sales of Company's products and shall be furnished regularly with sales literature, technical data, and sample products by the Company in reasonable quantities and without charge.

C. [Broker name] shall not participate in the sale of any product that would conflict with the products of the Company included in this agreement without the authorization of the Company.

Article VII

EXPENSES Except as herein provided, [broker name] agrees to assume all expenses of its own employees, and all expenses of maintaining its organization as the sales representatives of the Company's products within the Territory and all expenses of sales agents or brokers retained by [broker name]. [Broker name] will identify and recommend advertising and promotional opportunities which, if agreed to by the Company, will be paid for by the Company.

Article VIII

COMPANIES REPRESENTED [Broker name] will provide to the Company a list of all companies that it represents.

Article IX

DURATION OF AGREEMENT: TERMINATION This agreement shall be effective from the execution hereof and shall be binding on the parties hereto and their assigns, representatives, heirs, and successors. This agreement shall continue in effect for one year and be automatically renewable annually thereafter until terminated by either party on thirty (30) days' written notice to the other, provided that in the event of insolvency or adjudication in bankruptcy or on the filing of a petition therefore by either party, this agreement may be terminated immediately at the option of either party on written notice to the other. Termination shall be without prejudice to the rights and obligations of the parties hereto that have vested prior to the effective date of termination, except that, on termination, the Company shall pay [broker name] the commissions provided only on orders received by the Company prior to the effective date of such termination and delivered to customers within ninety (90) days following the effective date of such termination. The acceptance, however, of such orders and the liability of the Company for the payment of commissions thereon are to be subject to the terms and conditions herein before provided.

Article X

CHANGES; ALTERATIONS No change, alteration, modification, or amendment to this agreement shall be effective unless in writing and properly executed by the parties hereto.

Article XI

APPLICABLE LAW This agreement and any disputes relating thereto shall be construed under the laws of [your state], United States of America.

Article XII

CONTRACT TERMS EXCLUSIVE This agreement constitutes the entire agreement between the parties hereto, and the parties acknowledge and agree that neither of them has made any representation with respect to the subject matter of this agreement or any representations inducing the execution and delivery hereof except as specifically set forth herein, and each of the parties hereto acknowledges that it has relied on its own judgment in entering into the same.

IN WITNESS WHEREOF, the parties have executed this agreement:

This _____ day of _____, 20_____

By: _____   By: _____
      (your company name)   (broker name)

By: _____   By: _____
        (your title)   (broker title)

Catalog Sheet Preparation

These companies offer a complete package, from photography to printed sheets. You can order 2,000 to 2,500 catalog sheets with a color photograph, up to 50 words of designed copy, electronic art, and full-color printing on one side of an 80-pound coated stock for $375 to $500, depending upon which supplier you select. Each of the following companies was invited to provide particulars as to its services. Only those that responded have descriptions beyond the name, address, and telephone number. This list is neither all-inclusive, nor is it meant to serve as an endorsement. Please see *www.specialtyfoodresource.com* for updates.

Colorlith Corporation
900 Jefferson Street
Fall River, MA 02721
508-837-6100, 800-556-7171;
Fax: 508-677-4466
email: rpelletier@colorlith.com
Website: *http://colorlith.com*

Cosmos Communications
11-05 44th Drive,
Long Island, NY 11101
800-969-2676, x 225

email: info@cosmoscommunications.com
Website: *http://cosmoscommunications.com*

GenoaGraphix
3485 Sacramento Drive, Suite F
San Luis Obispo, CA 93401
800-258-6164, (805) 546-8494;
Fax: 508-677-4466
Website: *http://genoagraphix.com*

GenoaGraphix specializes in creating professional and high-quality catalogs of all sizes. Its creative team has over 16 years of experience in catalog design and management and offers a comprehensive catalog management service that includes the following:

- Digital photography
- Copywriting
- Complete layout and design
- Index creation
- One- through six-color printing
- Fulfillment and mailing

MegaColor Corporation
1571 Heil Quaker Boulevard
Nashville, TN 37086
888-333-8507 or 800-859-9599,
   (615) 280-5600
email: scohen@megacolor.com
Website: *http://megacolor.com*
Contact: Stan Cohen

Studios for photography are in California, Florida, New York, Georgia, North Carolina, Illinois, Massachusetts, Tennessee, Texas

Primary focus: MegaColor specializes in photography and full-color printing of brochures, catalog sheets, posters, business cards, and postcards. It guarantees the best prices and quality in the country.

Appendix G
Packaging Design

· ·

These companies supply and design packages. This list is not all-inclusive, nor is it meant to serve as an endorsement. Please see *www.specialtyfoodresource. com* for updates.

Can Creations Inc.
POB 84876
Pembsroke Pines, Florida 33084
800-272-0235, (954) 581-3312;
Fax: (954) 581-2523
email: orders@cancreations.com

Since 1985, we have made it our purpose to provide you with the tools and inspiration you need to make your gift basket business a success.

Institute of Packaging Professionals
1601 N. Bond Street, Suite 101
Naperville, IL 60563
(630) 544-5050; Fax: (630) 544-5055
email: info@iopp.org
Website: *www.iopp.org*

Krepe-Kraft
4199 Bay View Road

Blasdell, NY 14219-2732
888-826-8581, (716) 826-7086
Fax: (716) 826-7239
email: sales@krepekraft.com
Website: *www.krepekraft.com*

Packaging Graphics
5732 Milentz Avenue
St. Louis, MO 63109
(314) 457-9095
email: salesdept@packaginggraphics.net
Website: *www.packaginggraphics.net*

Presentation Packaging
870 Louisiana Avenue S.
Minneapolis, MN 55426-1614
800-818-2698 or (763) 540-9544;
Fax: (763) 540-9522
email: customerservice@presentation
    packaging.com

Website: *http://presentationpackaging.com*

Contact: Carol Sylvester, Connie Maloney, and/or Lori Pearson

Primary focus: Presentation Packaging designs and manufactures imaginative corrugated packaging for the food, mail order, retail, gift-ware, and direct mail industries. The company reports that its stock collection is the largest available in the industry, combining colorful preprints, litho-label, and direct print patterns with a huge selection of shapes and sizes. All boxes ship and store flat.

Packaging and Labeling Materials

. . . .

These companies provide specialty food containers, labeling services, and related materials. There are hundreds of others (more than five dozen exhibited at the 2007 NASFT Summer Fancy Food Show), and you should check available listings for some near you. This list is not meant to serve as an endorsement. Please see *www.specialtyfoodresource.com* for updates.

AKM Packaging Inc.
4054 Mountain Road
West Suffield, CT 06093
800-836-6256, (860) 668-6930:
Fax: (860) 668-6931
email: akm5253@aol.com
Website: *http://akmpackaging.com*

No glass jars.

Allstate Can Corporation
1 Wood Hollow Road
Parsippany, NJ 07054-2821
(973) 560-9030; Fax: (973) 560-9217
email: ddagostino@allstatecan.com
Website: *www.allstatecan.com*

Berlin Packaging
111 N. Canal Street, Suite 300
Chicago, IL 60606
800-2-BERLIN (800-223-7546):
Fax: 800-423-7545
email: marketing@berlinpackaging.com
Website: *http://berlinpackaging.com*

Specific focus: Berlin Packaging is the largest U.S. distributor of glass, plastic, and metal containers plus accompanying closure systems with more than 3,100 bottles, jars, tubs, etc. All orders placed before 3:00 PM are shipped the same day. There are no minimum quantity requirements. Professional customer service representatives are available to answer packaging questions and help you locate the ideal container for your product. There are 18 field offices around the United States. Call 800-4-BERLIN for a free catalog.

CCW Products Inc.
5861 Tennyson Street
Arvada, CO 80003
(303) 427-9663, x 308; Fax: (303) 427-1608
email: don.j@ccwproducts.com
Website: *www.ccwproducts.com*

Dispensa-Matic Label Dispensers
28220 Playmor Beach Road
Rocky Mount, MO 65072
800-325-7303, (573) 392-7684
Fax: (573) 392-1757
email: richard@dispensamatic.com
Website: *http://dispensamatic.com*

Driscoll Label Co. Inc.
1275 Bloomfield Avenue, Building 8, Suite 66
Fairfield, NJ 07004-2708
(973) 575-8492; Fax: (973) 575-8345
email: info@driscolllabel.com
Website: *www.driscolllabel.com*

Independent Can Company
Western Specialty Container Division
2040 S. Lynx Place
Ontario, CA 91761
(909) 923-6150; Fax: (909) 923-6052
email: sales@independentcan.com
Website: *http://independentcan.com*

Label Graphics Manufacturing
175 Patterson Avenue
Little Falls, NJ 07424-1607
(973) 890-5665; Fax: (973) 890-1164
email: labels@labelgraphicsmfg.com
Website: *http://labelgraphicsmfg.com*

Labels Plus
2407 106th Street SW
Everett, WA 98204
800-275-7587, (206) 523-0477;
Fax: (206) 523-1973
email: tracy@labelsplus.com
Website: *http://labelsplus.com*

LabelTronix
1097 N. Batavia Street
Orange, CA 92867
800-429-4321; Fax: 800-419-1555
email: tbishop@labeltronix.com
Website: *http://labeltronix.com*

Lightning Labels Inc.
Mr. Steve Smith
2369 S. Trenton Way, Unit C
Denver, CO 80231
Website: *www.lightninglabels.com*

Steve Smith has published *An Introduction of Product Labeling,* which is extremely helpful for new-to-industry specialty food producers.

MARFRED Industries
26599 Corporate Avenue
Hayward, CA 94545-3920
(510) 887-3000, x 154; Fax: (510) 784-0295
email: phil.footlik@marfred.com
Website: *https://ecommerce.marfred.com*

MOD-PAC Corporation
Custom Sales/Manufacturing
1801 Elmwood Avenue
Buffalo, NY 14207-2496
(716) 873-0640; 800-666-3722;
Fax: (716) 873-6008
email: sales@modpac.com
Website: *www.modpac.com*
or
Stock Box Sales Office
4199 Bayview Road

Blasdell, NY 14219-1907
800-666-3722

Primary focus: Quality paperboard folding cartons for every day and every season. Special stock run and custom run programs.

Olshen's Bottle Supply Co.

2331 NE Argyle Street, Suite A
Portland, OR 97211-9998
800-258-4292, (503) 290-0000;
Fax: (503) 290-4270
email: trooper731@aol.com
Website: *www.richardspackaginginc.com*

Primary focus: A family-owned business since 1925, Olshen's distributes stock glass and plastic containers and closures. It also offers special order and custom-designed items.

Pohlig Bros.

8001 Greenpine Road
Richmond, VA 23237
(804) 275-9000; Fax: (804) 275-9900
Website: *http://pohlig.com*

Specific focus: Manufacturer of custom-designed paperboard boxes, specialty packaging, and point-of-sale packaging.

ThermoSafe Brands

2320 S. Foster Avenue
Wheeling, IL 60090
800-800-0359, (847) 398-0110;
Fax: (847) 398-0653
Website: *www.thermosafe.com*

Specific focus: Products for the shipment, storage, and distribution of perishables.

Presentation Packaging

870 Louisiana Avenue S.
Minneapolis, MN 55426
800-818-2698, (763) 540-9544;
Fax: (763) 540-9522
email: customerservice@presentation
  packaging.com
Website: *http://presentationpackaging.com*

Specific focus: Decorative tins, glass, and plastic containers, including PET wide-mouth jars and bottles, tamper-evident bands, and a wide assortment of packaging concepts.

Primera Technology Inc.

1 Carlson Parkway N.
Plymouth, MN 5547-4446
(763) 475-6676, x 219; Fax: (763) 475-6677
email: jstein@primera.com
Website: *www.primera.com* or
  http://primeralabel.com

Professional Image Printing and Packaging

12437 E. 60th Street
Tulsa, OK 74146
800-722-8550, (918) 461-0609;
Fax: (918) 249-9800
email: jjarzen@calvertco.com
Website: *http://pi-pkg.com*

Zenith Specialty Bag Company Inc.

17625 E. Railroad Street
City of Industry, CA 91748-0445
(626) 912-2481; Fax: 800-284-8493
email: p.lubbers@zenithbag.com
Website: *http://zsb.com*

Appendix I
Internet Resources

．．

The following list is neither all-inclusive nor meant to serve as an endorsement. Please see *www.specialtyfoodresource.com* for updates.

Reference Material

Advertising Age/*American Demographics*
Website: *http://adage.com/american demographics/*

A good source of consumer trends information for business leaders.

Easy World Wide Web With Netscape
by Jim Minatel
800-428-5331; Fax: (203) 866-0199

An easy-to-follow, step-by-step guide with full-color illustrations and screen shots on every page. Very useful if you are browsing the Internet.

The Food Channel
Website: *www.foodchannel.com*

This Internet forum provides trend information, reports, and other food industry facts plus online forums, links to other food sites, and a direct link to Food Channel staff. The Food Channel will offer a new publication called *FoodWire*. It will be targeted to the general public and contain food news, trends, and recipes with interactive links to *www. foodchannel.com*.

TrendWire is currently published every two weeks. *FoodWire* will be published monthly. Both will be free publications (advertising supported).

NASFT
Website: *www.specialtyfood.com*

NASFT produces an online specialty food catalog that helps consumers find the products they're looking for. It does not offer the products directly but connects the consumer with a search capability more than 200 listings of specialty food companies' websites.

National Minority Supplier Development Council Inc. (NMSDC)
1040 Avenue of the Americas, 2nd Floor
New York, NY 10018
(212) 944-2430; Fax: (212) 719-9611
Website: *http://nmsdc.org*

Organic Industry Resources

Key industry resources including certifiers, associations, and support services can be found on *The Organic Pages Online*. To learn about acquiring an organic farm or how to start an organic business, see *http://howtogoorganic.com*.

The Food Network
Website: *www.foodnetwork.com*

This combination of lifestyle network and website is committed to exploring new and different ways to view food.

Poor Richard's Email Publishing
Chris Pirillo and Peter Kent

Covers everything about email publishing, including the mechanics of publishing and an extensive resource directory. Published by Top Floor Publishing. Available from Amazon.com.

Website Development and Directory

Deep River Production
Website: *http://swardlick.com*

Deep River Interactive is a wholly owned subsidiary of Swardlick Marketing Group and works with companies and organizations to create new business models based on the transformative power of the Internet. It helps businesses reinvent themselves using new

technologies and integrated marketing solutions to achieve powerful and measurable results.

SnapMonkey.com
POB 37163
Denver, CO 80237
(303) 338-1552; Fax: (303) 200-8552
email: info@snapmonkey.com
Website: *www.snapmonkey.com*

The firm offers a robust searchable multimedia directory program. Any organization can add a SnapMonkey directory to its existing website. SnapMonkey will categorize and allow each member of the directory to showcase its product or service. Members have their own control panel, allowing them to update their content 24/7. They may add a video or a flash presentation to their listing, as well as photos, a 500-character description of their product and service, a Web link, and more. In addition, the SnapMonkey program is designed to be a profit center for the organization. The directory administrator may set pricing for different types of listings. The collection of funds each month from the members is automated, and funds are deposited into the administrator's account. Directory administrators also have the option of putting the entire directory presentation, complete with member profiles, onto a CD. They can then duplicate this CD and use it as a marketing tool to hand out at trade shows, to add to the back of books or publications, etc.

E-Zine University: Learn to Make and Promote Email Publications
Website: *http://ezineuniversity.com*

An electronic magazine that provides information on creating and maintaining an online newsletter. Comprehensive newsletter.

Kellen Interactive (Formerly HQ Cyberservices)
Josh Linard, Business Development Manager
1100 Johnson Ferry Road, Suite 300
Atlanta, GA 30389
(404) 836-5050; Fax: (404) 252-0774
Website: *http://kelleninteractive.com*

Offices in Atlanta; Washington, DC; New York; Tucson; and Brussels. From conceptualization of strategies and budgets to implementation and ongoing support, Kellen Interactive is committed to exceeding your expectations. It provides daily services as webmaster and Internet consultant for over 200 companies and organizations. Kellen offers one-on-one customer service and project management every step of the way. It is committed to client budget, objectives, and deadlines for every project.

OpSys
Miami, FL
(305) 503-3000
Website: *www.opsys.com*
Yahoo! Merchant Solutions
Website: *http://smallbusiness.yahoo.com*

Offers a service that helps you build, manage, and market an online store.

ZeroMillion.com Entrepreneur's Library
Website: *www.zeromillion.com*

This is a free resource developed to help website owners, advertisers, and marketing professionals get the most from their marketing activities. The site includes details of the latest Web marketing techniques being used by many of the most successful sites on the Net and features articles, reviews, and links to hundreds of the best website promotion resources available.

Online Legal Resource

LegalZoom.com
Website: *www.legalzoom.com*

LegalZoom.com helps you create reliable legal documents from your home or office. Simply answer a few questions online, and your documents will be prepared within 48 hours. A good source for assistance in setting up incorporations, LLCs, trademarks, and so forth.

General/Business

***Inc.* Magazine**
Website: *http://inc.com*

An online resource center with a wide variety of resources for small businesses.

SnapMonkey.com
Website: *www.snapmonkey.com*

Provides a full resource center full of ideas on how to bring your small business online and grow it to success.

U.S. Chamber of Commerce
Website: *http://chamberbiz.com*

Listing of all chambers in the United States.

U.S. Small Business Administration
Website: *http://sba.gov*

Provides information and guidelines for small businesses.

U.S. Patent and Trademark Office
Website: *http://uspto.gov*

Provides information on applying for and researching patents and trademarks.

WebTrends
851 SW Sixth Avenue, Suite 1600
Portland, OR 97204
877-932-8736, (503) 294-7025; Fax: (503)
   294-7130
Website: *www.webtrends.com*

Provides Web analytics services and website statistics and is the leading provider of Web analysis and consumer-centric marketing intelligent solutions.

Marketing/Promotion

Directory of Associations
Website: *www.marketingsource.com/associations/*

Provides a comprehensive list of associations for trade industries.

PR Newswire
810 Seventh Avenue, 32nd Floor
New York, NY 10019
800-832-5522, (201) 360-6700
Website: *http://prnewswire.com*

An informational site on how to create press releases and have them distributed to your target market.

SearchEngineWatch.com
Website: *searchenginewatch.com*

Search engine marketing and optimization techniques.

SmallBusiness.com
Website: *http://smallbusiness.com*

An incredible resource directory listing all kinds of advice for small businesses.

Alltop: Small Business
Website: *http://smallbusiness.alltop.com*

A website for anyone interested in the setup and operation of a small business. It offers various discussions and blogs covering many topics.

Gourmet Food Online

Foodlocker.com
5920 S. Loop East
Houston, TX 77033
888-465-1377; Fax: 888-467-5581
email: info@foodlocker.com
Website: *http://foodlocker.com*

This website allows you to order gourmet foods by region and imported and hard-to-find foods by type, brand name, or region. Sales are conducted by online ordering only.

Federal Government Sources

· ·

Federal small business agencies are listed first, followed by the state Small Business Development Center listings. Please see *www.specialtyfoodresource.com* for updates.

Federal Agencies

Code of Federal Regulations
Website: *http://ecfr.gpoaccess.gov*

The Code of Federal Regulations (CFR) contains the specific laws governing labels and ingredient statements for food products. Copies of the appropriate chapters may be purchased from your local government printing office.

Small Business Administration (SBA)
1441 L Street NW
Washington, DC 20416
800-368-5855, (202) 653-7561
Website: *http://sba.gov*

The SBA provides business counseling and has a government-guaranteed loan program for small businesses. You can only qualify for such loans if you have been refused by your local bank. Don't hold your breath. Very few food entrepreneurs are able to access these funds. Ask for the address of the regional office nearest you.

SCORE "Counselors to American Small Business"
409 Third Street SW, 6th Floor
Washington, DC 20024
or
1175 Herndon Parkway, Suite 900
Herndon, VA 20170
800-634-0245, (703) 487-3612;
Fax: (703) 487-3066
Website: *www.score.org*

Founded in 1964, this all-volunteer nonprofit association with 389 chapters throughout the United States and Territories offers free advice to all entrepreneurs. It is a valuable resource partner with the Small Business Administration and offers free consulting and low-cost workshops to prospective and current entrepreneurs. Visit the website to research various topics such as business planning, e-business, finance and capital, human resources, leadership, legal, marketing and public relations, office management, sales and customer service, taxes, and training and to receive advice from a matched mentor.

Small Business Development Centers (SBDC)

Website: *www.sba.gov/aboutsba/sbaprograms/ sbdc/*

The U.S. Small Business Administration (SBA) administers the Small Business Development Center (SBDC) Program to provide management assistance to current and prospective small business owners. SBDCs offer one-stop assistance to small businesses by providing a wide variety of information and guidance at centrally located branch locations.

Not all states have a listing for a specialty food association. Please check with that state's department of agriculture for guidance.

U.S. Department of Commerce (DOC)

14th and Constitution Avenue
Washington, DC 20230
(202) 377-2000
Website: *http://osec.doc.gov*

You can forget about any substantive marketing assistance from this department. Food marketing (domestic and international) is not conducted by the DOC. Check instead with the Department of Agriculture and its Foreign Agricultural Service.

U.S. Food and Drug Administration (FDA)

International Activities Branch Center for Food Safety and Applied Nutrition FDA (HFS-585) 200 C Street SW
Washington, DC 20204
Website: *www.fda.gov*

Request a free copy of information on how to start a food business. The website contains a lot of information, including a *Food Labeling Guide*.

FDA State Health Agencies

Website: *www.fda.gov/oca/sthealth.htm*

The website will get you to a complete listing of all state departments of health. These include food safety sections.

Small Business Administration Offices and Small Business Development Centers

Alabama District Office SBA

801 Tom Martin Drive, Suite #201
Birmingham, AL 35211
(205) 290-7101; Fax: (205) 290-7404

Alabama SBDC

M. William Campbell, State Director
1500 First Avenue N., R118
Birmingham, AL 35203
(205) 307-6510; Fax: (205) 307-6511
email: williamc@uab.edu
Website: *www.asbdc.org*

Alaska District Office SBA

510 L Street, Suite 310
Anchorage, AK 99501-1952
(907) 271-4022

Alaska SBDC

University of Alaska Anchorage

Jason Dinneen, State Director

430 W. Seventh Avenue, Suite 110

Anchorage, AK 99501

(907) 274-7232; Fax: (907) 274-9524

Website: *www.aksbdc.org*

American Samoa Community College SBDC

Herbert Thweatt, Director

Pago Pago, AS 96799

(684) 699-4830; Fax: (684) 699-8636

email: info@worldnet.att.net

Website: *http://as-sbdc.org*

Arizona District Office SBA

2828 N. Central Avenue, Suite 800

Phoenix, AZ 85004-1093

(602) 745-7200; Fax: (602) 745-7210

Arizona SBDC

Maricopa County Community College

Janice Washington, State Director

2411 W. 14th Street, Suite 114

Tempe, AZ 85281

(480) 731-8722; Fax: (480) 731-8729

email: janice.washington@domail.
    maricopa.edu

Website: *www.maricopa.edu/sbdc/*

Arkansas District Office SBA

2120 Riverfront Drive, Suite 250

Little Rock, AR 72202-1796

(501) 324-7379; Fax: (501) 324-7394

Arkansas SBDC

University of Arkansas—Little Rock

Janet Roderick, State Director

2801 S. University Avenue, Room 260

Little Rock, AR 72204

(501) 683-7700; Fax: (501) 683-7720

email: jmroderick@ualr.edu

Website: *http://asbdc.ualr.edu*

California District Offices SBA

455 Market Street, 6th Floor

San Francisco, CA 94105-2420

(415) 744-6820

San Francisco SBDC

Albert Dixon, Director

300 Montgomery Street, Suite 789

San Francisco, CA 94104

(415) 908-7501

Website: *www.sfsbdc.org*

Central California SBDC Fresno

Fresno District Office SBDC

Tom Burns, Director

3302 N. Blackstone Avenue, Suite 225

Fresno, CA 93726

(559) 230-4056

email: tombu@csufresno.edu

Website: *www.ucmerced.edu*

Los Angeles District Office SBDC

330 N. Brand, Suite 1200

Glendale, CA 91203

(818) 552-3215

Website: *http://lasbdcnet.lbcc.edu*

Los Angeles Regional SBDC

Constance Anderson, Director

3255 Wilshire Boulevard, Suite 1501

Los Angeles, CA 90010

(213) 674-2696; Fax: (213) 739-0639

email: constance.anderson@pcrcorp.org
Website: *http://pcrcorp.org*

Sacramento District Office SBA
650 Capitol Mall, Suite 7-500
Sacramento, CA 95814
(916) 930-3700; Fax: (916) 930-3737

Sacramento SBDC
Panda Morgan, Director
1410 Ethan Way
Sacramento, CA 95825
(916) 563-3220; Fax: (916) 563-3266
email: morganp@losrios.edu
Website: *www.sbdc.net*

San Diego District Office SBA
550 W. C Street, Suite 550
San Diego, CA 92101
(619) 557-7250; Fax: (619) 557-5894;
TTY: (619) 557-6998

San Diego—Imperial Counties SBDC
Debbie Trujillo, Regional Director
Southwestern College
900 Otay Lakes Road, Suite 1601
Chula Vista, CA 91910
(619) 482-6388; Fax: (619) 216-6692
email: dtrujillo@sweed.edu
Website: *http://sbditc.org*

Santa Ana District Office SBA
200 W. Santa Ana Boulevard, Suite 700
Santa Ana, CA 92701
(714) 550-7420; Fax: (714) 550-0191

Santa Ana—Tri County Regional SBDC
TriTech SBDC (High-Tech/High-Growth
   Specialty Center)

Mark Mitchel, Director
2 Park Plaza, Suite 100
Irvine, CA 92614
(949) 794-7229
Website: *www.leadsbdc.org*

Silicon Valley SBDC
84 W. Santa Clara, Suite 100
San Jose, CA 95113-1815
(408) 494-0240
Website: *www.siliconvalley-sbdc.org*

Colorado District Office SBA
721 19th Street, Suite 426
Denver, CO 80202
(303) 844-2607

Colorado SBDC
Kelly Manning, State Director
1625 Broadway, Suite 1700
Denver, CO 80202
(303) 892-3864; Fax: (303) 892-3848
email: kelly.manning@state.co.us
Website: *http://coloradosbdc.com*

Connecticut District Office SBA
330 Main Street, 2nd Floor
Hartford, CT 06106
(860) 240-4700

Institute of Technology and Business Development
Ginne Rae Clay-Gilmore, State Director
185 Main Street
New Britain, CT 06051
(860) 832-0650; Fax: (860) 832-0656
email: gilmoregin@ccsu.edu
Website: *www.ccsu.edu/sbdc/*

Connecticut Specialty Food Association
195 Farmington Avenue, Suite 200
Farmington, CT 06032

Delaware District Office SBA
1007 N. Orange Street, Suite 1120
Wilmington, DE 19801-1232
(302) 573-6294

Delaware SBDC
Clinton Tymes, State Director
Delaware Technology Park
1 Innovation Way, Suite 301
Newark, DE 19711
(302) 831-1555; Fax: (302) 831-1423
email: tymesc@udel.edu
Website: *www.delawaresbdc.org*

Washington, D.C., District Office SBA
Washington Metropolitan Area District Office
740 15th Street NW, Suite 300
Washington, DC 20005-3544
(202) 272-0345

District of Columbia SBDC
Henry Turner, Executive State Director
Howard University
2600 Sixth Street NW, Room 128
Washington, DC 20059
(202) 806-1550; Fax: (202) 806-1777
email: hturner@howard.edu
Website: *http://dcsbdc.org*

Florida District Offices SBA
7825 Baymeadows Way, Suite 100B
Jacksonville, FL 32256-7504
(904) 443-1900
or
100 S. Biscayne Boulevard, 7th Floor

Miami, FL 33131
(305)-36-5521; Fax: (305)-536-5058

Florida SBDC
Jerry Cartwright, State Director
University of West Florida
401 E. Chase Street, Suite 100
Pensacola, FL 32502
(850) 473-7800, x 7801; Fax: (850) 473-7813
email: jcartwright@uwf.edu
Website: *http://floridasbdc.com*

Georgia District Office SBA
233 Peachtree Street NE, Suite 1900
Atlanta, GA 30303
(404) 331-0100

Georgia SBDC
Allan Adams, State Director
University of Georgia
1180 E. Broad Street
Athens, GA 30602
(706) 542-6762; Fax: (706) 542-7935
email: aadams@georgiasbdc.org
Website: *www.sbdc.uga.edu*

UGA Extension Food Science Outreach Program
The University of Georgia
Food Science Building, Suite 240
Athens, GA 30602-7610
(706) 542-2574; Fax: (706) 542-9066,
Website: *http://efsonline.uga.edu*

Hawaii District Office SBA
300 Ala Moana Boulevard, Room 2-235
Box 50207
Honolulu, HI 96850
(808) 541-2990; Fax (808) 541-2976

Hawaii SBDC
William Carter, State Director
308 Kamehameha Avenue, Suite 201
Hilo, HI 96720
(808) 974-7515; Fax: (808) 974-7683
email: bill.carter@hawaii-sbdc.org
Website: *http://hawaii-sbdc.org*

Idaho District Office SBA
380 E. Parkcenter Boulevard, Suite 330
Boise, ID 83706
(208) 334-1696; Fax: (208) 334-9353

Idaho SBDC
James Hogge, State Director
Boise State University
1910 University Drive
Boise, ID 83725
(208) 426-3799; Fax: (208) 426-3877
email: jhogge@boisestate.edu
Website: *www.idahosbdc.org*

Idaho Specialty Foods Association
PO Box 5231
Boise, ID 83705
(208) 433-0603

Illinois District Office SBA
500 W. Madison Street, Suite 1250
Chicago, IL 60661-2511
(312) 353-4528; Fax (312) 886-5688
or
3330 Ginger Creek Road, Suite B
Springfield, IL 62711
(217) 793-5020; Fax (217) 793-5025

Illinois SBDC
Mark Petrilli, State Director

Department of Commerce and Economic
  Opportunity
620 E. Adams Street, 4th Floor
Springfield, IL 62701
800-252-2923; Fax: (217) 524-0171
email: ienconnect@mailnj.custhelp.com
Website: *http://ilsbdc.biz*

Indiana District Office SBA
8500 Keystone Crossing, Suite 400
Indianapolis, IN 46240-2460
(317) 226-7272

Indiana SBDC
Jeff Heinzmann, State Director
1 N. Capitol Avenue, Suite 900
Indianapolis, IN 46204
(317) 234-2086; Fax: (317) 232-8872
email: jheinzmann@isbdc.org
Website: *http://isbdc.org*

Iowa District Offices SBA
Des Moines Office
210 Walnut Street, Room 749
Des Moines, IA 50309-4106
(515) 284-4422
or
Cedar Rapids Office
2750 First Avenue NE, Suite 350
Cedar Rapids, IA 52402-4831
(319) 362-6405

Iowa SBDC
Jim Heckmann, State Director
Iowa State University
340 Gerdin Business Building
Ames, IA 50011
(515) 294-2030; Fax: (515) 294-6522

email: jimh@iastate.edu
Website: *http://iowasbdc.org*

Kansas District Office SBA
271 W. Third Street N., Suite 2500
Wichita, KS 67202
(316) 269-6616

Kansas SBDC
Wally Kearns, State Director
214 SW Sixth Street, Suite 301
Topeka, KS 66603
(785) 296-6514; Fax: (785) 291-3261
email: ksbdc.wkearns@fhsu.edu,
Website: *www.ksbdc.biz*

Kentucky District Office SBA
600 Dr. Martin Luther King Jr Place,
    Room 188
Louisville, KY 40202-2254
(502) 582-5971

Kentucky SBDC
Becky Naugle, State Director
University of Kentucky
225B Gatton College of Business
    & Economics
Lexington, KY 40506
(859) 257-7668 Fax: (859) 323-1907
email: lrnaugo@uky.edu
Website: *http://ksbdc.org*

Louisiana District Office SBA
365 Canal Street, Suite 2820
New Orleans, LA 70130
(504) 589-6685

Louisiana SBDC
Mary Lynn Wilkerson, State Director

University of Louisiana—Monroe
College of Business Administration 2-101
700 University Avenue
Monroe, LA 71209
(318) 342-5506; Fax: (318) 342-5510
email: mlwilkerson@lsbdc.org
Website: *http://lsbdc.org*

Maine District Office SBA
Edmund S. Muskie Federal Building, Room
    512
68 Sewall Street
Augusta, ME 04330
(207) 622-8274

Maine SBDC/SBTDC
John Massaua, State Director
University of Southern Maine
School of Business
96 Falmouth Street
PO Box 9300
Portland, ME 04104
(207) 780-4420; Fax: (207) 780-4810
email: jrmassaua@maine.edu
Website: *http://mainesbdc.org*

Maryland District Office SBA
City Crescent Building, 6th Floor
10 S. Howard Street
Baltimore, Maryland 21201
(410) 962-6195

The Maryland District Office does not serve
Montgomery and Prince Georges Counties.
Please visit the Washington, D.C., District
Office for assistance.

Maryland SBDC
Renee Sprow, State Director
7100 Baltimore Avenue, Suite 401

College Park, MD 20740
(301) 403-8300, x 15; Fax: (301) 403-8303
Website: *www.mdsbdc.umd.edu*

Massachusetts District Offices SBA
10 Causeway Street, Room 265
Boston, MA 02222
(617) 565-5590
or
Springfield Branch Office
STCC Technology Park
1 Federal Street, Building 101-R
Springfield, MA 01105
(413) 785-0484

Massachusetts SBDC
Georgianna Parkin, State Director
227 Isenberg School of Management
121 President's Drive
Amherst, MA 01003
(413) 545-6301; Fax: (413) 545-1273
email: gep@msbdc.umass.edu
Website: *www.msbdc.org*

Massachusetts Specialty Food Association
PO Box 34
Groton, MA 01450
800-813-5862, (508) 457-5346
Website: *http://msfa.net*

Michigan District Office SBA
477 Michigan Avenue
McNamara Building, Suite 515
Detroit, Michigan 48226
(313) 226-6075

Michigan SBDC
Carol Lopucki, State Director
Grand Valley State University

510 W. Fulton Street
Grand Rapids, MI 49504
(616) 331-7480; Fax: (616) 331-7485
email: sbtdchq@gvsu.edu
Website: *www.gvsu.edu/misbtdc/region7/*

Minnesota District Office SBA
100 N. Sixth Street
Suite 210-C Butler Square
Minneapolis, MN 55403
(612) 70-2324; Fax: (612) 70-2303

Northwest Regional Center SBDC
Jorge Prince, Regional Director
Bemidji State University
1500 Birchmont Drive NE, #32
Bemidji, MN 56601
(218) 755-4255
email: jprince@bemidjistate.ed
Website: *http://mnsbdc.com*

Minnesota SBDC: There are nine regional
offices throughout the state.

Mississippi District Office SBA
Regions Plaza
210 E. Capitol Street, Suite 900
Jackson, MS 39201
(601) 965-4378; Fax: (601) 965-5629,
    (601) 965-4294

Gulfport Branch Office SBA
Hancock Bank Plaza
2510 14th Street, Suite 103
Gulfport, MS 39501
(228) 863-4449; Fax: (228) 864-0179

Mississippi SBDC
Walter D. Gurley Jr., State Director
B-19 Jeanette Phillips Drive

PO Box 1848
University, MS 38677
(662) 915-5001; Fax: (662) 915-5650
email: wgurley@olemiss.edu
Website: *www.olemiss.edu/depts/mssbdc/*

Missouri District Offices SBA
1000 Walnut, Suite 500
Kansas City, MO 64106
(816) 426-4900
or
200 N, Broadway, Suite 1500
St. Louis, MO 63102
(314) 39-6600; Fax: (314) 39-3785

Missouri SBDC
Max Summers, State Director
410 S. Sixth Street, 200 Engineering N.
Columbia, MO 65211
(573) 884-1555; Fax: (573) 884-4297
email: summersm@missouri.edu
Website: *www.missouribusiness.net*

Montana District Office SBA
10 W. 15th Street, Suite 1100
Helena, MT 59626
(406) 441-1081; Fax: (406) 441-1090

Montana SBDC
Ann Desch, State Director
301 S. Park Avenue, Room 116
Helena, MT 59620
(406) 841-2746 Fax: (406) 841-2728
email: adesch@mt.gov
Website: *http://sbdc.mt.gov*

Nebraska District Office SBA
10675 Bedford Avenue, Suite 100

Omaha, NE 68134
(402) 221-4691

Nebraska SBDC
Omaha Business & Technology Center SBDC
University of Nebraska at Omaha
505 N. 24th Street, Suite 103
Omaha, NE 68110
(402) 595-3511; Fax: (402) 595-3832
Website: *http://nbdc.unomaha.edu*

Nevada District Office SBA
400 S Fourth Street, Suite 250
Las Vegas, NV 89101
(702) 388-6611; Fax: (702) 388-6469

Nevada SBDC
Sam Males, State Director
Reno College of Business
University of Nevada—Reno Campus
Ansari Business Building, 4th Floor, Room 411
Reno, NV 89557
(775) 784-1717; Fax: (775) 784-4337
email: males@unr.edu
Website: *http://nsbdc.org*

New Hampshire District Office SBA
JC Cleveland Federal Building
55 Pleasant Street, Suite 3101
Concord, NH 03301
(603) 225-1400; Fax: (603) 225-1409

New Hampshire SBDC
Mary Collins, State Director
University of New Hampshire,
Whittemore School of Business & Economics
108 McConnell Hall
Durham, NH 03824
(603) 862-2200; Fax: (603) 862-4876

email: mary.collins@unh.edu
Website: *http://nhsbdc.org*

New Jersey District Office SBA
2 Gateway Center, 15th Floor
Newark, NJ 07102
(973) 645-2434

New Jersey SBDC
Brenda Hopper, State Director
Rutgers University
49 Bleeker Street
Newark, NJ 07102
(973) 353-1927; Fax: (973) 353-1110
email: bhopper@njsbdc.com
Website: *http://njsbdc.com*

New Mexico District Office SBA
625 Silver SW, Suite 320
Albuquerque, NM 87102
(505) 248-8225; Fax: (505) 248-8246

New Mexico SBDC
Roy Miller, State Director
Santa Fe Community College
6401 Richards Avenue
Santa Fe, NM 87508
(505) 428-1362; Fax: (505) 428-1469
email: rmiller@sfccnm.edu
Website: *www.nmsbdc.org*

New York District Office SBA
26 Federal Plaza, Suite 3100
New York, NY 10278
(212) 264-4354; Fax (212) 264-4963

Niagara Center
130 S. Elmwood Avenue, Suite 540

Buffalo, New York 14202
(716) 551-4301; Fax: (716) 551-4418

Syracuse District Office
401 S. Salina Street, 5th Floor
Syracuse, NY 13202
(315) 471-9393; Fax: (315) 471-9288

New York State SBDC
James King, State Director
State University of New York
Corporate Woods, 3rd Floor
Albany, NY 12246
(518) 443-5398; Fax: (518) 443-5275
email: j.king@nyssbdc.org
Website: *http://nyssbdc.org*

North Carolina District Office SBA
6302 Fairview Road, Suite 300
Charlotte, NC 28210-2227
(704) 344-6563; Fax: (704) 344-6769

North Carolina SBTDC
Scott Daugherty, Executive Director
5 W. Hargett Street, Suite 600
Raleigh, NC 27601
(919) 715-7272; Fax: (919) 715-7777
email: sdaugherty@sbtdc.org
Website: *http://sbtdc.org*

North Carolina Association of Specialty Foods
2 W. Edenton Street
Raleigh, NC 27601

North Dakota District Office SBA
657 Second Avenue N., Room 218
PO Box 3086
Fargo, ND 58108-3086

(701) 239-5131; Fax: (701) 239-5645
Website: *north.dakota@sba.gov*

North Dakota SBDC

Bonita Wilkenheiser, State Director
1600 E. Century Avenue, Suite 2
Bismarck, ND 58502
(701) 328-5375; Fax: (701) 328-5381
email: bon@ndsbdc.org
Website: *www.ndsbdc.org*

Ohio District Offices SBA

1350 Euclid Avenue, Suite 211
Cleveland, OH 44115
(216) 522-4180; Fax: (216) 522-2038;
TDD: (216) 522-8350
or
401 N. Front Street, Suite 200
Columbus, OH 43215
(614) 469-6860

Ohio SBDC

Michele Abraham, State Director
77 S. High Street, 28th Floor
PO Box 1001
Columbus, OH 43216
(614) 466-5102; Fax: (614) 466-0829
email: mabraham@odod.state.oh.us
Website: *www.ohiosbdc.com*

Oklahoma District Office SBA

Federal Building
301 NW Sixth Street
Oklahoma City, OK 73102
(405) 609-8000

Oklahoma SBDC

Grady Pennington, State Director
Southeastern Oklahoma State University

1405 N. Fourth Avenue, PMB 2584
Durant, OK 74701
(580) 745-7577, x2955; Fax: (580) 745-7471
email: gpennington@sosu.edu
Website: *http://osbdc.org*

Oregon District Office SBA

601 SW Second Avenue, Suite 950
Portland, OR 97204-3192
(503) 326-2682; Fax: (503) 326-2808

Oregon SBDC

Christine Krygier, State Director
Lane Community College
99 W. Tenth Avenue, Suite 390
Eugene, OR 97401
(541) 463-5250; Fax: (541) 345-6006
email: krycierc@lanecc.edu
Website: *http://bizcenter.org*

Northwest Specialty Food Association

1200 NW Naito Parkway, #290
Portland, OR 97209
(503) 241-1487; Fax: (503) 274-4019
email: info@nwspecialtyfoods.org
Website: *www.nwspecialtyfoods.org*

Pacific Islands SBDC Network

Casey Jeszenka, Regional Director
UOG Station Mangilao
PO Box 5014
Mangilao, GU 96923
(671) 735-2590; Fax: (671) 734-2002
email: casey@pacificsbdc.com
Website: *http://pacificsbdc.com*

Pennsylvania District Offices SBA

Robert N. C. Nix Federal Building
900 Market Street, 5th Floor

Philadelphia, PA 19107
(215) 580-2SBA; Fax: 215-580-2722
or
411 Seventh Avenue, Suite 1450
Pittsburgh, PA 15219
(412) 395-6560

Pennsylvania SBDC
Christian Conroy, Interim State Director
University of Pennsylvania
Vance Hall, 4th Floor, Room 423
3733 Spruce Street
Philadelphia, PA 19104
(215) 898-1219; Fax: (215) 573-2135
email: cconroy@wharton.upenn.edu
Website: *http://pasbdc.org*

Puerto Rico District Office SBA
252 Ponce de Leon Avenue
Citibank Tower, Suite 200
San Juan, PR 00918
800-669-8049, (787) 766-5572;
Fax: (787) 766-5309

St. Croix Post of Duty
Almeric L. Christian Federal Building &
    U.S. Court House
3013 Estate Golden Rock, Room 167
Christiansted, St. Croix, VI 00820
800-669-8049, (340) 778-5380;
Fax: (340) 778-1102

Puerto Rico SBTDC
Union Plaza Building, 10th Floor
416 Ponce de Leon Avenue
Hato Rey, PR 00918
(787) 763-6811; Fax: (787) 763-6875
email: inegron@inter.edu
Website: *http://prsbtdc.org*

Rhode Island District Office SBA
380 Westminster Street, Room 511
Providence, RI 02903
(401) 528-4561

Rhode Island SBDC
John Cronin, Executive Director
Johnson & Wales University
270 Weybosset Street
Providence, RI 02903
(401) 598-2702; Fax: (401) 598-2722
email: john.cronin@jwu.edu
Website: *http://risbdc.org*

South Carolina District Office SBA
1835 Assembly Street, Room 1425
Columbia, SC 29201
(803) 765-5377; Fax: (803) 765-5962

South Carolina SBDC
John Lenti, State Director
University of South Carolina
Darla Moore School of Business
Hipp Building
1710 College Street
Columbia, SC 29208
(803) 777-4907; Fax: (803) 777-4403
email: lenti@darla.moore.sc.edu
Website: *http://scsbdc.moore.sc.edu*

South Dakota District Office SBA
2329 N. Career Avenue, Suite 105
Sioux Falls, SD 57107
(605) 330-4243; Fax: (605) 330-4215;
TTY/TDD: (605) 331-3527

South Dakota SBDC
John Hemmingstad, State Director
University of South Dakota

414 E. Clark Street
Vermillion, SD 57069
(605) 677-5287; Fax: (605) 677-5427
email: jshemmin@usd.edu
Website: *www.usd.edu/sbdc/*

Tennessee District Office SBA

50 Vantage Way, Suite 201
Nashville, TN 37228
(615) 736-5881; Fax: (615) 736-7232;
TTY/TDD Number: (615) 736-2499
or
555 Beale Street
Memphis, TN 38103
(901) 526-9300; Fax: (901) 544-3201

Middle Tennessee State University SBDC

Patrick Geho, Interim State Director
Rutherford County Chamber of Commerce
615 Memorial Boulevard
Murfreesboro, TN 37129
(615) 898-2745; Fax: (615) 893-7089
email: pgeho@mail.tsbdc.org
Website: *www.tsbdc.org*

Tennessee Specialty Foods Association

Website: *tsfagourmet.com*

Texas District Offices SBA

4300 Amon Carter Boulevard, Suite 114
Fort Worth, TX 76155
(817) 684-5500; Fax: (817) 684-5516
or
201 N. Florence Street, 2nd Floor, Suite 201
El Paso, TX 79901
(915) 834-4600; Fax: (915) 834-4689
or

222 E. Van Buren Avenue, Suite 500
Harlingen, TX 78550
(956) 427-8533; Fax: (956) 427-8537

Corpus Christi Branch Office

3649 Leopard Street, Suite 411
Corpus Christi, TX 78408
(361) 879-0017; Fax: (361) 879-0764

Lubbock Branch Office

8701 S. Gessner Drive, Suite 1200
Houston, TX 77074
(713) 773-6500; Fax: (713) 773-6550
or
1205 Texas Avenue, Room 408
Lubbock, TX 79401-2693
(806) 472-7462; Fax: (806) 472-7487
or
17319 San Pedro, Suite 200
San Antonio, TX 78232-1411
(210) 403-5900; Fax: (210) 403-5936;
TDD: (210) 403-5933

North Texas SBDC

Elizabeth Klimback, Regional Director
Bill J. Priest Campus of El Centro College
1402 Corinth Street, Suite 2111
Dallas, TX 75215
(214) 860-5835; Fax: (214) 860-5813
email: emk9402@dcccd.edu
Website: *www.ntsbdc.org*

University of Houston SBDC Network

Mike Young, Regional Director
University of Houston
2302 Fannin, Suite 200
Houston, TX 77002
(713) 752-8444; Fax: (713) 756-1500

email: fyoung@uh.edu
Website: *http://sbdcnetwork.uh.edu*

Texas—Northwest SBDC

Craig Bean Regional Director
Texas Tech University
2579 S. Loop 289, Suite 114
Lubbock, TX 79423
(806) 745-3973; Fax: (806) 745-6207
email: c.bean@nwtsbdc.org
Website: *www.nwtsbdc.org*

South-West Texas Border SBDC Network

Al Salgado, Regional Director
501 W. Durango Boulevard
San Antonio, TX 78207
(210) 458-2450; Fax: (210) 458-2425
email: albert.sagado@usta.edu
Website: *http://txsbdc.org*

Utah District Office SBA

125 S. State Street, Room 2227
Salt Lake City, UT 84138
(801) 524-3209

Utah Lead Center SBDC—Administration

Greg Panichello, State Director
Salt Lake Community College
9750 S. 300 West—LHM
Salt Lake City, UT 84070
(801) 957-3481; Fax: (801) 957-2007
email: greg.panicello@slcc.edu
Website: *http://utahsbdc.org*

Vermont District Office SBA

87 State Street, Room 205
Montpelier, VT 05601
(802) 828-4422

Vermont SBDC

Lenae Quillen-Blume, State Director
Vermont Technical College
1 Main Street
PO Box 188
Randolph Center, VT 05061
(802) 728-9101; Fax: (802) 728-3026
email: lquillen@vtsbdc.org
Website: *http://vtsbdc.org*

Vermont Specialty Foods Association

135 N. Main Street
Rutland, VT 05701-3238
(802) 747-0365; Fax: (802) 773-2242

Virgin Islands SBDC

Charlotte Amalie
Leonor Dottin, State Director
8000 Nisky Center, Suite 720
St. Thomas, VI 00802
(340) 776-3206; Fax: (340) 775-3756
email: ldottin@uvi.edu
Website: *http://sbdcvi.org*

Virginia District Office SBA

The Federal Building
400 N. Eighth Street, Suite 1150
Richmond, VA 23219-4829
(804) 771-2400; Fax: (804) 771-2764
email: richmond.va@sba.gov

Virginia SBDC

Jody Keenan, State Director
Mason Enterprise Center
George Mason University
4031 University Drive, Suite 200
Fairfax, VA 22030
(703) 277-7727; Fax: (703) 352-8518

email: jkeenan@gmu.edu
Website: *http://virginiasbdc.com*

Washington District Office SBA

2401 Fourth Avenue, Suite 450
Seattle, WA 98121
(206) 553-7310

Washington SBDC

Brett Rogers, State Director
Washington State University
534 E. Spokane Falls Boulevard
PO Box 1495
Spokane, WA 99210
(509) 358-7765; Fax: (509) 358-7764
email: barogers@wsu.edu
Website: *http://wsbdc.org*

Washington Specialty Food Association

PO Box 8226
Spokane, WA 99203

West Virginia District Office SBA

320 W. Pike Street, Suite 330
Clarksburg, WV 26301
(304) 623-5631; Fax: (304) 623-0023
email: wvinfo@sba.gov

West Virginia SBDC

M. E. Yancosek Gamble, State Director
1900 Kanawha Boulevard, Building 6,
    Room 652
Charleston, WV 25305
(304) 558-2960, x11; Fax: (304) 558-0127
email: mgamble@wvsbdc.org
Website: *http://sbdcwv.org*

Wisconsin District Office SBA

740 Regent Street, Suite 100

Madison, WI 53715
(608) 441-5263; Fax (608) 441-5541

310 W. Wisconsin Avenue, Room 400
Milwaukee, WI 53203
(414) 297-3941; Fax: (414) 297-1377

Wisconsin SBDC

Gayle Kugler, State Director
University of Wisconsin
432 N. Lake Street, Room 423
Madison, WI 53706
(608) 263-7794; Fax: (608) 263-7830
email: gayle.kugler@uwex.edu
Website: *www.wisconsinsbdc.org*

Wisconsin Cheese & Specialty Food Merchants Association

111 South Hamilton
Madison, WI 53703
(608) 255-0373

Wyoming District Office SBA

Federal Building, Room 4001
100 E. B Street
PO Box 44001
Casper, WY 82602-5013
800-776-9144, x1, (307) 261-6500, x1

Wyoming SBDC

Diane Wolverton, State Director
University of Wyoming
1000 E. University Avenue, Department 3922
Laramie, WY 82071
(307) 766-3405; Fax: (307) 766-3406
email: ddw@uwyo.edu
Website: *http://wyomingentrepreneur.biz*

Appendix K
State Resources, Associations, and Agencies

This list is not all-inclusive nor meant to serve as an endorsement. Where only state departments of agriculture are listed, be prepared to receive limited assistance. Most such departments are devoted to commodity marketing, not retail-packaged, high-value food products. In those instances where no state association is listed, you may wish to consult Appendix M: Export Assistance, for a listing of state departments of agriculture. Please see the website *www .specialtyfoodresource.com* for updates.

Every state has a department of commerce and business development, usually located at the state capital. Its sole purpose is to promote and develop business within the state and offer new businesses information on state regulations and any legal requirements that apply.

Each state also has a department of agriculture, which may be of assistance. See appendix M—Export Assistance.

Arizona

Flavors of Arizona
(480) 473-0285
email: kenbarry@desertrosefoods.biz or
   membership@flavorsofarizona.org
Website: *http://flavorsofarizona.org*

This organization is composed of eight Arizona food manufacturers. The Sonoran desert is an incubator for creative food products; ranging from Sonoran-grown pecans and prickly pear cactus products to succulent salsas and southwest condiments. Contact Ken Barry.

Connecticut

Connecticut Department of Agriculture
Bureau of Agricultural Development and
    Resource Preservation
765 Asylum Avenue
Hartford, CT 06106
(860) 713-256938; Fax: (860) 677-8418
email: ctfood@ctfood.org
website: *www.ct.gov/doag/*

Connecticut Food Association
195 Farmington Avenue, Suite 200
Farmington, CT 06032
(860) 677-8097; Fax: (860) 677-8418
email: info@ctfood.org
Website: *www.ctfood.org*

This association has published a directory of
resources essential to food producers. The book
includes listings of glass manufacturers, box
manufacturers, basket companies, packaging
and bag businesses, printers, label designers,
copackers, truckers, food technologists, public
relations agencies, etc.

Idaho

Marketing Idaho Food and Agriculture
Idaho State Department of Agriculture
PO Box 790
Boise, ID 83701-0790
(208) 332-8530; Fax: (208) 334-2879
Website: *http://agri.state.id.us*

Ask for a copy of the publication *Starting a
Specialty Food Business.*

Louisiana

**Louisiana Department of Agriculture
and Forestry**
PO Box 3334
Baton Rouge, LA 70821-3334
(225) 922-1277; Fax: (225) 922-1289
email: info@ldaf.state.la.us;
Website: *www.ldaf.state.la.us*

Massachusetts

**Massachusetts Department of Agricultural
Resources**
251 Causeway Street, Suite 500
Boston, MA 02114
(617) 626-1700; Fax: (617) 626-1850
Website: *www.mass.gov/agr/*

The department provides an array of marketing
support services to both value-added specialty
food and agricultural producers. Options
are provided for participation in Massachusetts pavilions at trade shows, special events,
seminars, and referrals. Ask for a copy of *The
Massachusetts Food Processors Resource Manual.*

**Massachusetts Specialty Foods Association
(MSFA)**
PO Box 34
Groton, MA 01450
800-813-5862, (508) 457-5346
Website: *http://msfa.net*

The association supports and strengthens specialty producers to enhance the Massachusetts
economy and promotes the interest of food
producers and processors in the state. It serves
as an umbrella organization to assist its members in obtaining financial, scientific, management, marketing, and technical assistance.

The association has access to consultation in many fields, including research and development, business and financial management, marketing, and technical and scientific areas.

Dartmouth (MA) Grange Shared-Use Kitchen

1133 Fisher Road
Dartmouth, MA 02747
(508) 636-1900
email: becky@dartmouthgrange.org
Website: *http://dartmouthgrange.org*

A state-certified, commercial, state-of-the-art kitchen with all the amenities that a specialty food producer, grower, or caterer might need, including a 40-gallon tilting skillet, a 40-gallon steam-jacketed kettle, 2 convection ovens, a 6-burner range with two conventional ovens, a 20 and 40-quart stand mixer with grinding attachment, an automated filling machine, a 4-quart commercial food processor, an industrial stick blender, digital scales, and assorted small wares.

Minnesota

Minnesota Department of Agriculture

625 Robert Street N.
St. Paul, MN 55155-2538
800-967-2474, (651) 201-6000
email: info@state.mn.us
Website: *www.mda.state.mn.us*

Nebraska

The Food Processing Center, University of Nebraska—Lincoln

Jill D. Gifford

Food Entrepreneur Assistance Program
  Manager
143 Filley Hall
Lincoln, NE 68583-0928
(402) 472-2819; Fax (402) 472-1693
email: jgifford1@unl.edu
Website: *http://fpc.unl.edu*

New Mexico

New Mexico Department of Agriculture

MSC 3189, corner of Gregg and Espina,
  Box 30005
Las Cruces, NM 88003-88005
(505) 646-3007; Fax: (505) 646-8120
email: nmagsec@nmda.nmsu.edu
Website: *http://nmdaweb.nmsu.edu*

A producer-consumer service and regulatory department under the New Mexico State University (NMSU) Board of Regents. Its Marketing and Development Division assists in the development of new markets and expansion of existing markets, both domestic and international, for farm products and livestock produced or processed in the state. It also assists commodity commissions in organizing and implementing commodity promotions.

New York

New York State Agricultural Experiment Station

Cornell University College of Agriculture
  and Life Sciences
630 W. North Street
Geneva, NY 14456
(315) 787-2273
email: necfe@nyaes.cornell.edu
Website: *www.nysaes.cornell.edu*

North Carolina

North Carolina Department of Agriculture & Consumer Services
2 W. Edenton Street
Raleigh, NC 27601
(919) 733-7125
Website: *www.ncagr.com*

Northwest Specialty Foods Association and Agri-Business Council of Oregon
1200 NW Naito Parkway, #290
Portland, OR 97209
(503) 241-1487; Fax: (503) 274-4019
email: info@nwspecialtyfoods.org
Website: *www.oregongourmetfoods.org;*
www.aglink.org

Ohio

Ohio Department of Agriculture
8995 E. Main Street
Reynoldsburg, OH 43068
800-467-7683; Fax: (614) 728-6201
email: agri@agri.ohio.gov
Website: *www.ohioagriculture.gov*

South Carolina

South Carolina Specialty Food Association
1301 Gervais Street, Suite 710
Columbia, SC 29201-3326
866-340-7105, (801) 771-0131;
Fax: (803) 771-7660
email: mridge@sc.gov
Website: *www.scsfa.org*

Tennessee

Appalachian Spring Cooperative
PO Box 555
Sneedville, TN 37869
(423) 733-2095
Website: *www.apspringcoop.com*

Texas

Texas Department of Agriculture
PO Box 12847
Austin, TX 78711
800-835-5832, (512) 463-7476;
Fax: 888-835-5832
email: sdunn@agr.state.tx.us
Website: *http://agr.state.tx.us*

This agency has access to a large database called the Texas Agriculture Marketing Exchange (TAME).

Vermont

Vermont Agency of Agriculture
116 State Street, Drawer 20
Montpelier, VT 05620-2901
(802) 828-2416; Fax: (802) 828-2361
email: agr-webmaster@state.vt.us
Website: *www.vermontagriculture.com*

Ask for a copy of the very thorough *Vermont Specialty Food Resource Directory.*

Vermont Cheese Council
2088 E. Main Street
Richmond, VT 05477
866-261-8595
email: info@vtcheese.com
Website: *http://vtcheese.com*

Vermont Specialty Food Association
135 N. Main Street, Suite 5
Rutland, VT 05701-3238
(802) 747-0365; Fax: (802) 773-2242
email: info@vermontspecialtyfoods.org
Website: *http://vermontspecialtyfoods.org*

Virginia

Virginia Department of Agriculture and Consumer Services
102 Governor Street
Richmond, VA 23219
(804) 786-2373; Fax: (804) 371-6097
email: webmaster.vdacs@vdacs.virginia.gov
Website: *http://vdacs.virginia.gov*

Washington

Washington Specialty Foods Association
1200 NW Naito Parkway, #290
Portland, WA 97209
(503) 241-1487; Fax: (508) 274-4019
Website: *www.nwspecialtyfoods.org*

Wisconsin

Wisconsin Cheese and Specialty Food Merchants Association
111 S. Hamilton
Madison, WI 53703
(608) 255-0373; Fax: (608) 255-6600
email: info@wispecialcheese.org

Wisconsin Specialty Cheese Institute
PO Box 15
Delevan, WI 53115
(262) 740-2180; Fax: (262) 740-2175
Website: *http://wisspecialcheese.org*

Wisconsin Department of Agriculture, Trade and Consumer Protection
Division of Marketing
PO Box 8911
Madison, WI 53708-8911
(608) 224-5115; Fax: (608) 224-5111
email: info@savorwisconsin.com
Website: *http://datcp.state.wi.us*

Wisconsin Cheese Makers Association
8030 Excelsior Drive, Suite 305
Madison, WI 53717-1950
(608) 828-4550; Fax: (608) 828-4551
email: office@wscheesemakersassn.org
Website: *www.wischeesemakersassn.org*

Appendix L
Specialty Food Trends Resource List

Please see our website *www.specialtyfoodresource.com* for updates.

Analyzing and predicting trends in any market is a multilayered task. Trends affecting the food industry as a whole can usually be seen in each specific market, as in the case of convenience and better-for-you foods in the specialty trade. Trends also have a tendency to feed and play off of one another, with each lasting a varied amount of time before either falling off the consumer's radar or becoming a staple.

Trends in the marketplace influence every consumer's behavior. Trends affect the food industry on a zillion levels, from specific food choices to changing meal patterns. Not all trends are the same. Some are pervasive, influencing the whole social landscape; others are really just fads.

Trends have a life cycle, and the particular stage of a trend is critical in determining its connection to a particular product or service.

Trends can exist on many levels. For instance, we can talk about a growing penchant for "spicy" foods or dining at home. If both are trends, might one explain the other? Does an understanding of a general sociological trend help explain a specific food trend?

Successful businesses are market driven when they design their products and services to fulfill consumer needs. They can define the marketplace through demographics (identifiable, measurable characteristics such as age, economic status, ethnic background, etc.) and psychographics (lifestyle or attitude characteristics).

Knowledge of today's trends can help you develop products and promotions for the future. The world is changing at an accelerated pace. Not much looks as it did 50 years ago. Like every other industry, the food industry has had to adapt to consumer demands driven by changing lifestyles.

How to Find Out about Underlying Forces and Changing Trends

Good sources of trend information appear in the media. This includes the Internet, which is being used with increasing frequency as a communication means. Several resources look at what's going on in the marketplace. Targeted to varying audiences, they each have their own focus and format. What they have to say is extremely valuable for developing staying power in the food world. Make your job easier by learning what the experts are saying. In addition to the professional trade journals listed in appendix A, the following may be useful in developing a deeper understanding of consumer trends and their impact on specialty food marketing.

Publications

ACNielsen
770 Broadway
New York, NY 10003
(646) 654-5000; Fax: (646) 654-5002
Website: *http://acnielsen.com*

This global market research company provides sales data and analysis, mainly of supermarket product activity.

Advertising Age/American Demographics Magazine
American Demographics
711 Third Avenue
New York, NY 10017-4036

(212) 210-0100; Fax: (212) 210-0200
Website: *adage.com/americandemographics/*

Advertising Age/American Demographics is a tool for marketing strategists. Readers gain vital insight into the connections between age, education, geography, income, wealth, lifestyles, and spending. They find clues as to what consumers want now and what they're likely to want tomorrow. Every issue includes cutting-edge marketing techniques, helpful diagrams, and usually exclusive data that help readers to maximize opportunities in key market segments. Annual subscriptions for U.S. subscribers are $99 annually; Canadian and Mexican subscriptions are $229 annually.

The Food Channel Newsletter

Strategic Foods Resources Division of
   Noble Associates
Springfield, MO and Chicago, IL
(417) 875-5302; Fax: (417) 875-5051
email: info@foodchannel.com
Website: *http://foodchannel.com*

Formerly the *Food Channel HotBytes* newsletter, the *Food Channel TrendWire* newsletter has been the food industry's source for food trends since November 1988. It's published 52 times a year and distributed electronically to subscribers. Individual e-letter subscriptions are $195 per year. Corporate subscriptions are $895. For subscription inquiries, contact Debbie Merritt.

Food Network

Website: *www.foodnetwork.com*

The Food Network is a unique lifestyle network and website that strives to be about way more than cooking. The network is committed to exploring new and different ways to approach food—through pop culture, competition, adventure, and travel—while also expanding its repertoire of technique-based information. The *Food Network* email newsletter is distributed to more than 90 million U.S. households and averages more than 7 million website users monthly. It is part of Scripps Network with headquarters in New York City and offices in Atlanta, Los Angeles, Chicago, Detroit, and Knoxville. Food Network can be seen internationally in Canada, Australia, Korea, Thailand, Singapore, the Philippines, Monaco, Andorra, Africa, France, and the French-speaking territories in the Caribbean and Polynesia. To receive the *Food Network* email newsletter, visit the website and subscribe.

Foodwatch

Eleanor Hanson and Linda Smithson,
   coeditors/publishers
6800 Galway Drive
Edina, MN 55439
(615) 819-1052
email: info@foodwatchtrends.com
Website: *http://foodwatchtrends.com*

Foodwatch specializes in trend identification and analysis based on two proprietary databases of food media and restaurant menu information. The Media Database consists of editorial and recipe information from 21 consumer magazines and 12 major metropolitan newspapers. The Menu Database is comprised of item information from more than 450 innovative chain and independent restaurant menus. Both databases are designed and indexed to focus on food trend output. Client projects include category reviews, new product ideation, trend presentations to management, Web recipe research and development, and new product concept development. Clients include major food manufacturers, commodity associations, and advertising and public relations firms. Published monthly in electronic form only. Subscriptions are $60 per year.

Hot Product News

2901 Juan Tabo NE, #114
Albuequerque, NM 87112
877-296-1898
Website: *www.hotproductnews.com*

Comment: This resource covers new products of all kinds; it may or may not be of value to the specialty foods marketer.

Mintel's Global New Products Database (GNPD)
email: helpdesk@mintel.com
Website: *www.gnpd.com*

Providing the world's premier editorial coverage of new product development, Mintel's GNPD is a comprehensive database that monitors worldwide product innovation in consumer packaged goods. Mintel's GNPD offers unrivaled coverage of new product activity for monitoring competitors and generating new product ideas. Does not publish any rates.

Appendix M
Export Assistance

••

Export assistance is available from private, federal, and state sources. Below are representatives from all three.

Private

One:Deux International LLC
Mr. Douglas Resh, President
International Business Consulting
Export Management Company
428 E. Thunderbird Road, Suite 745
Phoenix, AZ 85022
(484) 955-3674
email: doug@one-deux-international.com
Website: *www.one-deux-international.com*

One:Deux International is the source for all of your international operations. Welcome to a world of opportunities!

Federal

U.S. Department of Commerce (USDOC)
Industry and Trade Administration (ITA)
14th and Constitution Avenue NW
Washington, DC 20230
(202) 377-2000

Website: *http://trade.gov*
Useful for economic and general marketing data. No food-related assistance.

Small Business Administration (SBA)
1441 L Street NW
Washington, DC 20416
800-368-5855 or (202) 653-7561

As with U.S. Department of Commerce, offers generic, not food-specific, small business export assistance.

U.S. Department of Agriculture
Foreign Agricultural Service (FAS)
1400 Independence Avenue SW
Washington, DC 20250
Website: *www.fas.usda.gov*

The Foreign Agricultural Service (FAS) maintains a global network of agricultural counselors, attachés, and officers covering more than 100 countries to help build markets overseas and gather and assess information on world agricultural production and trade. Its traditional focus has been on agricultural commodities, but it has recently developed a sensitivity to the market potential and larger profits associated with high-value, retail-packaged food products.

State

Export assistance: The following organizations work with the U.S. Department of Agriculture's Foreign Agriculture Service and are involved actively in the overseas promotion of value-added food products. Please see our website *specialtyfoodresource.com* for updates.

National Association of State Departments of Agriculture (NASDA)
1156 15th Street NW, Suite 1020
Washington, DC 20005
(202) 296-9680; Fax: (202) 296-9686
email: nasda@nasda.org
Website: *www.nasda.org*

NASDA focuses exclusively on promoting U.S.-made food products in overseas markets. It sponsors an annual show in Chicago in concert with the Global Food and Style Expo at Chicago's McCormick Place in conjunction with the Food Marketing Institute's Supermarket Industry Exposition, which attracts supermarket industry executives from around the world.

Food Export USA—Northeast
150 S. Independence Mall W., Suite 1036
Philadelphia, PA 19106
(215) 829-9111
Website: *http://foodexportusa.org*

Food Export USA—Northeast is a nonprofit organization that promotes the export of food and agricultural products from the northeast region of the United States. The organization has been helping exporters of northeast food and agricultural products sell their goods overseas since 1973, when it was first created as a cooperative effort between ten northeastern state agricultural promotion agencies and the U.S. Department of Agriculture's Foreign Agricultural Service (FAS). Food Export USA, in conjunction with its member states, provides a wide range of services to facilitate trade between local food companies and importers around the world. These services include export promotion, customized export assistance, and a cost-share funding program. Food Export USA member states include Connecticut, Delaware, Maine, Massachusetts, New Hampshire, New Jersey, New York, Pennsylvania, Rhode Island, and Vermont.

Connecticut Department of Agriculture
765 Asylum Avenue
Hartford, CT 06106
(860) 566-4667; Fax: (860) 566-6576
Website: *www.ct.gov/doag/*

Delaware Department of Agriculture
2320 S. DuPont Highway
Dover, DE 19901
(302) 698-4500; Fax: (302) 697-6287
Website: *http://dda.delaware.gov*

Massachusetts Department of Agricultural Resources
251 Causeway Street, Room 500
Boston, MA 02114
(617) 626-1700; Fax: (617) 626-1850
Website: *www.mass.gov/agr/*

Maine Department of Agriculture, Food and Rural Resources
28 State House Station
90 Blossom Lane
Augusta, ME 04333
(207) 287-3419 Fax: (207) 287-7548
Website: *http://maine.gov/agriculture/*

New Hampshire Department of Agriculture, Markets & Food
25 Capitol Street, 2nd floor
Concord, NH 03301
(603) 271-3551; Fax: (603) 271-1109
Website: *http://agriculture.nh.gov*

New Jersey Department of Agriculture
PO Box 330
Trenton, NJ 08625
(609) 984-2279; Fax: (609) 984-5367
Website: *www.state.nj.us/agriculture/*

New York State Department of Agriculture and Markets
108 Airline Drive
Albany, NY 12235
(518) 457-4188; Fax: (518) 457-3087
Website: *www.agmkt.state.ny.us*

Pennsylvania Department of Agriculture
2301 N. Cameron Street
Harrisburg, PA 17110-9408
(717) 772-2853; Fax: (717) 705-8422
email: aginfo@state.pa.us
Website: *www.agriculture.state.pa.us*

Rhode Island Department of Environmental Management
Division of Agriculture
235 Promenade Street, Room 370
Providence, RI 02908-5767

(401) 222-2781, x4500; Fax: (401) 222-6047
Website: *www.dem.ri.gov/programs/bnatres/ agricult/*

Vermont Agency of Agriculture
120 State Street
Montpelier, VT 05620-2901
(802) 828-2430; Fax: (802) 828-2361
Website: *www.vermontagriculture.com*

Western United States Agricultural Trade Association (WUSATA)
4601 NE 77th Avenue, Suite 120
Vancouver, WA 98662
(360) 693-3373; Fax: (360) 693-3464
Website: *www.wusata.org*

Alaska Department of Natural Resources
PO Box 949
Palmer, AK 99645-0949
(907) 745-7200; Fax: (907) 745-7112
Website: *www.dnr.state.ak.us*

Arizona Department of Agriculture
1688 W. Adams Street
Phoenix, AZ 85007
(602) 542-0998; Fax: (602) 542-5420
Website: *www.azda.gov*

California Department of Food & Agriculture
1220 N Street, 4th Floor
Sacramento, CA 95814
(916) 654-0433; Fax: (916) 654-0403
email: 74404.273@compuserve.com
Website: *www.cdfa.ca.gov*

Colorado Department of Agriculture
700 Kipling Street, #4000
Lakewood, CO 80215-8000

(303) 239-4100; Fax: (303) 239-4125
Website: *www.colorado.gov/ag/*

Hawaii Department of Agriculture
1428 S. King Street
Honolulu, HI 96814
(808) 973-9560; Fax: (808) 973-9613
Website: *http://hawaii.gov/hdoa/*

Idaho State Department of Agriculture
PO Box 790
Boise, ID 83701
(208) 332-2411; Fax: (208) 32-8500
Website: *www.agri.state.id.us*

Montana Department of Agriculture
303 N. Roberts Street
POB 200201
Helena, MT 59620-0201
(406) 444-3114; Fax: (406) 444-5409
email: agr@mt.gov
Website: *http://agr.mt.gov*

New Mexico Department of Agriculture
Box 30005, Dept. 3189
Las Cruces, NM 88003-0005
(505) 646-3007; Fax: (505) 646-8120
Website: *http://nmdaweb.nmsu.edu*

Oregon Department of Agriculture
635 Capitol Street NE
Salem, OR 97310
(503) 986-4552; Fax: (503) 986-4750
Website: *www.oregon.gov/ODA/*

Utah Department of Agriculture and Food
PO Box 146500
350 N. Redwood Road
Salt Lake City, UT 84116

(801) 538-7101; Fax: (801) 538-7126
Website: *http://ag.utah.gov*

Washington Department of Agriculture
PO Box 42560
1111 Washington Street SE
Olympia, WA 98504-2560
(360) 902-1801; Fax: (360) 902-2089
Website: *http://agr.wa.gov*

Wyoming Department of Agriculture
2219 Carey Avenue
Cheyenne, WY 82002-0100
(307) 777-6569; Fax: (307) 777-6593
Website: *http://wyagric.state.wy.us*

Food Export Association of the Midwest USA (formerly MIATCO)
309 W. Washington Street, Suite 600
Chicago, IL 60606
(312) 334-9200; Fax: (312) 334-9230
Website: *http://miatco.org*

Illinois Department of Agriculture
PO Box 19281
Springfield, IL 62794-9281
(217) 782-6675; Fax: (217) 524-5960
Website: *www.agr.state.il.us*

Indiana State Department of Agriculture
150 W. Market, Suite 414
Indianapolis, IN 46204
(317) 232-8770; Fax: (317) 232-1362
Website: *www.in.gov/isda/*

Iowa Department of Agriculture and Land Stewardship
Wallace Building
502 E. 9th Street
Des Moines, IA 50319

(515) 281-5322; Fax: (515) 281-7046
Website: *www.iowaagriculture.gov*

Kansas Department of Agriculture
109 SW 91st Avenue, 4th Floor
Topeka, KS 66612-1280
(785) 296-3556; Fax: (783) 296-8389
Website: *www.ksda.gov*

Michigan Department of Agriculture
PO Box 30017
525 W. Allegan
Lansing, MI 48909
(517) 373-1052; Fax: (517) 335-1423
Website: *www.michigan.gov/mda/*

Minnesota Trade Office: Export Minnesota
1st National Bank Building, 5th Floor
332 Minnesota Street
St. Paul, MN 55101-1351
(651) 297-3291; Fax: (612) 297-5522
Website: *www.exportminnesota.com*

Missouri Department of Agriculture
PO Box 630
Jefferson City, MO 65102
(314) 751-3359; Fax: (314) 751-1784
Website: *www.mda.mo.gov*

Nebraska Department of Agriculture
PO Box 94947
301 Centennial Mall, 4th Floor
Lincoln, NE 68509
(402) 471-4876; Fax: (402) 471-2759
Website: *www.agr.state.ne.us*

North Dakota Department of Agriculture
600 E. Boulevard Avenue, Dept. 602
Bismark, ND 58505-0020

(701) 328-2231; Fax: (701) 328-4567
Website: *www.agdepartment.com*

Ohio Department of Agriculture
International Trade Program
8995 E. Main Street
Columbus, OH 43068
(614) 466-2732; Fax: (614) 466-6124
Website: *www.ohioagriculture.gov*

South Dakota Department of Agriculture
523 E. Capitol Avenue
Pierre, SD 57501-3182
(605) 773-5425; Fax: (605) 773-5926
email: agmail@state.sd.us
Website: *www.state.sd.us/doa/*

**Wisconsin Department of Agriculture,
Trade and Consumer Protection**
2811 Agriculture Drive
Madison, WI 53708
(608) 224-5012; Fax: (608) 224-5045
Website: *http://datcp.state.wi.us*

**Southern United States Trade
Association (SUSTA)**
World Trade Center
2 Canal Street, Suite 1540
New Orleans, LA 70130-1408
(504) 568-5986
Website: *http://susta.org*

Arkansas
1 Natural Resources Drive
Little Rock, AR 72205
(501) 683-4851
Website: *http://aad.arkansas.gov*

Florida Department of Agriculture &
Consumer Services
The Capitol, PL10
Tallahassee, FL 32339-0800
(850) 488-3022; Fax: (850) 488-7583
Website: *www.doacs.state.fl.us*

Georgia Department of Agriculture
204 Agriculture Bldg.
19 Martin Luther King Drive
Atlanta, GA 30334
(404) 656-3600; Fax: (404) 651-8206
Website: *http://agr.georgia.gov*

Kentucky Department of Agriculture
Capital Annex Room 188
500 Mero Street, 7th Floor
Frankfort, KY 40601
(502) 564-5126; Fax: (502) 564-5016
Website: *www.kyagr.com*

Louisiana Department of Agriculture
& Forestry
PO Box 631
5825 Florida Boulevard
Baton Rouge, LA 70821-0631
(225) 922-1234; Fax: (225) 922-1253
Website: *www.ldaf.state.la.us*

Maryland Department of Agriculture
50 Harry S. Truman Parkway
Annapolis, MD 21401
(410) 841-5880; Fax: (410) 841-5914
Website: *www.mda.state.md.us*

Mississippi Department of Agriculture and
Commerce
121 N. Jefferson Street
Jackson, MS 39201

(601) 359-1100; Fax: (601) 354-7710
Website: *www.mdac.state.ms.us*

North Carolina Department of Agriculture
& Consumer Services
PO Box 27647
1 Edenton Street
Raleigh, NC 27611
(919) 733-7125; Fax: (919) 733-1141
Website: *www.ncagr.com*

Oklahoma Department of Agriculture
2800 N. Lincoln Boulevard
Oklahoma City, OK 73105-8804
800-580-6543, (405) 521-3864;
Fax: (405) 522-0909
Website: *www.oda.state.ok.us*

South Carolina Department of Agriculture
Wade Hampton State Office Building
    Capitol Complex
PO Box 11280
Columbia, SC 29211
(803) 734-2210; Fax: (803) 734-2192
Website: *http://agriculture.sc.gov*

Tennessee Department of Agriculture
PO Box 40627
Nashville, TN 37204
(615) 837-5100; Fax: (615) 837-5333
Website: *www.tennessee.gov/agriculture/*

Virginia Department of Agriculture
1100 Bank Street, Suite 219
Richmond, VA 23219
(804) 786-3501, Fax: (804) 371-2945
Website: *www.vdacs.virginia.gov*

Appendix N
Miscellaneous Resources

The following list is not all-inclusive, nor is it meant to serve as an endorsement. Please see *www.specialtyfoodresource.com* for updates.

Business Development

FastTrac National Headquarters
4747 Troost
Kansas City, MO 64110
800-689-1740; Fax: (816) 235-6216;
    For orders/customer service:
    877-450-9800
email: info@fasttrac.org
Website: *www.fasttrac.org*

FastTrac is a comprehensive entrepreneurship-educational program that provides entrepreneurs with business insights, leadership skills, and professional networking connections so they are prepared to create a new business or expand an existing enterprise. The nine FastTrac programs include practical, hands-on business development programs and workshops for existing and aspiring entrepreneurs, as well as entrepreneurship curricula for college students. FastTrac is designed to help entrepreneurs hone the skills needed to create, manage, and/or grow successful businesses.

Food Marketing International
10001 N. 77th Place
Scottsdale, AZ 85258
(480) 778-0640
email: steve@specialtyfoodresource.com
Website: *www.specialtyfoodresource.com*

Primary focus: Establishing strategic frameworks for specialty food entrepreneurs; business development consulting. Contact Steve Hall.

Green Harbor Associates
4 Calypso Lane
Marshfield, MA 02050
(781) 837-1664; Fax: (781) 837-8304
email: green.harbor@comcast.net

Primary focus: The firm offers a marketing-consulting service to manufacturers of specialty foods, from assisting in label design to picking a distribution channel to implementing an extensive marketing strategy. In addition, the firm handles all aspects of trade advertising and public relations. Interested parties are invited to contact the firm's principal, Ronald M. Cardoos.

Gourmet Business Solutions

129 N. Garden Avenue
Clearwater, FL 33755
800-975-7068, x703
email: info@gourmetbusinesssolutions.com
Website: *http://gourmetbusinesssolutions.com*

Gourmet Business Solutions is a management consulting firm specializing in brand and business development, marketing, and Internet/technology solutions for companies in the gourmet food and specialty food industry. We offer the highest level of solutions and sales programs specifically for companies manufacturing and selling gourmet and specialty food. Contact Ryan Montague.

Specialty Food Resource LLC

10001 N. 77th Place
Scottsdale, AZ 85258
(480) 778-0640
email: steve@specialtyfoodresource.com
Website: *www.specialtyfoodresource.com*

Primary focus: Produces and manages website and discussion forum/blog devoted to connecting specialty food processors, distributors, brokers, suppliers, and retailers. Contact Steve Hall.

LegalZoom.com

7083 Hollywood Boulevard, Suite 180
Los Angeles, CA 90028
800-773-0888, (323) 962-8600;
Fax: (323) 982-8800
Website: *www.legalzoom.com*

Online legal document service for incorporations, LLCs, trademark, patents, and copyrights.

Northeast Center for Food Entrepreneurship (NECFE) at Cornell University

New York State Food Venture Center
Cornell University NYS Agricultural
   Experiment Station
630 W. North Street
Geneva, NY 14456
(315) 787-2274
email: necfe@nysaes.cornell.edu
website: *www.nysaes.cornell.edu/necfe/*

The Resource Center provides access to information about

- Available facilities;
- Equipment for the food processing business;
- Business and marketing basics;
- Terms and definitions common in the food processing industry;
- Regulatory information;
- Links to trade groups and agencies associated with the food production industry;
- NECFE business and marketing services; and
- NECFE product-processing development services;

NXLeveL Training Network

800-873-9378; Fax: 800-860-0522
email: info@nxlevel.org
Website: *http://nxlevel.org*

The NxLeveL Entrepreneurial Training Programs are practical, hands-on business development courses designed to help entrepreneurs advance their skills in starting, growing, and managing their business. NxLeveL classes are offered throughout the United States through the NxLeveL Training Network®. The NxLeveL Training Network is a group of organizations engaged in entrepreneurial training, the purpose of which is to develop the best training curricula possible and to share best practices among network partners, including effective operational, funding, and management strategies.

Pennsylvania State University Food Entrepreneur Resources

email: ifl5@psu.edu
Website: *http://foodsafety.cas.psu.edu/processor/
resources.htm*

This resource offers an extensive listing of links that can answer your questions about starting a food processing business.

Business Lists

Info USA Inc.

5711 S. 86th Circle
Omaha, NE 68127
800-321-0869, (402) 331-7169
email: help@infousa.com
Website: *http://infousa.com*

Sells business listings compiled from nationwide Yellow Pages.

Gourmet News

PO Box 1056
Yarmouth, ME 04096
(207) 846-0800
Website: *http://gourmetnews.com*

Rents its extensive listing of specialty food decision makers.

Catalog Sales

5th Food Group

Internet and Catalog Marketing
4412 Copper Mountain Lane
Richardson, TX 75082
(972) 907-1464; Fax: (972) 907-1466
email: tony@5thgroupmarketing.com
Website: *www.5thfoodgroup.com*

5th Food Group (formerly Catalog Solutions) serves as an outsourced mail order and online marketing department for specialty food companies. "The 7 Habits of the Highly Ineffective Cataloger" available online. Subscribe to its "Food by Mail Industry Updates" via email.

Liability Insurance

DeWitt Stern Insurnace Services of California LLC

Ms. Rochelle Brotter
(818) 933-2737

Mikkelsen, Kelly & Kipp Insurance Inc.

Scott Mikkelsen
553 Cal Sag Road
Alslip, IL 60803
(708) 389-6330

This insurance agency can sell coverage in Illinois, Indiana, Minnesota, Wisconsin,

Michigan, California, Idaho, Arizona, Oklahoma, Connecticut, and Washington.

Nutritional Analysis and Label Content

Food Consulting Company

Karen Duester
13724 Recuerdo Drive
Del Mar, CA 92014
800-793-2844, 858-793-4658;
Fax: 800-522-3545
email: info@foodlabels.com
Website: *www.foodlabels.com*

Specializes in nutritional analysis, food nutrition facts labels, food labeling content, and information on FDA regulations for nutrition labels. Promises 100 percent FDA compliance. Publishes a monthly newsletter, *Food Label News,* that offers timely and in-depth coverage of any and all labeling questions and concerns. Ms. Duester is a monthly contributor to *FoodEntrepreneur* ezine.

Lawrence-Allen Group NutriLABEL

2031 Fairmont Drive
San Mateo, CA 94402-3925
800-345-2909, (650) 345-2909;
Fax: (650) 345-9723
email: support@nutrilabel.com
Website: *http://nutrilabel.com*

Primary focus: Provides fast, low-cost services, including food product nutritional analysis, camera-ready nutrition facts panel art, FDA labeling compliance assistance, ingredient statement preparation, trademark research, and new specialty food product development and consulting services. This is a confidential

service with more than 50 years' experience. Contact Larry Imes.

On the Menu LLC

Ms. Julie Bush
1805 S. Bellaire Street, Suite 305
Denver, CO 80222
(655) 757-1333, (303) 757-1739
email: julie@on-the-menu.net
Website: *www.otmenu.com*

On the Menu is committed to delivering quality products and services with integrity.

Strasburger & Siegel Inc.

7249 National Drive
Hanover, MD 21076-1324
800-875-6532, (410) 712-7373;
Fax: 410-712-7378
email: info@sas-labs.com
Website: *http://sas-labs.com*

Strasburger and Siegel is just one of many laboratories that offer competitively priced analytical services, including microbiological and microanalytical services, consulting services (project design, product stability, shelf life evaluation, thermal process engineering, etc.), and customized product development services.

Produce Marketing

Sell What You Sow! The Grower's Guide to Successful Produce Marketing

New World Publishing
11543 Quartz Drive, #1
Auburn, CA 95602
(530) 823-3886

Sell What You Sow! by Eric Gibson is a guide to profitable produce marketing that covers marketing plans, research, crop selection, and selling through farmers' markets, restaurants, roadside markets, pick-your-own operations, and retail outlets. It is a comprehensive how-to book of high-value produce marketing.

Quality Issues

The Deming Route to Quality and Productivity
by William W. Scherkenbach

CEEPress Books, George Washington University, Washington, DC, 1992

The Memory Jogger II
by Michael Brassard and Diane Ritter
GOAL/QPC, Salem, NH, 1994
800-643-4316

This is a pocket guide of tools for continuous improvement and effective planning.

Uniform Product Code

GS1 United States
Princeton Pike Center
209 Lenox Drive, Suite 202
Lawrenceville, NJ 08648
(609) 620-0200; Fax: (609) 620-1200
email: info@gs1us.org
Website: *www.gs1us.org*

This company offers UPC barcodes at a lower cost with no annual fees, no disclosure of federal tax ID, and no release of annual sales figures. It provides barcode graphics at no charge. Please note: If you plan to sell to The Kroger Company and/or Wal-Mart, you must obtain your barcodes from GS1.

Resources for Women and Minority Entrepreneurs

U.S. Small Business Administration
Office of Women's Business Ownership (OWBO)
1110 Vermont Street NW
Washington, DC 20416
800-827-5722, (202) 606-4000
Website: *www.sba.gov/aboutsba/sbaprograms/onlinewbc/*

The Office of Women's Business Ownership is the primary advocate for the interests of women business owners and provides current and potential women business owners access to the following services and programs:

- Technical, financial, and management information
- Information about selling to the federal government
- Access to capital
- Women's Prequalification Loan Program

Online Women's Business Center
Website: *www.sba.gov/aboutsba/sbaprograms/onlinewbc/*

With over 60 centers nationwide, the Women's Business Centers program provides long-term training, counseling, networking, and mentoring to all types of potential and existing women entrepreneurs.

Office of Minority Enterprise Development
(202) 205-6410
Website: *www.sba.gov/aboutsba/sbaprograms/8abd/*

The main objective of this office is to foster business ownership by individuals who are socially and economically disadvantaged and to promote the competitive viability of such firms. The SBA has combined its efforts with those of private industry, banks, local communities, and other government agencies to meet these goals. The following programs or services are offered:

- Management and technical assistance
- Section 8(a) Business Development Program certification
- Federal procurement opportunities
- Bonding

Council for Entrepreneurial Development (CED)

(919) 549-7500
Website: *http://cednc.org*

CED provides educational courses, networking opportunities, mentoring, and capital formation resources for new and existing entrepreneurs.

Count Me In for Women's Economic Independence (Women and Money)

email: info@count-me-in.org
Website: *www.count-me-in.org*

Count Me In for Women's Economic Independence is a national nonprofit organization that will raise money from women to be lent to women. Count Me In is a lending and learning organization dedicated to strengthening women's position in the economy. The concept is straightforward: millions of women across America will be asked—and inspired—to contribute a minimum of $5 to Count Me In to create a national loan fund for women. The money will be redistributed to qualifying women in the form of small business loans ranging from $500 to $10,000

and scholarships for business training and technical assistance.

National Association of Women Business Owners (NAWBO)

1100 Wayne Avenue, Suite 830
Silver Spring, MD 20910
301-608-2590
email: national@nawbo.org
Website: *www.nawbo.org*

Annual dues: $75 to $125, depending on chapter location. Members: 80,000.

NAWBO is a lobbying organization aimed at promoting policies that encourage female entrepreneurship. NAWBO also established the National Foundation for Women Business Owners (NFWBO), a nonprofit research foundation. NFWBO publishes a wide range of research studies and reports on statistical trends among women-owned firms. Its *Compendium of National Statistics on Women-Owned Businesses in the U.S.* brings together all the publicly available statistical information on women-owned businesses.

American Business Women's Association (ABWA)

9100 Ward Parkway
Kansas City, MO 64114
800-228-0007, (816) 361-6621
email: abwa@abwa.org
Website: *www.abwahq.org*

Annual dues: $35 ($32 for retired entrepreneurs).

The ABWA's primary focus is to promote entrepreneurial ventures by women. It offers member discounts ranging from car rentals and office products to long-distance phone services. The ABWA also provides education and skill-building services to assist members just starting out.

American Woman's Economic Development Corp. (AWED)

71 Vanderbilt Avenue
New York, NY 10169
800-222-2933

Annual dues: $55 for new members, $49 for renewals Members: 2,000.

AWED's experts have experience in every area of small business—from financing and wholesale distribution to public relations. They offer classes in the New York City area but also dispense advice and coaching to members nationwide over the telephone. Four regional conferences are held annually to encourage networking among members

National Women's Business Council (NWBC)

409 Third Street SW
Washington, DC 20024
(202) 205-3850; Fax: (202) 205-6825
email: info@nwbc.gov
Website: *www.nwbc.gov*

The National Women's Business Council is a bipartisan federal advisory council created to serve as an independent source of advice and policy recommendations to the president, congress, and the U.S. Small Business Administration on economic issues of importance to women business owners. The Council's mission is to promote bold initiatives, policies, and programs designed to support women's business enterprises at all stages of development in the public and private sector marketplaces—from start-up to success to significance.

National Minority Supplier Development Council Inc. (NMSDC)

1040 Avenue of the Americas, 2nd Floor
New York, NY 10018
(212) 944-2430; Fax: (212) 719-9611
Website: *http://nmsdc.org*

Providing a direct link between corporate America and minority-owned businesses is the primary objective of the National Minority Supplier Development Council, one of the country's leading business membership organizations. It was chartered in 1972 to provide increased procurement and business opportunities for minority businesses of all sizes. The NMSDC Network includes a National Office in New York and 39 regional councils across the country. There are 3,500 corporate members throughout the network, including most of America's largest publicly owned, privately owned, and foreign-owned companies, as well as universities, hospitals, and other buying institutions. They certify and match more than 15,000 minority-owned businesses (Asian, Black, Hispanic, and Native American) with member corporations that want to purchase goods and services.

National Women Business Owners (NWBOC)

1001 West Jasmine Drive, #G
Lake Park, FL 33403
800-675-5066; Fax: (561) 881-7364
email: info@nwboc.org
Website: *www.nwboc.org*

NWBOC was established in 1995 to increase competition for corporate and government contracts through implementation of a pioneering economic development strategy for women business owners. NWBOC is a national 501(c)(3) not-for-profit corporation and is the first third-party, national certifier providing "Woman Business Enterprise" (WBE) Certification for women-owned businesses. The certification ensures that a private, for-profit company is truly owned and controlled by a woman or women.

Mothers' Home Business Network (MHBN)
PO Box 423
East Meadow, NY 11554
(516) 997-7394
Website: *www.homeworkingmom.com*

Annual Dues: $39.95. Membership: 6,000.

One of the largest groups for women home-based business owners. MHBN provides information, ideas, and inspiration to moms who choose to work at home. Publishes two newsletters, *Home Working Mothers* (annual) and *Kids and Career* (twice a year). MHBN provides literature on how to juggle your time between raising children and running a successful business as well as a "fraud detector" for evaluating home business opportunities.

Miscellaneous

Find a Freelancer
www.findafreelancer.com

This is a good online source for freelance writing and editing, graphic design, development and programming, artwork and illustration, Web design, and photography

Appendix O
State of the Industry Report: Prime Time for Fancy Foods

by A. Elizabeth Sloan

The economic downturn and heightened interest in at-home cooking and entertaining are contributing to an uptick in gourmet/specialty food sales.

With consumers watching cooking shows like soap operas, gourmet/specialty/fancy food sales in the United States topping $63 billion in 2007, and celebrity chefs like Emeril Lagasse creating personal empires in excess of $150 million, the "foodie" revolution shows no signs of slowing down (Schoenfeld 2005). More than 5 million Americans download recipes from the Food Network's website each month. Moreover, it's a global movement; "superchef" Martin Yan has hosted more than 1,800 cooking shows aired around the world.

So despite a sluggish economy, high gasoline prices, and a weakened dollar globally—specialty foods will likely continue to enjoy strong sales. In fact, historically, when times get tough, consumers turn to food as an affordable luxury and view fancy foods as a way to add a bit of adventure to daily life.

During the current downturn, the opportunity for specialty food growth may be even greater than before. More than 39 million consumers tried to eat gourmet every day last year (Packaged Facts 2007). Nearly three-quarters (73 percent) already purchase specialty foods, almost two thirds (65 percent) buy such products to treat themselves, and 64 percent use them in everyday meals at home (Tanner 2007).

Moreover, the industry will get an additional push from the nation's 72 million Gen Yers ages 15–30, who are now entering the workforce and becoming consumers in their own right. Those ages 18–24 and 25–34 rank equally as the top purchasers of specialty foods, spending 30 percent of their weekly food dollars on specialty items (Tanner 2007). Gen Yers have the highest preference for gourmet, ethnic, and natural foods and for food being presented as an "art form." They're also the most likely to try new foods, drinks, and health food items (Experian 2007).

As the economy forces today's culinary-savvy consumers to cut back on away-from-home eating and take-out meals—35 percent are visiting restaurants less often than they were three months ago—they'll be more likely than previous generations to want to continue to experience and experiment with new foods and flavors, despite cooking and eating more at home (Technomic 2008). Some consumers already consider certain specialty foods to be staples, as evidenced by the large number of trips made to gourmet, natural, and ethnic food stores to pick up just one or two items (FMI 2008b).

Economic constraints have also created a boom in home entertaining, fueling the demand for more elegant and unique fancy foods. One third (36 percent) of consumers buy specialty foods for a birthday or holiday celebration; 24 percent do so when having a party or dinner guests (Tanner 2007).

Those who purchase fair trade, green, local, or cage-free products as a means of personal or social expression are unlikely to be deterred by rising prices. Organic food sales across all channels topped $18.8 billion in 2007, up 17 percent over 2006 (*Nutrition Business Journal* 2008). Mainstream retailer Wal-Mart carries gourmet and organic foods, and 89 percent of supermarkets offer private label versions of specialty and/or organic foods (FMI 2008b). Thus, it appears that the price gap between traditional and fancy foods is closing, and the availability of more affordable options may well make natural and specialty foods more accessible than ever, even in economically troubling times.

Specialty Foods Sizzle

Specialty foods accounted for 12.5 percent of all retail food sales in 2007, reaching $47.9 billion in sales—up 8.7 percent over 2006 and 24 percent over 2005. Fancy foods sold through food service/restaurants, such as Starbucks or Panera Bread, added another $15 billion (Tanner 2008).

Retail sales accounted for 76 percent of specialty foods sales in 2007; food service 24 percent. Of the retail sales, traditional supermarkets enjoyed 70 percent, specialty stores 19 percent, and natural food stores 11 percent. More than 180,000 specialty products were in the marketplace last year (Tanner 2008/Mintel 2008).

Nearly nine in ten supermarket chains (87 percent) reported putting more emphasis on natural/organic products in 2008; 61 percent added emphasis to ethnic products (FMI 2008a). In addition, nearly nine in ten chains (87 percent) now offer natural/organic foods, and 67 percent offer gourmet foods. More than half (52 percent) feature an expanded gourmet cheese section, and 29 percent have a coffee bar, 23 percent a sushi station, and 22 percent an olive bar (FMI 2008a). More than one third (36 percent) of primary grocery shoppers visit an ethnic food store at least occasionally, and 31 percent patronize organic/natural food stores (FMI 2008b).

But competition for the specialty food dollar is fierce. Combined new product introductions in gourmet, health food, and specialty stores reached 3,535 in 2007 (Mintel 2008). Beverages topped the list with 678 new specialty products unveiled, followed by sauces and seasonings with 561 new products and confectionery with 529 (table O.1). With dollar sales of $3.3 billion, cheese and cheese alternatives are the largest specialty food category, up 12 percent in 2007 versus 2005, followed by condiments at $2.5 billion, up 6.4 percent, and bread and baked goods at $1.9 billion, up 19.8 percent (table O.2; Tanner 2008/Mintel 2008).

Among specialty segments with annual sales in excess of $1 billion, unit sales of snacks jumped 22.9 percent, frozen/refrigerated/entrees 19.5 percent, and meat/poultry 18 percent. For categories with sales of less than $1 billion, candy and individual snacks soared 51.5 percent; milk, half and half, and cream

	Table O.1

Specialty Food and Beverage Product Launchesby Category, in Gourmet, Health Food, and Specialty Retailers in 2007 (from Mintel 2008)

Category	Number of Products Introduced
Beverages	678
Sauces and seasonings	561
Confections	529
Bakery products	468
Snacks	373
Spreads	90
Meals and meal centers	161
Dairy products	123
Processed fish, meat, and egg products	104
Fruits and vegetables	98
Desserts and ice cream	85
Breakfast cereals	61
Side dishes	56
Soups	38
Sweeteners and sugar	9

29.7 percent; refrigerated juice/functional beverages 29.7 percent; energy bars and gels 29.1 percent; cold cereals 24 percent; yogurt and kefir 20.7 percent; shelf-stable entrées and mixes 18.7 percent; frozen fruits/vegetables 18.4 percent; hot cereals 17.6 percent; ready-to-drink (RTD) tea/coffee and carbonated functional beverages 15.8 percent; refrigerated sauces, salsas, and dips 14.7 percent; and shelf-stable juices/drinks 14.3 percent (Tanner/Mintel 2008). In specialty food stores, the most frequently purchased items are cold beverages, bought by 62 percent of all shoppers; coffee/tea, purchased by 61 percent; chocolate, 58 percent; cheese, 54 percent; and olive/specialty oils, 51 percent.

Table O.2

Sales of Top Ten Specialty Food Categories in 2007
(From Mintel 2008)

Category	Sales ($ Million)	% Change from 2005
Cheese and cheese alternatives	3,302	2.4
Condiments	2,479	6.4
Bread and baked goods	1,927	19.8
Chips, pretzels, and snacks	1,723	30.9
Frozen and refrigerated entrees, pizzas, and convenience foods	1,433	39.4
Frozen desserts	1,253	5.1
Frozen and refrigerated meats, poultry, and seafood	1,251	22.3
Cookies and snack bars	1,151	16.1
Coffee, coffee substitutes, and cocoa	1,007	18.9
Refrigerated juices and functional beverages	960	54.3

Those ages 18–24 are the most likely to buy specialty treats, meats, and products that require limited cooking skills, such as items for grilling. Among these young consumers, 65 percent purchase specialty chocolates, 56 percent purchase specialty meats, 51 percent gourmet cookies, and 40 percent specialty salty snacks (Tanner 2008). Those ages 25–34, who are more likely to cook meals than their younger counterparts, are the top buyers of specialty beverages, with 73 percent purchasing these products. Among purchasers 25–34, cheese is bought by 61 percent, bread 52 percent, pasta sauce 49 percent, salad dressing 48 percent, frozen entrées 48 percent, and condiments 45 percent. It's important to note that older boomers (those ages 55–64)—commonly mistaken for the "gourmet generation"—did not rank highest on purchases of any specialty food item. Those ages 65+ were the number-one purchasers of specialty oils; those ages 45–54 led in specialty coffee and tea purchases (Tanner 2007).

Gourmet Megatrends

With specialty foods historically setting the pace for the consumer food products industry, it's ironic that two mainstream megatrends—convenience and health—are creating lucrative new opportunities in the fancy food world.

Because "young gourmets" frequently have limited cooking skills and older gourmets limited time, it's not surprising that gourmet frozen/refrigerated entrées, pizzas, and convenience foods, such as Kahiki's Szechuan Peppercorn Beef or Manchester Farms' Premium Seasoned Quail are turning in torrid sales. Celebrity chef food kits, such as Westwego's Sauté Your Way kits with Louisiana Gulf wild shrimp and sauces by Chef Paul Prudhomme, are enjoying skyrocketing sales.

Délice gourmet, slow-cooked crock pot dinners and soup kits include Southern Italian Pasta e Aioli. Capitalizing on the popularity of U.S. Southern cooking, Simply Southern introduced fully cooked Southern sides and vegetables such as Homestyle Okra & Tomatoes and Blackeye Peas.

Dessert mixes are another fast-growing gourmet convenience category. Lollipop Tree mixes include Lemon Poppy Seed and Raspberry White Chocolate Bars. Simmering sauces are another emerging product category. Private Harvest offers Orange Teriyaki Simmering Sauce, and from Made in the Napa Valley™ there is Wine Country Simmering Sauce.

Other products just make preparation easier. Fabrique Délices' Cassoulet includes pork and duck and does not require long hours of preparation. Lactalis USA's President Brie is sold in log form designed to fit on round crackers when sliced. Sorrento's Fresh Mozzarella Ciliengini are mini cheese pearls that can easily be added to a salad or pasta.

Lighter and lower-fat versions of high-end products represent an important trend that is just beginning in specialty foods. Laughing Cow Light French Onion Cheese from Bel Brands USA contains just 35 calories per wedge. Foxtail's gourmet pies, including Chocolate Coconut, boast "no added sugar." Green County Foods has introduced Sugar-Free Petits Fours.

In the past, specialty items were almost always imported, but today the trend is toward quality products produced in the United States, which also aligns well with the interest in locally sourced foods. Birmingham, Alabama's, Porchetta Primata LLC produces "Ariccian" porchetta from an ancient Roman recipe, and the company prides itself on the fact that, unlike some imported products, its porchetta is antibiotic- and hormone-free. BelGioioso Cheese Company's new Burrata is a cream-filled mozzarella based on the classic Italian cheese from the Puglia region but now is being made in Wisconsin.

Products formulated with very old recipes represent another emerging trend. Vienna Beef's all-natural franks are made with a century-old recipe and smoked with hardwood hickory. Walkers Shortbread touts the fact that the company follows an original recipe and production methods first employed in Joseph Walker's bakery, which opened in 1898. Britain's West Country Farmhouse cheddar is produced where cheddar originated more than 500 years ago and is "still made on family farms, by hand."

With high-spending boomers' penchant for partying, it's not surprising that gourmet cocktail snack companions, sophisticated drink mixes, and foods and sauces with wine and spirits flavorings are also enjoying brisk sales. Earth & Vine's new concentrated Meyer Lemon Elixir creates terrific Italian sodas, martinis, lemonades, and sangrias.

Wine and other alcoholic beverage flavors are popping up everywhere. Kerrygold's Aged Cheddar Cheese comes in Irish Whisky and Irish Stout. Finger Lakes Strawberry Chardonnay from Yancey's Fancy New York Artisan Cheese marries fruit and wine flavors. American Vintage Wine Biscuits from American Vintage are made with wine as their name suggests; the line includes varieties such as Chianti Oregano with Crushed Red Peppers.

And with at-home dinner parties taking the place of going out to eat for all age and income groups, easy-to-make gourmet meals and appetizers will find a welcome market. Sweetypepp are Peruvian mini red peppers with a thick shell that can be filled for a unique appetizer. Jennie-O Turkey Store's new Artisan Roasted Sage Dressing Stuffed Turkey Roasts make any meal into a gourmet feast.

Small bites and single-serve offerings have also found a place in the gourmet arena. Rising Sun Farms' mini-cheese Tortlettes come in Key Lime topped with cranberries and other flavors. Corbin Kitchens' new Mini Tamales, Mini Patty Melts, and Mini Grilled Cheese Sandwiches are a perfect snack or appetizer. Don Miguel Mexican Foods introduced mini Breakfast Empanadas. Van Holten's Big "O" Snack Olives packaged in a stand-up pouches contain only 40 calories per pouch.

With American Culinary Federation chefs naming bite-sized desserts the hottest culinary trend for 2008, gorgeous gourmet dessert shots and single-serve cakes, such as those created by Galaxy Foods, are single-handedly bringing back dessert. Petites fours are also getting renewed attention (NRA 2007). Sugar Bowl Bakery's all-natural Petite Brownie Bites are made from a blend of nine cocoas.

Italian artisan confections, such as marzipan, panforte, and torrone, are also gaining momentum in the United States, as is gelato. Cia Bella Gelato Company's Select Series Gelato is available in Key Lime Graham Cracker and Maple Ginger Snap flavors. Cia Bella also introduced Gelato Dessert Bars, all-natural round gelato sandwiches. Churros with fruit fillings are another hot ethnic sweet trend. PhillySwirl broke new ground with its Ice Cream Cupcakes.

Crunchiness is another fast-growing gourmet product attribute. John Wm. Macy's SweetSticks are one of the first crunchy dessert companions; they are sourdough twists designed to complement ice cream in Java Cinnamon or Dutch Chocolate varieties. TH Foods Inc.'s Crunchmaster multiseed crackers are crunchy and oven baked. Nonni Food Company's New York Style brand introduced Focaccia Sticks in Roasted Garlic.

Functional shapes are another interesting twist. For example, King's new Hawaiian Snackers' Rolls are made for mini sandwiches or sliders. Rubschlager Rye-Ola whole rye breads are round for perfect snacks or hors d'oeuvres. Sara Lee created a round sandwich croissant—Twister Croissant Rolls.

Old Favorites/New Ideas

When it comes to innovation, the gourmet cheese category is on fire. Woolwich Dairy Inc. markets a hard goat cheese, goat cheddar, and goat mozzarella; Meyenberg Farms has a goat cream cheese, and Mt. Sterling offers a Goat Raw Milk Mild Cheddar and Whey Cream Goat Butter. Cabot's Tuscan Cheddar has layers of Tuscan herbs and spices throughout. Lactalis USA's P'Tit Pyrenees is 50 percent sheep's milk and 50 percent cow's milk cheese. Scotland and Wales are the hot import countries. *Cave-aged,* such as Emmi's Kaltbach Cave-Aged Cheese, is a new premium label term.

And the flavors are unprecedented. Montchevre-Betin added Fresh Goat Cheese with Honey. Sartori Foods' Signature Blends of grated/shaved cheeses come in Sicilian and other flavors. Sartori Foods also is among the cutting-edge cheese makers offering olive oil cheese in Basil or Rosemary Olive Oil flavors. Bel Brands USA's Kaukauna Connoisseur Cheese Wheels come in Mango Peach and Asiago Pesto. Blazer's cheeses are offered in Capers & Black Peppercorn and Garlic Chive & Spring Dill varieties.

Duck in any way, shape, or form is the new favorite in the gourmet meat case. King Cole offers fully cooked Peppered Duck Breast and comfit. Alexian™ introduced French rilette prepared with 100 percent duck meat; Fabrique Délices offers Cured Duck Salami.

Slow-cooked roasted meats are all the rage in gourmet delis. William Fischer Premium Deli meat is now available in Roast Loin of Pork and Roast Eye of Beef Round for slicing. King's Command Foods introduced a Certified Angus Beef Meatloaf for takeout.

Fancy deli salads have been upgraded, too. Tryst Gourmet introduced premium Chicken Salads, including Mandarin Orange and Cranberry Apple, in single-serve tubs with the mix-ins on top. Sandridge Food Corporation offers a Grilled Chicken and Fennel Salad; Reser's has a Wild Rice Waldorf.

Superfruits are making their way into the gourmet meat case. Fabrique Délices introduced an all-natural pheasant sausage with goji berries. Balatoni

Jus's Fructa Salami from Hungary contains bits of apricot and has a fruit casing made of apricots, papaya, pear, and pineapple.

Flavor Gone Wild

When you talk about gourmet foods, it's really all about unique flavors. For at-home gourmets, McCormick's 2008 Gourmet Collection includes Lavender, Cocoa Chile Blend, and Toasted Sesame Seed; new peppers include Smoke-house and Worcestershire flavors. Saltworks offers Applewood and Chardonnay Smoked Sea Salts.

Sandwich dressings are another hot category. Deano's Deli Bistro sandwich sauces come in Hot Ginger and Cilantro & Lime. Flavored olive oil spreads are also moving into the spotlight, as are chutneys. Baxters offers all-natural chutneys in Spanish Tomato & Black Olive and Cranberry & Caramelized Red Onion.

With outdoor grilling at an all-time high, rubs, marinades, and barbecue sauces are proliferating. Robert Rothschild Farm markets sauces in a variety of flavors from Plum Garlic to Harissa Moroccan and Tandoori Indian. Hot dip mixes, such as Gourmet du Village Hot Parmesan & Artichoke, are also coming on strong.

Flavors are also taking the snack scene by storm. Flavored nuts are hot. The Peanut Shop of Williamsburg offers Crab'in Nuts, Salsa, and B-B-Q Nuts. Umpqua Indian Foods introduced Indian-flavored jerky. Flavors also continue to infuse gourmet staples, such as Honey Ridge Farms' Balsamic Honey Vinegar.

With gourmet food marketers often taking their cues from high-end res-taurant chefs, it is important to note that *fresh* is the most frequent descriptor on fine-dining menus; it has nearly three times more mentions than the second claim, *homemade*. In descending order, other top claims include *crispy, creamy, seasonal, crisp, house/house-made, prime, tender, garden-fresh, special, imported, and classic,* according to Mintel Menu Insights (2008).(Figure O.1 shows the impor-tance of various descriptors.)

To create a healthy food halo, fine-dining restaurants are most likely to use an *organic* descriptor, followed by *pesticide-free, natural, low-fat, naturally raised,*

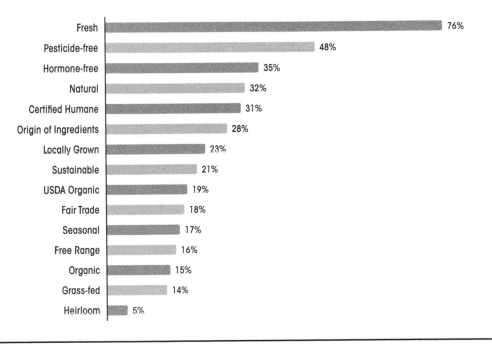

Figure O.1

Importance Of Various Labels/Phrases When Shopping for Foods and Beverages (From The Hartman Group 2008)

Label/Phrase	Percentage
Fresh	76%
Pesticide-free	48%
Hormone-free	35%
Natural	32%
Certified Humane	31%
Origin of Ingredients	28%
Locally Grown	23%
Sustainable	21%
USDA Organic	19%
Fair Trade	18%
Seasonal	17%
Free Range	16%
Organic	15%
Grass-fed	14%
Heirloom	5%

lean, light, vegetarian, USDA-approved, cholesterol-free, milk-fed, low calorie, and sugar-free (Mintel Menu Insights 2008).

Natural Products Retailers

Retailers of natural products sold $17.4 billion worth of organic and natural foods in 2007; mass-market sales of organic and natural foods totaled $12.4 billion. However, growth was faster in the mass market, up 15.2 percent versus 8.7 percent in natural products retailers (Rea and Spencer 2008). Produce remained the largest food category in natural products stores in 2007, with sales of $3.6 billion, up 8.8 percent over 2006, followed by packaged grocery products at $3 billion, up 7.7 percent; dairy $1.5 billion, up 11.1 percent; and frozen/refrigerated $1.4 billion, up 9.9 percent.

Among those categories with less than $1 billion in sales by natural products retailers, snacks, at $846 million in 2007, grew 8.9 percent; fresh meat/seafood at $962 million was up 15.3 percent; beer/wine at $665 million was up 15 percent; and nondairy beverages (e.g., soy, rice, oat) at $657 million were up 6 percent (Clute 2008).

The four fastest-growing food categories in natural foods supermarkets were carbonated, functional, and ready-to-drink (RTD) tea/coffee drinks, up 29.4 percent; pet food, up 21.9 percent, sweeteners, up 18.8 percent; and beans, grains, and rice, up 18.5 percent (Rutberg 2008).

Organic food sales in natural products retailers hit $8.1 billion in 2007, up 11.3 percent. Produce was the largest organic category with sales of $2.6 billion in 2007, up 9.5 percent over 2006. Packaged grocery items posted sales of $1.7 billion, up 10.9 percent; dairy $1.1 billion, up 12.1 percent; nondairy beverages $548 million, up 6.3 percent; and frozen/refrigerated meals/entrées $389 million, up 12.3 percent (Clute 2008).

The top ten fastest-growing organic categories in natural products retailers were pet food, with sales growth of 65.6 percent; carbonated, functional, and RTD tea/coffee beverages, up 59.2 percent; meal replacements/supplement powders, up 37.5 percent; sweeteners, up 27.9 percent; frozen/refrigerated meats, poultry, fish, up 26.8 percent; candy/individual snacks, up 26.1 percent; condiments, up 20.8 percent; nuts, seeds, dried fruits, trail mixes, up 20.8 percent; energy bars/gels, up 20 percent; and cookies/snack bars, up 19.7 percent.

More than half of organic bread/baked goods (56 percent) and shelf-stable fruits/vegetables (52 percent) are still sold in the natural channel (Soref 2008). According to the Hartman Group's *Organics 2008 Report,* 42 percent of consumers now buy organic foods occasionally, 12 percent do so weekly, and 7 percent daily; 37 percent never purchase them. Among recent purchasers of organic foods, 71 percent bought them in the grocery store, 24 percent in a supercenter, 20 percent in a natural food store, and 10 percent in a club store (Hartman Group 2008).

The benefits that consumers associate with organics are also changing. Hartman (2008) reports that the absence of pesticides, artificial flavors, colors, preservatives, and herbicides most define *organics* to consumers. However, 75 percent of consumers also cite the absence of growth hormones, 69 percent cite the absence of antibiotics, and 67 percent the absence of genetically modified organisms (GMOs).

Two thirds (65 percent) of consumers say they're willing to pay a premium of more than 30 percent for organic meat, poultry, and deli meats. A total of 64 percent are willing to do so for fresh fruit, 61 percent for milk, 61 percent for fish/seafood, 60 percent for fresh vegetables, and 60 percent for eggs (Hartman Group 2008). When selecting foods and beverages, *fresh* still tops the list of the most important food labels or phrases for three quarters (76 percent) of consumers (Hartman Group 2008). As seen in figure O.1, *pesticide-free* and *hormone-free* are now more important than a *natural food* claim.

Products that are of high quality have always fared well in the marketplace, and so will specialty foods. Moreover, the gap between nationally branded prices and fancy foods is narrowing. Perhaps, if history repeats itself, consumers won't feel guilty for spending extra dollars on foods and beverages they really enjoy.

References

Clute, M. 2008. Retailers respond to turning tide. *Natural Foods Merchandiser* 27, no. 6:22–24.

Experian. 2007. *Simmons consumer research study* (November). New York: Experian Research Services. *www.experianconsumerresearch.com*

Food Marketing Institute (FMI). 2008a. *The food retailing industry speaks 2008. annual state of the industry review.* Arlington, VA: Food Marketing Institute. *www.fmi.org*

Food Marketing Institute (FMI). 2008b. *U.S. grocery shopper trends 2008.* Crystal City, VA: Food Marketing Institute. *www.fmi.org*

Hartman Group. 2008. *Organics 2008 report* (June). Bellevue, WA: The Hartman Group. *www.hartmangroup.com*

Information Resources. 2008. *Consumer trend watch* 2008. *Times & Trends* (February). *www.gmaonline.org/publications/gmairi/2008/february/february.pdf*

Mintel. 2008. *Speciality foods: The NASFT state of the industry report; The market US 2008*. Chicago: Mintel. *www.mintel.com*

Mintel Menu Insights. 2008. *Gourmet descriptors in fine dining restaurants: First quarter 2008*. Chicago: Mintel. *www.mintel.com*

Nutrition Business Journal. 2008. Organic markets overview. *Nutrition Business Journal* 1 (March/April): 3–46. *www.nutritionbusiness.com*

NPD Group. 2008. NPD reports year round BBQ grilling at all-time high (May 16 press release). Port Washington, NY: NPD Group. *www.npd.com*

Packaged Facts. 2007. *Gourmet, specialty, and premium foods and beverages in the U.S.* (November). New York: Packaged Facts. *www.packagedfacts.com*

Rae, P., and M. Spencer. 2008. NFM's market overview. *Natural Foods Merchandiser* 27, no. 6:1.

Rutberg, S. 2008. Customers roll over for healthy pet treats and toys. *Natural Foods Merchandiser* 27, no. 6:40–42.

Schoenfeld, B. 2005. Emeril's empire. *Cigar Aficionado*, November.

Soref, A. 2008. Move over Goldfish: Natural kids' snacks are in the house. *Natural Foods Merchandiser* 27, no. 6:46.

Tanner, R. 2007. Today's specialty food consumer. *Specialty Food Magazine* 37, no. 10:49–64.

Tanner, R. 2008. The state of the specialty food industry. *Specialty Food Magazine* 38, no. 4:34–48.

Technomic. 2008. Consumers report trading out dining occasion. *American Express Market Brief* (March). Chicago: Technomic. *www.technomic.com*

A. Elizabeth Sloan, a professional member of the Institute of Food Technologists and contributing editor of *Food Technology*, is president of Sloan Trends Inc., 2958 Sunset Hills, Suite 202, Escondido, CA 92025 (sloan@sloantrend.com).

Appendix P
The New Entrepreneurial Spirit:
Breaking Down the Barriers to Personal and Business Success!

One of the challenges to an entrepreneur is to be able to get a good night's sleep. This involves an ability to delude oneself from time to time. For example, you must not lose sleep over not knowing exactly when or where your next mortgage payment will come in.

With the profusion of new and highly entrepreneurial food enterprises, I thought it would be helpful to seek expert advice about what it is to be a specialty food entrepreneur. The following information is based on an article by Robert Ruotolo, DSW. "Dr. Bob" is a senior partner with the Quantum Performance Group and has an extensive background and accomplishment in organizational development. You can find the full article, The New Entrepreneurial Spirit in the New Millenium on his website: *www.quantumperformancegroup.com.*

Today's world of work is different, and, therefore, our response to it must be different. Self-management and self-sufficiency are concepts that apply equally to individuals in the workplace, in their own business, and at any level of an enterprise. The need and ability to be responsive, adaptable, and even at times resilient are called for in the realm of being competitive and successful in today's specialty food world.

Preparing Yourself and Others for Such a Work Environment

A certain set of characteristics and behaviors can be developed in people who want to compete and succeed. By adopting these characteristics and behaviors, food entrepreneurs can create and sustain a work environment that can ensure long-term business viability and success.

What Are the Entrepreneurial Qualities and Characteristics?

The phrase *new entrepreneurial spirit* embodies what is required. The word *entrepreneur* connotes self-directed and ownership, and the ability to focus on health and wealth creation—to be able to stand back and view the wholeness of one's decisions and their potential impact before taking action. It also means to include others who are needed to effect change or who may be impacted by whatever changes will take place. The word *spirit* means purposeful, passionate, transforming, and connected. These are powerful words!

What Are the Added Dimensions That Make This Concept New?

The new dimension is the need to partner and work in harmony with others rather than being the lone star against the world! One must be principle centered—that is, one must be clear about a few principles that govern one's behavior and communicate them so others will support them. These are the qualities that you want to adopt to bring your products successfully into the marketplace.

Four Characteristics and Five Principles

Here is a description of how to identify and develop the four characteristics and five principles upon which you can build your business culture in yourself and others who work with you (from the book *Inspiration at Work: Igniting a New Entrepreneurial Spirit in the Individual and the Corporation* by Robert Ruotolo, DSW).

Four characteristics of the new entrepreneurial spirit:

1. The power of being self-directed
2. Establishing a sense of ownership and partnership
3. Focus on health and wealth creation, wholeness, and inclusion
4. Being principle centered

These characteristics are linked to the following five principles for personal and business success:

1. Know yourself.
2. Establish your own values and beliefs.
3. Be responsible for your own behavior.
4. You are the codesigner of your present and future.
5. Give thanks and celebrate life!

The Power of Being Self-Directed

The hallmark of the entrepreneur is to be self-directed, to be in tune and aligned with one's purpose and passion. This does not mean standing alone, though it is sometimes better to do so than to give up your "sense of being" to be accepted by others. Becoming self-directed is enabled by the first two principles—know yourself and establish your own values and beliefs.

There are some simple questions to ask to assess a sense of being self-directed:

• Do you have a three- to five-year plan for your life and your business?
• Do you know where you want to be and how you will get there?
• If you had to define and describe what is most important to you in your life/business, what would it be?
• What are the three to five key areas in your life that you need kept in balance to sustain your short- and long-term well-being?

In business, these questions are usually referred to collectively as strategic planning.

If you take these same questions and make sure you are addressing them in your specialty food business, you will be creating the culture to be self-directed. It needs to become a way of life!

Establishing a Sense of Ownership and Partnership

Adopting a new entrepreneurial spirit requires you to take responsibility for your own behavior and your contribution to the relationships of which you are a part. These relationships can be business related or family and friendship related. Have these discussions with your significant others. Use a facilitator/counselor if necessary. Don't leave these dialogues to chance!

Ownership and partnership link to the third and fourth principles: be responsible for your own behavior and being a codesigner of your present and future.

Focusing on Health and Wealth Creation, Wholeness, and Inclusion

Focus is an essential ability to be successful in today's specialty food business environment. You should focus on your "purpose and passion" and how to make it come alive through your work. Your business needs to focus on how to direct its talents and resources as efficiently and effectively as possible to the marketplace and your customers.

A powerful, dynamic synergy is established in the entire workplace if we can get individuals and teams to focus on these three elements: health and wealth creation, wholeness, and inclusion. Creation is what we are all about! All of what we do either contributes to or takes away from health and wealth creation. We also sometimes sacrifice one for the other. Our challenge is to optimize both. A characteristic of success can be defined as "to the extent we can contribute positively to both." Besides monitoring physical well-being, we can measure social and emotional well-being. How are you managing your wealth creation?

Being Principle Centered

The characteristic of being principle centered serves as a guide that links our behavior to our vision, values, and beliefs. Being principled centered enhances the speed of our decision making and actions. The five principles of personal and business success stated above can help you behave in a manner consistent with the characteristics of being a new entrepreneur.

Here is a review of each principle. By following the principles, you are at the same time more in harmony with yourself, others, and the world around you. This is the essence of self-direction—and self-management!

The First Principle: Know Yourself.

This refers to the constant need for self-awareness, self-discovery, and continuous feedback. A need for self-awareness and self-renewal takes place at a group or team level in your business. This is why we conduct business performance audits.

Questions to answer are these:

- Who am I, or what am I?
- Why do I exist, or what is my purpose/mission?
- If this is who I am or what I am, then what should I be doing? How should I behave?

The Second Principle: Establish Your Own Values and Beliefs.

As you begin to know yourself, you soon realize that values and beliefs form an important part of your very being. You learn quickly that some things are more important than others. These "things" encompass everything. Knowing and believing affect how you see yourself in the world and how the world relates to you.

The Third Principle: Be Responsible for Your Own Behavior.

As you discover your interests and passions—what really excites you—and believe in their positive value for you and others, you are pulled toward them. They become your vision and driving force!

Will you do what it takes to be responsible for your own behavior? Do you just dream about it, or are you committed enough to do what it takes to fulfill your dream? Will you be self-disciplined around ownership and partnership and be focused? By acknowledging that we accept responsibility for our actions, we can take the first action step to doing something about changing our circumstances.

The Fourth Principle: You Are the Codesigner of Your Present and Future.

This is the result of and natural outcome of the first three principles. It supports the notion of a shared vision and values. It supports and promotes the notion of interdependence and the synergy and power of like-mindedness. This principle emphasizes the importance of association. Are the people with whom you live, play, and work going to help you be what you want to be? If not, why not? Is it because you have not shared your dreams and desires with them? Is it because they do not believe in you or your dreams?

The Fifth Principle: Give Thanks and Celebrate Life

This recognizes that life, and living it to the fullest, is a gift. We have no control over life itself, only how we choose to live it out, whether as an owner of our own behavior or as a victim of the world around us. A simple way of giving thanks and celebrating is through acknowledgment of the good and wonderful around us and in and through others. Make a practice of positively acknowledging others for what they have done! See what positive effects this has on your relationships with others and on improving their effectiveness.

Can you image what an impact these five principles can have if you apply all of them to all of the roles you carry out in life, especially as a business owner?

The Next Steps to Creating and Sustaining the New Entrepreneurial Spirit

Dr. Bob completes his advice with the following comment:

You can create an entrepreneurial spirit and now use this principle-centered framework to continue and improve your path of life and living it to its fullest! Bring these four new entrepreneurial characteristics and five principles into your specialty food business to create and nurture a powerful culture, one that can thrive in such turbulent times! Begin by working on a definition of your desired future place—your vision.

Acknowledgments

· ·

This is the fifth edition of this guide, and I wish to acknowledge all those good souls who have made it possible.

Someone once said, "By the time a book, any book, gets to its fourth edition, it becomes a classic." I wonder about this, and I remain in debt to all of those who assisted me in getting the book to its fourth edition. If it is a classic, it is because of them.

First, I could not have written this tome without the altogether unending good humor, editorial counsel, and exhaustive research of my wife, Patricia Teagle.

I am grateful for Encore Foods President Ron Johnson's level-headed and healthy enthusiasm about the specialty food trade. His observations have balanced well with some of the highly entrepreneurial processes we see among the new-to-market food processors.

I am indebted also to my older son, Tully, for his assistance in surfing the Internet to find and confirm extensive appendix information (and, to cover the bases, hello to my younger son, Colin).

I acknowledge gladly the advice and valuable counsel I received from Karen Cantor, the driving spirit and copublisher of *Food Entrepreneur Magazine,* the predecessor of *Food Entrepreneur eZine.*

I extend my appreciation to my colleagues in the specialty food business, particularly Elliot Johnson of Mark T. Wendell Company for the precision with which he assesses industry trends; Liz and Nick Thomas, founders of

Chalif Inc., who provided comprehensive and altogether helpful reviews of the first draft of this guide; the late Barry Raskin, a specialty food broker largely responsible for guiding me during my early education in this field; Ernie Fisher, an international food consultant who brought a real-world perspective to examining this industry; and Lee Robinson, who as president of The Ruffled Truffle provided me with the opportunity to learn about the gift segment of the specialty food business.

I am grateful, further, to my late friend Page Pratt, cofounder of Food Marketing International, with whom I shared many a rewarding marketing moment, and to my first editor, Jean Kerr, whose unflappable disposition eased the burden of perfecting the first edition of this book. Finally, I would like to acknowledge my late colleague, classmate, and best friend, Rolff Johansen, for bringing civility and wit to our hectic earlier years in specialty food marketing.

Index

About the Author

$\textbf{S}$ **tephen Farrelly Hall** is president of Food Marketing International, a firm that guides food entrepreneurs in planning for success. His services include helping new-to-market firms clarify and define their preferred futures. He provides practical and timely advice on how to equip new organizations with the tools needed for profitability. His hands-on organizational assessments explore the strategic frameworks of product distinctiveness and traction. He has spent more than 25 years in import/export, national brand management, and business development consulting for dozens of specialty/gourmet food firms. He has been quoted in the *Wall Street Journal, Entrepreneur Magazine,* and *Time Magazine* and has appeared as a principal guest on CNBC's *Money Talk.* A retired Navy intelligence officer (reserve), he resides in Scottsdale, Arizona, with his wife, Patricia, and two sons, Tully and Colin.